WHAT WERE WE THINKING

A BRIEF INTELLECTUAL HISTORY
OF THE TRUMP ERA

CARLOS LOZADA

SIMON & SCHUSTER

NEW YORK   LONDON   TORONTO   SYDNEY   NEW DELHI

Simon & Schuster
1230 Avenue of the Americas
New York, NY 10020

First Simon & Schuster hardcover edition October 2020

SIMON & SCHUSTER and colophon are registered
trademarks of Simon & Schuster, Inc.

For information about special discounts for bulk purchases,
please contact Simon & Schuster Special Sales at
1-866-506-1949 or business@simonandschuster.com.

The Simon & Schuster Speakers Bureau can bring authors to your live event. For
more information or to book an event, contact the Simon & Schuster Speakers
Bureau at 1-866-248-3049 or visit our website at www.simonspeakers.com.

Interior design by Ruth Lee-Mui

Manufactured in the United States of America

1   3   5   7   9   10   8   6   4   2

Library of Congress Cataloging-in-Publication Data has been applied for.

ISBN 978-1-9821-4562-0
ISBN 978-1-9821-4564-4 (ebook)

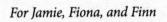

For Jamie, Fiona, and Finn

Many books have been written about me, some good,
some bad. Both happily and sadly, there will be more to come!
—Donald J. Trump, July 17, 2020

CONTENTS

HOW WE THOUGHT HERE

Early in Donald Trump's 2016 presidential campaign, I approached an editor at the *Washington Post* with what I considered an inspired proposal: What if, as the paper's new nonfiction critic, I binge-read a selection of the candidate's books published since the 1980s—including *Trump: The Art of the Deal*, that foundational text of Trump Studies—and explained to our readers whatever I learned about him? Even ghostwritten books still reveal much about the purported author's self-image, much as all propaganda divulges its intentions. The editor liked the idea, but he urged me to hurry. It wasn't clear how long interest in Trump would last.

That was in July 2015.

Interest in Trump has lasted far longer than may have seemed possible, if "interest" comes close to describing the hold that Trump, as candidate and president, would exert over American public life. Reading his books did offer a preview of "a world where bragging is breathing and insulting is talking, where repetition and contradiction come standard, where vengefulness and insecurity erupt at random," as I wrote at the time. "Elsewhere, such qualities might get in the way of the story. With Trump, they are the story."

In the years since, I've pored over books on the Trump era, trying to keep pace with the intellectuals, journalists, insiders, partisans, and activists who are grappling with the turmoil it has wrought. I've read some 150 of them thus far, and even that is just a fraction of the Trump canon. One of the ironies of our time is that a man who rarely reads, preferring the rage of cable news and Twitter for hours each day, has propelled an onslaught of book-length writing about his presidency.

Dissections of the white working class. Manifestos of political resistance. Works on gender and identity. Histories and memoirs of race and protest. Surveys of populism, authoritarianism, and anger. Investigations of political extremism. Polemics on the future of left and right. Debates and proposals on immigration. Studies on the institution of the presidency and the fate of democracy. And, of course, plenty of books about Trump himself—his values, his family, his businesses, and his White House.

There are still many more I want and expect to read, but this sample is enough to hazard some conclusions. These books, appearing between 2016 and 2020, have dominated the bestseller lists. As a publishing phenomenon, they have succeeded. Less so, I fear, as an intellectual project. The best of these works combine urgency and insight, timeliness and timelessness. But too many books of the Trump era are more knee-jerk than incisive, more posing than probing, more righteous than right, more fixated on calling out the daily transgressions of the man in the Oval Office—*this is not normal!*—than on assessing their impact. They are illuminating in part because they reflect some of the same blind spots, resentments, and failures of imagination that gave us the Trump presidency itself, and that are likely to outlast it. Individually, these books try to show a way forward. Collectively, they reveal how we're stuck.

Among the president's opponents, the response to Trump was born in disdain for his campaign, aversion toward his supporters, shock at his victory, and revulsion against his policies. Essay anthologies quickly sprouted, with activists, novelists, and politicians wallowing in their election night woes and calling for resistance to the new order. When expletives and all caps crowd out discernment, and when high-mindedness veers into dogmatism, the resistance lit can be among the least inspiring subgenres of this era.

On the right, Trump deepened a breach between opportunists and absolutists. The former offer books pandering to their new leader, ignoring or reveling in his more sordid traits and undemocratic impulses, captive minds seeking to retrofit Trumpism into something approaching a coherent ideology. The latter, meanwhile, publish hardcover breakup letters to their party and movement, without realizing that sometimes, when the love is gone, it really is you and not them.

Scribes and sociologists descended upon every small-town diner and rusted factory between the coasts, hoping to divine the mind of the white working-class Trump voter, seeking to adjudicate which shorthand motivation, whether economic deprivation or racial prejudice, explains the enduring devotion of Trump's base. The least convincing of these works insist on one answer alone; the most vivid are those that show how the two impulses can be intertwined—because people are human and humans are complicated—and how, rather than pushing voters toward a particular candidate, such feelings can leave them believing that politics has no place for them at all.

From the academy, packed bookshelves emerged to warn that Trump was killing off the American experiment, with the precise cause of death determined by each writer's expertise. Political scientists warned of the death of democracy. Philosophers and literary critics worried about the death of truth. Internationalists fretted over the death of global trade and alliances. Historians, meanwhile, shook their heads and explained to anyone who would listen that we'd all been here before.

Donald Trump may not read many books ("Actually, I'm looking at a book, I'm reading a book, I'm trying to get started," he replied in 2017 when a Fox News host asked him about his reading habits), but he understands their cultural and political allure. He has published more than a dozen books, and he launched his campaign in 2015 declaring that "we need a leader that wrote *The Art of the Deal.*" That 1987 memoir, whose true writer has since expressed regret for his role, is as much a part of Trump's image as *The Apprentice* or Trump Tower, maybe more. The president is certainly aware of the books covering him and his administration, publicly praising or trashing them depending on whether he thinks they are nice to him—no matter that his attention boosts their sales and reach either way.

Critics scoff at the president's literary indifference, often comparing it to his predecessor's reverence for the written word; Barack Obama receives rapturous coverage every time he promotes a new list of titles purchased from the local indie shop. To the extent that Trump relies on books at all, it is to confirm his instincts rather than to challenge his assumptions; to ratify, not edify. (In 2015, for instance, his initial campaign remarks insulting Mexican immigrants may have been partially inspired by Ann Coulter's *¡Adios, America! The Left's Plan to Turn Our Country into a Third World Hellhole*, which the candidate had hailed as a "great read" just three weeks earlier.) Yes, I would be delighted if our president read more books, even more so if they were good ones. But of the many concerns I have about Trump, a thin TBR pile is not foremost among them. I'd settle for him reading his briefing materials. Or the Constitution.

The books Americans buy, debate, and prize usually say something about how they feel about their prospects, their politics, and their leadership. *Hillbilly Elegy*, J. D. Vance's bestselling 2016 memoir, appealed to readers hoping for insight on the motivations of the communities backing Trump, even if the book never even mentions him. After the candidate won and took office, George Orwell's *1984* displaced Vance atop Amazon's sales ranking, meaning readers were suddenly less concerned with how we got here than with where we were headed. Ben Lerner's heralded 2019 novel *The Topeka School* drew upon the shifting tactics of high school debaters a generation ago to explain the rapid-fire rhetoric and macho posturing of right-wing politics in our time. And shortly after Trump pledged to "dominate the streets" of American cities where protesters were demonstrating against racism and police violence, books such as Robin DiAngelo's *White Fragility* (2018) and Ibram X. Kendi's *How to Be an Antiracist* (2019) became bestsellers.

Every book, it seems, can be a Trump book.

My own concern is not how we got here, but how we thought here. I'm not interested in identifying that *one book* from decades ago that supposedly saw it all coming. I focus on the books and debates of this moment—from the heartland to the border, from the resistance on the left to the civil war on the right, from the battles over truth to the fears about democracy—not out of some misplaced now-more-than-everism but to preserve a snapshot of how we grappled with the Trump era in real time. I want to remember what I thought about it, too.

Some of the ideas I explore here build on the essays and reviews

I have written in the *Washington Post* during the Trump years. Obsessive *Post* readers may recognize my views on particular authors or subjects from these earlier writings, but they may also notice that, on occasion, my conclusions about specific books have shifted during flight. Fresh arguments and events can place a book in a new light, whether brightened, dimmed, or filtered. And often a work reads differently when in dialogue with additional books over a longer timeline, or when it is read in a new circumstance in the life of the nation or the life of the reader. The most rewarding books are the ones I never stop reconsidering and reviewing in my mind, even if I never open them again.

I realize it may be early to judge the books of the Trump era; almost certainly, the most illuminating works about this period have yet to be written. Future memoirs will offer new details and settle old disputes (Don McGahn, Robert Mueller, Kirstjen Nielsen, and Anthony Fauci rank highest on my wish list), while official and reported investigations will deepen the record. I also understand that using nonfiction books alone to assess the intellectual output of this time may seem limiting. With so many relevant forms of expression available—newspaper and magazine reporting, novels, drama, music, poetry, film, television, speeches, podcasts, photography—there is something oddly nostalgic about relying solely on words that are printed and bound.

But if journalism is still history's first draft, then books remain the first draft of how we think about that history, how we seek our place in it. That is the spirit of this exercise, to which I bring nothing more than the discipline of a dedicated reader and the zeal of a new American. The 2016 presidential election was my first as a U.S. citizen and voter, and Trump's rise in national politics has coincided almost exactly with my time as a book critic. The demands of both literature and citizenship will forever shape the way I view this presidency.

As both reader and citizen, I believe that the early intellectual response to the Trump presidency is of enormous consequence. This president has challenged principles, practices, and standards of American life—on the accountability and legitimacy of our leaders, on who can take part in the American experiment. With that challenge in mind, the books that matter most right now are not necessarily those revealing White House intrigue, policy disputes, or official scandals, no matter how crucial those subjects. They are, instead, the books that enable and ennoble a national reexamination—one that Trump has attempted to carry out on his own and on our behalf. They are the books that show how our current conflicts fit into the nation's story, that hold fast to the American tradition of always seeing ourselves anew.

They are the books on the white working class that do not oversimplify its motives or its politics, and the resistance volumes that resist dogma and exclusion. They are the studies on the decline of truth that leave room for self-doubt, and the works on immigration that find newcomers changing America from within, and being changed by it, too. They are the memoirs of race and identity that see the individual behind every group struggle, and the reports of White House mayhem that reveal the long-term erosion of the office and our government. They are the volumes on democracy that identify today's battles as part of that endless fight to live up to our self-professed, self-evident truths, and that show that striving, while failing, to reach them is not just a feature of our system but its definition.

Such books are not beholden to this moment, which is why they reveal so much about it. The most essential books of the Trump era are scarcely about Trump at all.

ONE

HEARTLANDIA

I keep running into Ed Harry.

Harry, in his seventies, is a former labor organizer from Luzerne County, Pennsylvania, and an air force veteran who served in Vietnam. He's also a lifelong Democrat, even a delegate to the 1992 party convention that nominated Bill Clinton. "I wasn't just a guy who voted straight Democrat up and down the ballot, it was a religion to me, it was my identity," he told a reporter.

Then, in 2016, Ed Harry cast his ballot for Donald Trump.

Harry's shift, and that of other voters like him, became a subject of endless fascination for journalists, academics, intellectuals, and assorted authors exploring America's heartland to examine the politics of white grievance. Are Trump's working-class supporters driven mainly by their economic struggles or—in that politest euphemism of our age—their cultural anxieties? Who is to blame for their plight? Is Trump helping them or just using them?

A descendant of nineteenth-century Welsh immigrants and a son and grandson of coal miners, Harry is an especially popular emblem for the heartland set: he is featured in not one but two prominent books explaining the Trump voter, published five months apart in 2018. The overlap reveals more than the formulaic qualities of the genre. It turns out that Harry's political impulses vary significantly from one book to the other—in ways that neatly fit the authors' divergent explanations of how Trump won the presidency.

In *The Great Revolt*, by Salena Zito and Brad Todd, Harry is motivated mainly by economic and political concerns. He worries about trade deals that encourage companies to relocate jobs overseas and he despises political dynasties like the Clintons and Bushes. Harry mistrusts big anything—"big banks, big Wall Street, big corporations, the establishment of both parties and their lobbyists, and the big media corporations," he ticks off—and he attacks Democrats for abandoning the working class. "Blue-collar America essentially had the door shut in its face," he complains. Zito and Todd seem proud of their archetype. "If anyone went to central casting looking for blue-collar union boss type and Harry was in line, he would be the first man picked." He is, the authors say, "the kind of guy you want on your side."

In Ben Bradlee Jr.'s *The Forgotten*, however, Harry has more expansive motives. Sure, he rails against the North American Free Trade Agreement and the Trans-Pacific Partnership, but he also eagerly enlists in the culture wars. "To me there are more important issues than getting an extra door for transsexuals in public buildings," he tells Bradlee, complaining that the Democrats have gone "so far left." In the pages of *The Forgotten*, Harry morphs from central casting into a 9/11 truther ("you'll never convince me that two planes caused the buildings to collapse") who listens to conspiracy theorist Alex Jones, questions the official story behind the Oklahoma City bombing, and believes that Black Lives Matter protesters have secretly received tens of millions of dollars from George Soros. He accepts Trump's claim that 3 million undocumented immigrants voted illegally in 2016, and even considers that estimate too modest, because Barack Obama, Harry assures, urged immigrants to "come in and vote." In this book, Harry does seem like the kind of guy you want on your side, as long as you're on a very particular side.

So why does Ed Harry, salt of the earth in one volume, go scorched-earth in another?

The answer may say less about the politics of a single voter than about how a single voter can be politicized by those seeking to explain him. Yes, the white working class may have helped put Trump in the White House, but it has also become a literary and sociological device advancing the political interpretations of the writers and intellectuals suddenly fixated on this demographic.

For Bradlee, a former senior editor with the *Boston Globe*, Trump's campaign message constituted a "nostalgic paean to a simpler, whiter time in America," and it resonated with voters who felt that the country was being "inundated" with immigrants. He warns that Trump promotes a "retro-tribalism that is trending toward the old separate-but-equal ethos"—and naturally he emphasizes the parallel views he finds among Trump voters. (Part of Bradlee's book features a white nationalist and former Klansman in Luzerne County who considers Trump the greatest president of his lifetime.) By contrast, Zito and Todd relish Trump's efforts to tear down elite institutions, including political parties and the news media, and to defend traditional America as they see it. The Trump voters in their book are kindhearted people who speak in thoughtful, folksy, quotable paragraphs, whose smiles and laughs and love of life are all "infectious."

The debates over the Trump voter have produced a rush of such books examining, debunking, or somehow channeling the white working class. They include histories, memoirs, polemics, academic surveys, and near-fetishistic dispatches from writers pulling up to every chrome-counter diner (they must be chrome) and shuttered factory ("shuttered" is an obligatory adjective) in America. The books' individual literary merits vary widely; some are delightful, others insufferable. Analytically, they offer a mish-mash of insight, data, blame, poignancy, and condescension, with a generous helping of partisanship. As often as not, the heartland chroniclers interpret their subject through their prisms and biases, projecting onto the white working class their own wishes and wor-ries, confirming whatever they advocate or imagine.

The quest to assign blame is a powerful impulse of the heartland genre. Many of the writers appear driven to find one overriding culprit for the economic and even spiritual struggles of the white working class, and where they choose to attach culpability is a product of their research, reporting, and experience—and also their politics. Blame yourself or anyone but yourself; blame the community or distant politicians; blame job-stealing immigrants or soulless corporations or knee-jerk emotions. The possibilities are endless, overlapping, and conflicting.

J. D. Vance's eternal bestseller, *Hillbilly Elegy*, appeared in the summer of 2016, precisely when the Trump voter had become a subject of earnest cable-news hits and incessant cultural decon-struction. A memoir of the author's childhood in southwestern Ohio, his roots in the Appalachian region of Kentucky, and his path from deprivation to Yale Law School, *Hillbilly Elegy* is affect-ing and inspirational. "Americans call them hillbillies, rednecks, or white trash," Vance writes of his community. "I call them neigh-bors, friends, and family."

But he also calls them out. In Vance's telling, the spiritual and material poverty—the "hub of misery"—enveloping his child-hood in the 1980s and 1990s was almost always the fault of those suffering it. You could walk around his home of Middletown, Ohio, Vance writes, "and find not a single person aware of his own laziness." In towns such as his, "many folks talk about working more than they actually work." His explanation for that dissonance is damning: it is a culture that "encourages social decay instead of counteracting it," a multigenerational legacy perpetuating self-pity and recklessness. If Vance could change one thing about the white working class, he asserts, he would eradicate this pervasive helplessness, "a feeling that you have little control over your life and a willingness to blame everyone but yourself."

Vance identifies the guilty party—and his own worldview— early in life. He saw how people "gamed the welfare system," he writes, recalling his days as a grocery store cashier during high school. They would buy packs of soda with food stamps only to sell them at a discount for cash, or they'd ring up separate orders, using food stamps for food and their own money for booze. "Most of us were struggling to get by. . . . But a large minority was content to live off the dole," he complains. This willingness to point the finger inward helps explain the bipartisan appeal of *Hillbilly Elegy*: the book confirms liberal elites' suspicions about the pathologies of the deplorable pro-Trump white working class but also ratifies the bootstraps ethos of mainstream conservatism. Even Vance's path to Yale Law, with stops in the marine corps, Iraq and Ohio State, affirms the favored meritocracies of the Left (Ivy League, check) and of the Right (military service, check). As Mamaw, the tough-talking grandmother who helped raise Vance, reminds him, "Never be like these fucking losers who think the deck is stacked against them."

But you don't have to be a loser to blame a stacked deck—you just need to see the world through different politics. Sarah Smarsh also endured chronic poverty, the kind in which all your relatives' old letters are about looking for jobs, searching for homes, and hoping for money. In *Heartland*, her 2018 memoir, Smarsh, a fifth-generation Kansan with "roots so deep in the country where I was raised that I rode tractors on the same land where my ancestors rode wagons," argues that a poor work ethic was hardly their challenge. "Being as we got up before dawn to do chores and didn't quit until after dark," she notes wryly, "it was plain that the problem with our outcomes wasn't lack of hard work."

Smarsh probes more deeply than Vance into the cultural, personal, and economic identities vying for power over her. Being born both female and poor were "marks against my claims on respect," she writes, while the very concept of the white working class (a term she first encountered as an adult) mixes racial privilege and economic deprivation, "an obvious, apolitical fact for those of us who lived that juxtaposition every day." Yet the difference between *Hillbilly Elegy* and *Heartland* is more than the difference between the stories of a once-poor white man and a once-poor white woman, more than the distance between the mountains and the plains. It is an ideological divide.

Unlike Vance, Smarsh contends that the working poor blame themselves far too much. "If your life was a mess, we thought, you brought it on yourself," she writes, even if the offenders were big businesses or Wall Street or "things so far away and impenetrable to us that all we could do was shake our heads." And while Vance chastises those too quick to rely on government help, Smarsh recalls the shame of even considering such assistance. "The clearest evidence of America's contempt toward the struggling might be in its approach to welfare programs," she writes, "framed by public policy and commentary as something so detestable that my family refused to apply when they qualified."

That contempt has a name and a source. Smarsh notes that

she and her younger brother were born just weeks before each of Ronald Reagan's presidential election victories, and she lays much responsibility at the feet of the fortieth president. She derides theories of trickle-down economics—"as though we were standing outside with our mouths open praying for money to rain"—and excoriates Reagan's legacy. "We would be able to map our lives against the destruction of the working class: the demise of the family farm, the dismantling of public health care, the defunding of public schools, wages so stagnant that full-time workers could no longer pay the bills."

Blame can be found within the individual or in distant forces, but it can also be all around you. According to *Washington Examiner* columnist Timothy P. Carney, the problem is not insufficient federal assistance, personal shiftlessness, new immigrants, or lousy trade deals. Instead, the white working class is suffering from the death of community. "Much of America has been left abandoned, without the web of human connections and institutions that make the good life possible," Carney writes in *Alienated America*, published in 2019. Drawing inspiration from thinkers such as Alexis de Tocqueville and Robert Putnam as well as from contemporary survey data and personal interviews, Carney argues that regions of the country with weak family and community life were attracted to Trump's message of retrograde nostalgia, while regions with stronger social ties—more athletic leagues, churches, and charities—resisted it. His key contribution to the heartland genre is the distinction he makes between the lives of individual voters and the condition of their communities. "Trump's core supporters weren't necessarily poorer than other voters," he emphasizes. "But they lived in *places* that were worse off, culturally and economically, than other places."

Alienated America reads like *Bowling Alone II: The Revenge*, in

which the social, economic, and political consequences of a fray-
ing civil society are laid bare. Carney dwells on areas of the country with growing income gaps and rising deaths due to alcoholism,
drug overdoses, and suicide, particularly among non-college-
educated white men. "If you were studying Pennsylvania and Ohio
in the 2016 election, you could have predicted a county's swing to
Trump by looking at its rate of overdose deaths," he notes, and he
points to the prevalence of working-age men who seem to have
dropped out of the labor market, out of school, out of family—
out of life. "This looks like the 'American carnage' Donald Trump
lamented in his inaugural address," Carney worries. He acknowledges, too, that racism is an undeniable aspect of Trump's appeal,
especially for white native-born voters in areas with high inflows
of immigrants. Over time, Carney hopes, new cultures and norms
can develop, but in the meantime, "diversity makes trust and social
capital harder to come by."

This is a thoughtful work, and the author a sympathetic guide,
even if Carney's stirring call for strengthened civic and community ties always seems to track his own preference for religious
observance and conservative values. Carney blames the sexual
revolution, the retreat from marriage, out-of-wedlock births, an
overpowering federal government, and the decline of organized religion for distancing Americans from their communities. He longs
for "middle institutions" between the government and the individual and "third places" outside of work or home where Americans
can find one another. For Carney, who cites his own Christianity
as well as Judaism and Islam as intensely communal faiths, there
is no better third place than a house of worship, which serves as a
pillar of community and family life. "It's hard to have faith without
family," he writes. "It's hard to keep families strong without faith.

It's hard to keep families or faith strong without communities to support them."

Absent such efforts, Carney concludes, alienated locales will remain susceptible to politicians peddling grievance, division, and restoration. The irony of such communities throwing their lot in with Trump is that the problems afflicting the white working class "cannot be solved or even significantly ameliorated by any president, or by the central government at all," Carney argues. "America's illness—the condition making the American Dream seem so dead to so many—is by its nature a local malady."

In this telling, the true maladies of the heartland break through conventional explanations involving racism and poverty. "They tell a story that does mess up the 'economic anxiety' account of Trump and working class white woe," Carney writes, "but it also complicates the 'cultural resentment' story."

Yet both are stories that chroniclers of the heartland literature find irresistible.

No sooner had Trump begun winning primaries than writers analyzing the heartland began parsing two competing reasons for his ascent: race versus class. Does the president appeal to white working-class voters because he pledges to ease their economic struggles or because he stokes their prejudice? This has become one of the most enduring political debates of the era and a standard feature of the heartland lit. Yet the most compelling accounts are those that show how race and class offer reinforcing explanations rather than conflicting ones.

Memoirists such as Vance and Smarsh do not focus on racial strife in their stories and reflections. In *Hillbilly Elegy*, Vance writes that his community's animosity toward President Obama, for instance, was less about race than about the insecurities Obama elicited. The president's elite education and wholesome family made him seem alien to people in Vance's hometown "for reasons that have nothing to do with skin color," he contends. (It's not Vance's most convincing moment.) And in *Heartland*, Smarsh emphasizes class with the eloquence of the royally pissed off. "To be made invisible as a class is an invalidation," she writes. "With invalidation comes shame. A shame that deep—being poor in a place full of narratives about middle and upper classes—can make you feel like what you are is a failure."

That's a feeling America's white underclass has experienced for centuries, argues Louisiana State University historian Nancy Isenberg in *White Trash*, a thorough and gritty work published in 2016, just a few weeks before *Hillbilly Elegy*. For all the country's self-styled egalitarianism, Isenberg contends, America has always had a class system, with the white working class hanging on near the lower rungs. "We can no longer ignore the stagnant, expendable bottom layers of society in explaining the national identity," Isenberg writes, reciting the litany of pejoratives used to depict the white working class: Offscourings. Bogtrotters. Rascals. Rubbish. Squatters. Crackers. Clay-eaters. Hillbillies. Rednecks. And white trash.

In Isenberg's view, racial division is a tool that elites deploy to keep all lower classes down. "Poor whites are still taught to hate—but not to hate those who are keeping them in line," she writes. In her eagerness to elevate class as the nation's overriding divide, however, Isenberg sometimes reduces race's role in American life to fleeting asides or awkward equivalences. She emphasizes, for instance, that Lyndon Johnson's Great Society "targeted both urban ghettos *and* impoverished white areas of Appalachia," and she recasts the Civil War as a class struggle: Northerners looked down on poor Southern whites as proof that reliance on slavery weakened free white workers, while Confederates countered that the North debased itself by using white labor for menial tasks. "It is no exaggeration to say that in the grand scheme of things, Union and Confederate leaders saw the war as a clash of class systems wherein the superior civilization would reign triumphant," Isenberg argues. (Note: Whenever a formulation begins with "It is no exaggeration that . . . ," it is safe to assume that the rest of it contains an exaggeration.)

When considering the racial attitudes of their white working-class subjects, Zito and Todd are generous in giving them the benefit of the doubt. "The professional Left focuses heavily on race-related questions in analyzing the Trump vote," they write in *The Great Revolt*, "but race-tinged subjects were rarely cited by Trump voters interviewed for this book." I suppose waiting for interview subjects to forthrightly volunteer their racism is one way to find out. But in *Identity Crisis* (2018), political scientists John Sides, Michael Tesler, and Lynn Vavreck draw on survey data to argue that the economic insecurities of Trump voters, while real, mattered most when animated by racial vitriol. In other words, white working-class voters are less concerned about losing their own jobs than about seeing white workers losing their jobs to *those people*—immigrants or minority groups.

Racial anxieties drove economic ones, the authors contend, a fusing they refer to as "racialized economics." And because the 2016 campaign was fought over culture, race, religion, and immigration—rather than, say, entitlement spending—voters' underlying attitudes on those matters were suddenly "activated," they write. "It was not the voters who changed in 2016 so much as the choices they were given." Who truly belongs in America? That is what "Stronger Together" versus "Make America Great Again" was really all about.

Once activated, such attitudes are hard to shed; some Americans even give their lives to uphold them. That is the argument of *Dying of Whiteness*, a 2019 study by Jonathan Metzl, a medical doctor and sociology professor at Vanderbilt University. Through interviews and surveys, Metzl considers why low-income white men in Missouri, Tennessee, and Kansas oppose government policies and programs that could help them and their communities, such as expanded health insurance and greater education spending. His answer highlights how racism translates into support for self-defeating policies that worsen economic conditions and, in turn, further aggravate racial animosities.

White working-class men, worried that specific government programs help immigrants or gang members or welfare recipients, decide they'd rather forgo benefits themselves than share them with so many undesirables. "White America's investment in maintaining an imagined place atop a racial hierarchy—that is, an investment in a sense of whiteness—ironically harms the aggregate well-being of US whites as a demographic group," Metzl concludes. He speaks with men such as Trevor, a forty-one-year-old uninsured former cabdriver in Tennessee who uses a walker and suffers from hepatitis C yet derides the Affordable Care Act because, as he puts it, "no way I want my tax dollars paying for Mexicans or welfare queens." Racial anxieties and antigovernment mistrust are not just relevant to how particular individuals may feel, Metzl argues, but they also become institutionalized into laws and policies "in ways that carry negative implications for everyone."

Those negative health implications can include what Princeton University economists Anne Case and Angus Deaton call "deaths of despair"—a surge in fatalities over the past two decades due to suicides, drug overdoses, and alcoholism-related liver disease among the middle-aged white working class, especially those lacking college degrees. In their book *Deaths of Despair and the Future of Capitalism*, published in early 2020, Case and Deaton estimate that some 600,000 deceased Americans would still be alive today if the steadily declining mortality rates of the late twentieth century had not suddenly reversed direction. That number is close to the estimated U.S. deaths due to HIV/AIDS since the early 1980s, they write, or also "what we might see during the ravages of an infectious disease, like the Great Influenza Pandemic of 1918." Long before the first recorded coronavirus infection in the United States, white working-class America was experiencing a slow-moving pandemic of its own.

Case and Deaton completed this book before the onset of COVID-19, but their diagnosis is entirely relevant to the crisis. Mass unemployment and mass infection, occurring simultaneously in a nation where health insurance often depends on employment, threaten to both prove and aggravate the conditions Case and Deaton describe. "Jobs are not just the source of money; they are the basis for the rituals, customs, and routines of working-class life," they write. "Destroy work and, in the end, working-class life cannot survive."

The authors do not blame these deaths of despair on any personal or cultural failings of the dying. With echoes of Smarsh's and Carney's books, Case and Deaton instead point to the wreckage of manufacturing towns, falling wages, low levels of education, the dysfunction of the American health care industry, and the decline of community life. Well in advance of social distancing, Americans had already grown far too distant from one another.

Works such as *Identity Crisis* and *Dying of Whiteness* put prejudice closer to the center of Trump's political appeal, while *Deaths of Despair and the Future of Capitalism* emphasizes the macroeconomic and policy forces behind the suffering of middle-aged working-class white Americans. Yet they all succeed in showing how economic and cultural forces feed off one another. That may be why, in *Alienated America*, Carney attempts to obliterate the race-or-class debate altogether. "It becomes absurd to argue over whether Trump voters and angry blue-collar Americans are upset about economics or culture," Carney writes. "They're inextricable."

Many of the intellectuals who have traveled through Trump Country (because that's what you call a chunk of America when its only salience is electoral) often generalize what they encounter into a collective feeling. Anger? Despondence? Hope? Resentment? Naivete? The search for a blanket emotion is one of the animating principles of the heartland literature.

Feelings are the point of *Strangers in Their Own Land*, a 2016 work by Arlie Russell Hochschild, a sociologist at the University of California at Berkeley. Hochschild made ten trips to southwestern Louisiana from 2010 to 2016, aiming to understand "how life *feels* to people on the right—that is, the emotion that underlies politics." The unspoken assumption is that life for conservatives must necessarily feel quite different than for other Americans. That belief guides, and ruins, this book.

Consider that Hochschild prepped for her travels from Berkeley to the Bayou by reading *Atlas Shrugged*, because she figures conservatives are into that. "If Ayn Rand appealed to them, I imagined, they're probably pretty selfish, tough, cold people," she confides, and is pleasantly surprised to find them kind, even "charitable." Still, Hochschild suffers culture shock. "I felt like I was in a foreign country," she explains. Rural Louisiana was just so different! "No *New York Times* at the newsstand, almost no organic produce in grocery stores or farmers' markets, no foreign films in movie houses, few small cars, fewer petite sizes in clothing stores, fewer pedestrians speaking foreign languages into cell phones—indeed, fewer pedestrians." People even prayed before dinner, she noticed. It was all so weird.

Hochschild's conversations with residents of Lake Charles and other Louisiana towns are illuminating, yet the author cannot resist placing everyone she meets into clichéd, oversimplified categories that sound like they were dreamed up in the faculty lounge. There are the Team Loyalists, who stick with the Republican Party. The Worshippers, who have learned to live with disappointment. The Cowboys, who celebrate risk and squint at government regulation. And those daring to cut across categories are dubbed the Rebels. (This taxonomical obsession comes standard in the white-working-class books. In *The Great Revolt*, for instance, Zito and Todd list Rotary Reliables, Silent Suburban Moms, King Cyrus Christians, and other groupings that, as even the authors admit, sometimes "fit the familiar portraits of lower-income whites painted by journalists routinely since the election.")

Such oblivious reductionism would be harmless if it only rendered *Strangers in Their Own Land* annoying, which it does. But Hochschild also clutters her account with her capitalized and italicized theories of the Right, in which contrivance and condescension spar for supremacy. She hopes to scale the Empathy Wall (which makes us hostile to those with different beliefs) so she can resolve the Great Paradox (why low-income conservative voters support politicians who oppose programs and policies that could help them). Most important, Hochschild unveils the Deep Story, one that explains how life *feels* to people inhabiting that strange foreign land, the Right:

> You are patiently standing in a long line leading up a hill, as in a
> pilgrimage. You are situated in the middle of this line, along with

others who are also white, older, Christian, predominantly male, some with college degrees, some not.

Just over the brow of the hill is the American Dream, the goal of everyone waiting in line. . . .

You've suffered long hours, layoffs, and exposure to dangerous chemicals at work, and received reduced pensions. You have shown moral character through trial by fire, and the American Dream of prosperity and security is a reward for all of this, showing who you have been and are—a badge of honor. . . .

Look! You see people *cutting in line ahead of you!* You're following the rules. They aren't. As they cut in, it feels like you are being moved back. How can they just do that? Who are they? Some are black. Through affirmative action plans, pushed by the federal government, they are being given preference for places in colleges and universities, apprenticeships, jobs, welfare payments, and free lunches. . . . Women, immigrants, refugees, public sector workers—where will it end? Your money is running through a liberal sympathy sieve you don't control or agree with. . . .

But it's people like *you* who have made this country great. You feel uneasy. It has to be said: the line cutters irritate you. . . .

You are a stranger in your own land. You do not recognize yourself in how others see you. It is a struggle to feel seen and honored. . . . [Y]ou are slipping backward.

This is not a story anyone tells Hochschild outright; it is her own creation. "I constructed this deep story to represent—in metaphorical form—the hopes, fears, pride, shame, resentment, and anxiety in the lives of those I talked with," the author explains.

Hochschild may be right about her deep story. When she gets back in touch with her "Tea Party friends" in Louisiana, as she invariably calls them, and runs her theories by them, the charitable folk assure her she is correct. And in *Dying of Whiteness*, which was published two and a half years later, Metzl reaches similar conclusions in a different part of the country. But Hochschild seems so intent on finding support for the story that she disregards alternative explanations that don't rely on leading questions or imposed frameworks. For example, Hochschild wonders: Why, in a region where industrial contamination is such a problem for the health of residents and wildlife, do so many people support politicians promising to slash the Environmental Protection Agency?

This is one of Hochschild's great paradoxes, but it loses greatness when you consider the residents' wretched experience with environmental regulation. Louisiana authorities had given permits to a drilling outfit that ended up creating a massive local sinkhole, Hochschild reports. The state environmental agency had failed to properly oversee companies discharging hazardous waste into Louisiana waters. And health authorities had even issued guidelines on how best to eat polluted fish. ("Trimming the fat and skin on finfish, and removing the hepatopancreas from crabs, will reduce the amount of contaminants.") In this light, distrust of environmental regulators is hardly paradoxical. It is logical.

Hochschild attends a Trump rally in New Orleans just days before the candidate's victory in the Louisiana primary, and she is struck by the collective fervor. "His supporters have been in mourning for a lost way of life," she writes, divining the feelings of the crowd. "Joined together with others like themselves, they now feel hopeful, joyous, elated. . . . As if magically lifted, *they are no longer strangers in their own land*." Trump not only fits the deep story—he plays to his supporters' emotions and grievances—but also provides its neat resolution. "While economic self-interest is never entirely absent," the author concludes, "what I discovered was the profound importance of emotional self-interest."

But Hochschild is also captive to her own feelings, and her own politics, too, a condition that, depending on an author's degree of self-awareness, can lead to insight or delusion. In the book's preface, Hochschild laments that people on the right oppose government programs that assist working-class families, protect the environment, and combat homelessness. Such ideals all "face the same firmly closed door," she writes. "If we want government help in achieving any of these goals, I realized, we need to understand those who see government more as problem than solution. And so it was that I began my journey to the heart of the American right."

Strangers in Their Own Land, then, should not be read as simply a sociologist's effort to glimpse the lives and feelings of rural conservatives, but also as a means to a particular end—an end toward which the author sees conservatives as obstacles to overcome.

That's a deep story, too.

No matter how many times its author traveled to those distant wilds of Louisiana, *Strangers in Their Own Land* nonetheless reflects the perils of casting one's eye over the white working class with partisan preconception. So it's ironic that one of the tougher critiques of this approach would come from another California academic whose direct knowledge of the white working class seems based mainly on conversations with her eighth-grade-dropout father-in-law and her enthusiastic reading of J. D. Vance and, yes, Arlie Russell Hochschild.

In *White Working Class* (2017), Joan C. Williams excoriates the hypocrisy, condescension, and "class cluelessness" that characterize much of the fascination with her title demographic. A professor at the University of California's Hastings College of the Law in San Francisco and a graduate of Yale and Harvard, Williams organizes her book around those nasty little questions liberal elites supposedly mutter among themselves about the blue-collared folk. Why don't they move to where the jobs are or get more education? Don't they know that manufacturing work is gone for good? Why do they resent government benefits? Don't they realize the Democrats are trying to help? Why do they seem so attached to Trump? Is it racism, sexism, or what?

Williams believes that if such questions are posed today—and here we must take her word for that—it's because for decades left-leaning elites have been unconcerned about the white working class. "During an era when wealthy white Americans have learned to sympathetically imagine the lives of the poor, people of color, and LGBTQ people, the white working class has been insulted or ignored precisely during the period when their economic fortunes tanked," she writes.

On racial prejudice, Williams excuses no one. "Let's state right up front that racism is an issue in the white working class, and it goes back a long way," she writes. Working-class racism is "more explicit" than its elite variants, Williams contends, but today's upper classes are guilty of racism, too. "Among the professional elite, where the coin of the realm is merit, people of color are constructed as lacking in merit," she writes. "Among the white working class, where the coin of the realm is morality, people of color are constructed as lacking in that quality." Even worse, white elites happily distance themselves from white racism by dumping it all on the less privileged, dismissing their anger as racism and sexism, "beneath our dignity to take seriously," Williams writes. Such class condescension, she fears, has pushed portions of the white working class to the far right.

White Working Class is far from the most beautifully written work in this collection—Smarsh's *Heartland* gets my vote—and it indulges in some class condescension of its own, as when

Williams implies that a solution to working-class woes might be for the masses to take part in, effectively, a propaganda initiative. "We need a bipartisan campaign to educate the American public about the positive roles that government plays in their lives," she writes, proposing a video series in which ordinary Americans express gratitude for sewers, schools, and highways, shouting out "Thank you, Uncle Sam!" at the end of each installment. Even so, *White Working Class* is useful as a counterweight to works that reduce the white working class to one particular politics, problem, or story, however deep that story may be. "The working class doesn't want to be examined like some tribe in a faraway land," Williams warns.

It is hard to resist that impulse, but in *We're Still Here* (2019), sociologist Jennifer M. Silva does her best to look upon the rural working class without blame or pity. Silva spent two years interviewing working-class residents in Pennsylvania coal towns, a period that overlapped with the 2016 presidential campaign and election. She initially planned to study white working-class conservatives, but the political landscape she discovered there surprised her. "I had trouble finding people who felt strongly enough about politics to fully identify with a political party or advocate for specific policy platforms," Silva acknowledges. While many of the people she interviewed would vote for Trump, even more did not intend to vote at all, she reports. "They feel empowered by their knowledge that they have not been foolish enough to believe in something larger than themselves," Silva writes, a sentiment both poignant and tragic. To them, trusting the political system is a sign of foolishness; residents openly mock Silva for sporting her I VOTED sticker on Election Day, for "daring to believe that our democracy would be responsive to my voice."

Much has been made of how white heartlanders embraced

Trump for his outsider persona, but in *We're Still Here*, they see themselves as the permanent outsiders, beyond the reach or interest of the political system. More than embracing any party or politician, they resort to self-improvement manuals—books such as *You Can Heal Your Heart* by Louise Hay and David Kessler and *Codependent No More* by Melody Beattie were popular among Silva's interviewees—and conspiratorial thinking about a corrupt leadership class. The author's conversations with Graham, a white twenty-five-year-old nursing-home worker, veer from fraudulent elections to FEMA concentration camps to how the buildings really came down on 9/11 to how the Sandy Hook Elementary School massacre and the Boston Marathon bombing were "a bunch of bullshit." Graham repeatedly pauses to ask Silva if she is truly informed ("you know that, right?") and finds comfort in grasping realities no one else sees. "It's not conspiracy theory, it's conspiracy factual," he insists. Both the self-help industry and internet conspiracies so popular with local residents are "solitary strategies that serve to turn them inward or against each other," Silva explains. For all the obsession over how Pennsylvania, Michigan, and Wisconsin voted in 2016 and whether the states will go red or blue in 2020, it is this isolation from politics that looms as a pervasive force. It's not quite a Deep Story, just one told with depth.

Silva is one of the few students of the heartland who emphasizes that its residents are not, well, solely white, and she devotes her time and attention accordingly. "In my interviews with white residents of the coal region, I repeatedly heard about the 'newcomers,' black and Puerto Rican people who were moving into this rural, racially homogeneous area. . . . Rather than write about these ethnic minorities as silent 'others,' moral foils, and political scapegoats, I wanted to treat the newcomers as active participants." The African Americans and Latinos that Silva interviews originally hail from low-income, high-crime urban areas in the Northeast; they moved to find jobs they can keep and rents they can afford. They portray their new home as "a place where they can tirelessly transform their own shameful pasts—selling drugs, going to prison, perpetrating violence, being hurt or vulnerable— into their children's redeemed futures." Yet they seem even less likely than white residents to trust the political system enough to engage with it. "I'm a proud American," Eva, a twenty-one-year-old recovering heroin addict, tells Silva. "But I would be a lot more proud if America really stood for something."

We're Still Here is an odd title for this book. Silva's subjects hardly see themselves as a "we," as a class or a collective; their stories are individual narratives of pain and (occasional) uplift. Silva is frustrated by this—"we have to ask why disadvantaged people refuse to connect to others in the first place," she writes—but she does not judge them for it. Instead, Silva reserves her blame and judgment for those who blame and judge, and in so doing becomes that rare heartland writer to overtly criticize another voice of the genre.

"When I read *Hillbilly Elegy*, a memoir of upward mobility, I felt intense anger and protectiveness toward working-class people," Silva writes at the end of her book. To her, Vance's writing "smacks of self-righteousness, a harsh unwillingness to acknowledge how economic inequality produces real suffering, or how the barriers to mobility are devastatingly real." Her frustration is not that the people she meets lack individual agency, but that many of them have concluded that even their best efforts don't make much difference, and that any sense of collective interest or power—that "we" she longs to see—remains an illusion.

• • •

Perhaps it is too much to ask of any book to fully explain a contested and loosely defined demographic, one rediscovered and relitigated in a polarized time. In *The Heartland* (2019), University of Illinois historian Kristin Hoganson considers the contradictory notions Americans imagine when trying to describe the place. "Beset by disunity, they imagine their nation as a body with a protected, essential core: the heartland," she writes. It can be "the steadfast stronghold of the nation in the age of mobility and connectedness, the crucible of resistance to the global, the America of America First." But, Hoganson explains, it can also conjure a "provincial wasteland," a place that is "out of touch, out of date, out of style . . . the mythic past that white ethnonationalists wish to return to."

That's why, according to the varied authors and works of the heartland genre, the members of the white working class are overwhelmingly victims of their own culture, or invariably defrauded by amorphous external forces. They are either kind and goodhearted, or prejudiced and resentful. They are fooled by the stories they tell themselves about government and dependency, or imprisoned by class. They are abandoned by institutions, derided by self-involved elites, manipulated by opportunistic politicians—or energized by them.

Halfway through *Hillbilly Elegy*, when a young J. D. is living with his grandmother in Middletown and griping about the working-class types he sees standing in grocery lines with food stamps in one hand and cell phones in the other, he turns to big books for answers. Still in high school, he reads William Julius Wilson's *The Truly Disadvantaged* and Charles Murray's *Losing Ground*. Vance didn't entirely understand these texts at the time, he admits, yet he grasped enough to realize that "neither of these books fully answered the questions that plagued me." Why were drugs and strife and financial struggles so prevalent in his neighborhood? Why the desperate sadness that never seemed to lift? "It would be years," he concludes, "before I learned that no single book, or expert, or field could fully explain the problems of hillbillies in modern America."

No single book—and certainly no single voter. But that doesn't keep authors from trying. In a book published in November 2019, *When the Center Does Not Hold: Leading in an Age of Polarization*, David Brubaker begins his first chapter by introducing an old friend of ours:

"Ed Harry is the son of a coal miner, a veteran of the war in Vietnam, and a resident of Luzerne County. . . ."

BOOKS DISCUSSED

Ben Bradlee Jr. *The Forgotten: How the People of One Pennsylvania County Elected Donald Trump and Changed America.* Little, Brown, 2018.

Timothy P. Carney. *Alienated America: Why Some Places Thrive While Others Collapse.* Harper, 2019.

Anne Case and Angus Deaton. *Deaths of Despair and the Future of Capitalism.* Princeton University Press, 2020.

Arlie Russell Hochschild. *Strangers in Their Own Land: Anger and Mourning on the American Right.* The New Press, 2016.

Kristin L. Hoganson. *The Heartland: An American History.* Penguin Press, 2019.

Nancy Isenberg. *White Trash: The 400-Year Untold History of Class in America.* Viking, 2016.

Jonathan Metzl. *Dying of Whiteness: How the Politics of Racial Resentment Is Killing America's Heartland.* Basic Books, 2019.

John Sides, Michael Tesler, and Lynn Vavreck. *Identity Crisis: The 2016 Presidential Campaign and the Battle for the Meaning of America.* Princeton University Press, 2018.

Jennifer M. Silva. *We're Still Here: Pain and Politics in the Heart of America.* Oxford University Press, 2019.

Sarah Smarsh. *Heartland: A Memoir of Working Hard and Being Broke in the Richest Country on Earth.* Scribner, 2018.

J. D. Vance. *Hillbilly Elegy: A Memoir of Family and Culture in Crisis.* Harper, 2016.

Joan C. Williams. *White Working Class: Overcoming Class Cluelessness in America.* Harvard Business Review Press, 2017.

Salena Zito and Brad Todd. *The Great Revolt: Inside the Populist Coalition Reshaping American Politics.* Crown Forum, 2018.

TWO

RESISTIBLE

You saw them. You probably read a couple. You may have even written one.

They began invading in-boxes and Facebook feeds across the country in the early hours of November 9, 2016, and continued for days, weeks, even months to come, countless renditions of what became an instantly recognizable genre: the How Awful I Felt on Election Night essay. Aaron Sorkin, one of the nation's top renewable sources of sanctimony, exemplified the form in an open letter to his teenage daughter and his former wife, in which he pledged to "fucking fight" Trump and reassured his fellow citizens that "our darkest days have always—always—been followed by our finest hours." The theme to *The West Wing* didn't play only because it was implied.

The How Awful I Felt on Election Night essays soon morphed into the How Awful I Felt on Election Night books, collections featuring activists, artists, writers, and politicians spilling their feelings—a jumble of shock, despair, grief, fury, and resolve—about Trump's victory. Dread was an overriding response. "My husband and I would remain up for hours, alternately swearing and reaching for each other's hands in bleary and increasing panic," writer

Nicole Chung recalls in *How Do I Explain This to My Kids?*, a 2017 collection with a title that fit the angst of the time. Others went for all-caps anger. "Stay vigilant. Stay focused. Stay OUTRAGED," activist Linda Sarsour, who co-chaired the Women's March the day after Trump's inauguration, writes in the 2017 essay anthology *What We Do Now: Standing Up for Your Values in Trump's America*. "Perpetual outrage is what's going to fuel our movements right now." A few tried to stake out some shared terrain among opponents of the new order. "End the litmus tests that separate us," organizer M. Dove Kent urged in *What We Do Now*. "This doesn't mean we need to alter our core political convictions, but it does mean that the thinner lines in the sand that previously divided us must be erased."

This mix of emotions and impulses came to embody what was instantly dubbed, with a dash of melodrama but understandable zeal, the resistance against the Trump presidency.

In the years since, such responses have led to popular protests—including marches for women's rights and scientific inquiry, and widespread demonstrations against police brutality—and dedicated political action. "It's been decades since the country has seen this sort of wide-scale, locally led, nationally networked civic engagement," congressional-staffers-turned-activists Leah Greenberg and Ezra Levin exult in *We Are Indivisible* (2019). The book builds on the "Indivisible Guide" the authors created shortly after Trump's victory, a how-to manual for thwarting the new president's agenda. (Short version: Shame your congressional representatives.) The demonstrations and organizing that marked the early days of the Trump administration fostered a kind of self-validation among the resistance forces. "If Trump is a threat to our democracy and the product of its weaknesses, the citizen activism he has inspired is the antidote, the way to vindicate our long experiment in self-rule," write E. J. Dionne Jr., Norman J. Ornstein, and Thomas E. Mann in *One Nation After Trump* (2017). It is painful solace—that the nation's elected president would prove so abhorrent and dangerous that he propels the citizenry toward greater civic participation, a sort of democracy by desperation.

There is optimism, determination, insight, and even beauty in the resistance writings. Just as often, there is exclusion, self-righteousness, and opportunism—responses that can limit the power and appeal of a political project in search of allies to counter a dangerous and reckless opponent. The resistance literature looks inward, its impassioned calls for solidarity aimed at those already inclined to agree. It calls for conversations but restricts the speakers. It claims moral leadership, but to uncertain ends. It worries endlessly about Trump's America but betrays contempt for Trump's Americans.

The resistance, understandably, has tended to focus on countering Trump's more retrograde policies and proposals, but it is less engaged in battling or even comprehending the forces that propelled Trump to the presidency in the first place. That fight is not about declaring "this is not normal!" or "that's not who we are!" again and again, but about determining whether Americans, torn by politics, class, race, and identity, can still make common cause about anything—whether "we" is still a viable concept in the Trump era, or will remain so after it.

Much of the resistance writing stresses who can rightfully claim the label—who counts and who doesn't. It is about community and consensus, but also ostracism and difference. And excluded is anyone who fails to espouse the full worldview that the writers and activists champion.

The editors of *What We Do Now* introduce its contributors—

including Elizabeth Warren, Bernie Sanders, and various leaders from nonprofit, legal, and faith groups—somewhat presumptuously, as "some of the best and the brightest of America's progressive leaders—hereby announcing themselves as the new American resistance movement." Greenberg and Levin hail the network of Indivisible activists as "the largest anti-Trump 'resistance' operation in the country." (To truly belong, they explain, you must both "resist Trump's agenda" and "uphold progressive values," as though the two must always go together.) And in her 2019 book *American Resistance*, sociologist Dana Fisher defines the resistance as "people working individually and through organizations to challenge the Trump Administration and its policies." She includes what she calls the "violent fringe" antifa movement but emphasizes that anonymous Trump administration officials who "have challenged President Trump as a person but support his broader policy agenda are *not* part of the Resistance." It's a pointed dig at the senior government official who wrote an anonymous *New York Times* op-ed in the fall of 2018 describing resistance and consternation within the administration.* No room here for traditional conservatives or political moderates who may also want to stand up for their values in Trump's America, who find the president or his policies no less appalling. There is a difference, it turns out, between resisting and Resistance.

Of course, excluding political opponents is a natural instinct for those who feel under siege. "Our journey forward has to start with recommitting to our core values as progressives," writes Ilyse Hogue, president of NARAL Pro-Choice America, in *What We Do Now*. Progressives are the only intended audience for those

---

*The unnamed author later did detail significant substantive disagreements with President Trump—particularly on matters of trade and national security—in the 2019 book *A Warning*, published two weeks after Fisher's *American Resistance*.

books, perhaps the only possible audience. While criticizing Trump supporters for their "blinding privilege" and complicity with racism, activist Brittany Packnett pauses to acknowledge the obvious: "Chances are, if you're reading this you didn't even vote for him." In these books, the resistance writers rarely look beyond activist communities on the left. "This is the only way forward: local, intersectional organization across movements to protect our communities from hate, racism, and exploitation," writes Cristina Jiménez, cofounder of United We Dream.

The resistance literature also stresses racial grievance, its warnings prescient yet indiscriminate. In *Radical Hope*, feminist activist Kate Schatz blames white Americans—all of them—for Trump's rise. "I'm also going to make broad, sweeping statements that generalize our behavior as white people," she writes. "In many instances, you will think, *Not me!* I ask you to let that go. For example: we just elected Donald Trump. I know *I* didn't vote for him, and I know *you* didn't vote for him, but let's be real here: *we elected him.*" White women are something of a mystery in the resistance literature. "How could more than half of white women have endorsed [Trump's] bid?" Linda Sarsour asks in *We Are Not Here to Be Bystanders: A Memoir of Love and Resistance* (2020). "It made absolutely no sense to me." She later laments that so many women clearly voted "against their own interests" by supporting pro-Trump Republican candidates in the 2018 midterm elections. White resistance writers, meanwhile, resort to constant apologies and acknowledgment of their whiteness and status, even noting the white privilege it takes for them to discuss their white privilege with other privileged whites. "We talk about privilege in this chapter in a privileged-people-talking-to-other-privileged-people sort of way," Greenberg and Levin explain. "That's intentional! We're white people who drew on a ton

WHAT WERE WE THINKING

of privilege. . . . We generally find that our biggest contribution is talking to people with privilege about how we can all do better." *Do better* is a default admonition from resisters who encounter the uninitiated.

There is much talk of "conversations" in the resistance writings, but the outcome is more a monologue. "Ensuring dignity and a fair shake for all means engaging in authentic conversations to find real community-based solutions," Hogue explains in *What We Do Now*. "The values that unite our communities are not in conflict; they're intertwined." Such conversations, however, are restricted to the chosen. Aside from generalities about how Trump supporters may have voted for him out of a "depth of alienation," there is little effort in these pages to understand, let alone reach out to, communities beyond the ones the writers themselves represent. And white liberals' attempted dialogues on race are dismissed in mocking tones. "You don't get to just have conversations anymore," Packnett writes. "You don't get to just wear a safety pin and call yourself an ally. You don't get to just talk while the rest of us fear for our lives because discrimination, rape culture, and xenophobia just won the White House."

According to Fisher's surveys in *American Resistance*, however, the typical participant at the largest anti-Trump rallies of 2017 and 2018 were mostly white and female, leaning left but animated by a range of political issues, and unlikely to formally belong to the organizations leading the marches. So the intellectuals of the resistance seem to deliberately alienate prospective foot soldiers, prioritizing the purity of resistance over its expansion. "We will join together to become this nation's unshakable moral compass," Sarsour writes in *We Are Not Here to Be Bystanders*. She is describing a coalition of marginalized communities massing to resist the Trump agenda. It is an inspiring vision, but simply because

Trump's moral compass is broken does not mean that yours unerr-ingly points north. There is a difference between being righteous and being right.

Trump's relentless assault, in rhetoric and policy, against American racial minorities and immigrants from Latin America or Muslim-majority countries makes plain the prejudice animat-ing this administration and plenty of its supporters. But in the 2017 book *Rules for Resistance*, writers who have experienced populism and polarization in other countries warn the American resistance against dismissing Trump's supporters as dupes or de-plorables. They know where that leads. In Venezuela, for instance, those resisting former presidents Hugo Chávez and Nicolás Ma-duro treated the regime's partisans with disdain. "We wouldn't stop pontificating about how stupid Chavismo was, not only to international friends but also to Chávez's electoral base," writes economist Andrés Miguel Rondón. " 'Really, this guy? Are you nuts? You must be nuts,' we'd say." But such talk only further es-tranged citizens from each other. "Whole generations were split in two," Rondón explains. "A sense of shared culture was wiped out."

Such warnings capture the self-perpetuating tension between the resistance and the Trump base, the constant expectation that some catalytic moment—surely this offense, or that one, or the one over there—will break the Trumpian spell. "While denouncing Trump's supporters for 'voting against their interests' or for being 'backward' or 'reactionary' may be emotionally satisfying to his opponents, it will not persuade any of them to reconsider the choice they made," Dionne, Ornstein, and Mann write in *One Nation After Trump*.

Persuading the president's base is not their job, resistance writ-ers argue, and with good reason. Why should anti-Trump activists burden themselves with the moral or political transformation of Trump voters, men and women who won't pay attention to them in any case? The resistance has bigger worries. "If Trump gets his way, our very existence may become an act of civil disobedience," Jiménez warns.

But there are risks if resistance to Trump mainly means opposition to the president himself, or to his most reprehensible policies. "It would [be] a grave mistake to see the obliteration of the progressive policy agenda as the chief danger of a Trump presidency," political scientist N. Turkuler Isiksel writes in *Rules for Resistance*. "What we confront is not the usual dogfight between liberals and conservatives. It is a struggle between those who believe in preserving the imperfect but serviceable constitutional system of the republic, and those who will try to undermine it."

The greatest danger to be resisted, in other words, is not simply a change of policies, no matter how disgraceful the changes may be. It is the erosion of the very system of government that makes all resistance possible.

Such distinctions have tended to be uncommon in the resistance literature, which has focused far more on challenging specific administration policies and on promoting an ambitiously progressive agenda. In works such as Naomi Klein's *No Is Not Enough* and Greenberg and Levin's *We Are Indivisible*, Trump becomes not just a reason to resist every assault but an excuse to submit to every inclination.

Klein saw Trump—or at least something like him—coming long ago. Consider her books over the past two decades: *No Logo*, on the rise of corporate superbrands; *The Shock Doctrine*, on how governments and industries exploit the confusion of crises to impose pro-corporate policies; and *This Changes Everything*, on the battle between business interests and the environment. Klein looks upon the president with disdain and weary recognition. Trump the luxury lifestyle brand. Trump the neoliberal standard-bearer for the entitled rich. Trump the disaster-capitalist. Trump the climate-change denier.

It is a compulsion of resistance literature to see in the president the confirmation of all past fears, like a recurring childhood nightmare come to life. "Trump is not a rupture at all, but rather the culmination—the logical end point—of a great many dangerous stories our culture has been telling for a very long time," Klein writes. "That greed is good. That the market rules. That money is what matters in life. That white men are better than the rest. That the natural world is there for us to pillage. That the vulnerable deserve their fate and the one percent deserve their golden towers." It's a told-you-so book but, the thing is, Klein really did tell us.

In her view, there are two reasons for the constant chaos from the Trump White House, and both are self-serving. First, Trump's brand is synonymous with "winning," which means the president must always be fighting—whether against immigrants, China, the news media, the Democrats, the Never Trump Republicans, street demonstrators, or his own staff. Second, and more insidious, the constant waves of crisis and shock enable the administration to "push through the more radical planks of its agenda," Klein writes—the way, for instance, that a pandemic suddenly allows the administration to quietly implement restrictive immigration measures it had long pursued. This interpretation implies more forethought and strategy on the part of Trump than he might deserve, but it represents the shock doctrine of which Klein has warned for years.

The early calls for resistance, in Klein's mind, were encouraging but insufficient. Klein prefers a new kind of shock doctrine, one that capitalizes on the crisis of Trump's presidency to unite liberals in an ambitious policy platform. A $15 minimum wage.

A carbon tax. Demilitarization of police. Free college tuition. One hundred percent renewable energy. A Marshall Plan to fight violence against women. Reparations for slavery and colonialism. The abolition of prison. The abandonment of economic growth as a measure of social improvement. All these elements form the affirmative counterpoint to her book's title. Hey, Trump is going for it all, so why not her side, too? *No Is Not Enough* is a "road map for shock resistance," Klein asserts, one that celebrates the "rekindling of the kind of utopian dreaming that has been sorely missing from social movements in recent decades." For all her concerns about shock tactics, Klein is not above taking advantage of a crisis to push through radical ideas. They just need to be her ideas.

Greenberg and Levin explain that the slogan "Indivisible" spoke to them on a visceral level, far beyond its evocation of the Pledge of Allegiance. "We were up against an explicitly divide-and-conquer strategy from Trump," they write in *We Are Indivisible*. "That meant we had to treat an attack on one as an attack on all. . . . Our only hope was to stand together—indivisible." They write of indivisibility, but Greenberg and Levin offer a binary worldview: It is their side that must remain indivisible against an "unholy alliance" of white nationalists, Christian fundamentalists, and corporate influence on the other side, against opponents bent on undermining democracy to consolidate power. The division of America along economic, demographic, and cultural lines is a recurring vision among the resistance chroniclers, just as it is among Trump's acolytes. In her 2019 book *The Man Who Sold America*, MSNBC host Joy-Ann Reid, deemed a "heroine of the resistance" by the *New York Times*, also sees "two starkly different and disunited Americas" and fears a descent into a "new American civil war" over culture, race, and tribe. The resistance did not create this divide, but it now treats it as unavoidable and irreparable.

We Are Indivisible brims with good intentions and passionate thinking. Greenberg and Levin seek to end the filibuster; "democratize" the House (by introducing smaller districts, proportional representation, and ranked-choice voting) and the Senate (by admitting new states, such as the District of Columbia and, if its residents so choose, Puerto Rico); add new justices to the Supreme Court; expand voting for felons, immigrants, and teens; break up the tech giants; and give people vouchers to invest in local news media. "This can't be about putting power in the hands of Democrats," they insist. "This has to be about putting power in the hands of the people."

But it's a particularistic vision of the people and of the popular will. Levin and Greenberg fear Washington gridlock because "gridlock is just better for conservatives" than it is for the Left. The Senate needs rethinking because the chamber is "where progressive policy goes to die." And they rationalize reforming the high court on partisan grounds. "Republicans have appointed fifteen out of the last nineteen Supreme Court justices," Greenberg and Levin point out. "This just does not pass the smell test for a legitimate democracy." Would the court smell sweeter if Democrats had appointed a majority of the most recent justices? Would the authors still feel compelled to increase the number of justices and introduce term limits to their service? "You probably know the system doesn't respond to the people's will," the authors argue, as if that fact alone implied a mandate for progressive reform, as if the political system's unresponsiveness were not also one of the very reasons why tens of millions of Americans voted for Trump.

The original model for the "Indivisible Guide" is revealing. Both Greenberg and Levin witnessed the effectiveness of the Tea Party movement in stalling the Obama agenda, and they look back on it with dismay and envy. "What we needed was some sort of guide to replicating the Tea Party," they write, emphasizing that they seek to emulate not its racial politics but its advocacy skills and organizational prowess. The Tea Party launched with dubious calls for fiscal rectitude and soon degenerated into racist and nativist appeals—a lurch that produced voter suppression, alternative facts, and Trumpism. To imagine that you can adopt the ruthlessness of Tea Party–style tactics yet stop short of pursuing them to your own political endgame is to be enormously confident about your self-control.

"We can't keep playing the same game and expect different results," Levin and Greenberg say of their hope to adjust the rules of American democracy. But the game they prefer to play poses its own dangers, and threatens to open new divides.

Timothy Snyder's *On Tyranny* stays with you long after you've finished the last page. It is a quick read, but it takes far longer to absorb the implications. When I first read it, in the winter of 2017, just weeks after Trump's inauguration, I was taken by the Yale University historian's ominous exhortations and parallels. "To abandon facts is to abandon freedom. . . . Post-truth is pre-fascism," Snyder writes, just as the president's attacks on "fake news" and the White House's "alternative facts" were penetrating the national consciousness. "Americans today are no wiser than the Europeans who saw democracy yield to fascism, Nazism, or communism in the twentieth century," Snyder warns. "Our one advantage is that we might learn from their experience."

More than three years later, however, what strikes me most about *On Tyranny* are the actionable and prescient forms of resistance that it highlights, efforts that have proved vital in countering administration policies and in at least slowing Trump's assault on democratic practices and institutions. It is a work steeped in history yet imbued with the fierce urgency of what now.

Popular protests are an essential form of resistance. "Nothing is real that does not end on the streets," Snyder reminds, because leaders must see and feel that their actions have consequences. But resistance also entails steady, methodical pushback from institutions, professions, and bureaucrats. "It is hard to subvert a rule-of-law state without lawyers, or to hold show trials without judges," Snyder writes. "Authoritarians need obedient civil servants." Court challenges have delayed, altered, or overturned initiatives—think of the travel ban against Muslim-majority countries or the family separation policy on the U.S.-Mexico border—while civil servants and longtime diplomats, whether acting as whistleblowers or in open testimony during the impeachment hearings of 2019, were the ones who revealed the president's efforts to manipulate foreign policy for his political benefit. Snyder urges citizens to defend essential institutions. "Do not speak of 'our institutions' unless you make them yours by acting on their behalf," he admonishes. "Institutions do not protect themselves. . . . So choose an institution you care about—a court, a newspaper, a law, a labor union—and take its side."

Snyder also wants conversations, though not of the kind that other resistance writers often demand or deride. "Professions can create forms of ethical conversation that are impossible between a lonely individual and a distant government," he argues. Professional groups and institutions distinguish themselves by upholding their rules and behavior in extraordinary times, by staying predictable and normal amid chaos and abnormality. Indeed, it is in extraordinary moments that upholding ordinary practices matters most. "If members of the professions confuse their specific ethics with the emotions of the moment, however, they can find themselves saying and doing things that they might have previously thought unimaginable," Snyder writes. In *Rules for Resistance*, ACLU national legal director David Cole details the way legal, journalistic, and national-security professionals forced a national debate surrounding the Bush administration's counterterrorism and detention tactics—by filing lawsuits, writing and publicizing human rights reports, leaking classified documents, and condemning violations of constitutional and human rights. "As a result, the course of history changed," Cole writes.

It is not just professional conversations that matter. In *On Tyranny*, Snyder lingers on the importance of everyday language as a precursor of tyranny, or as a bulwark against it. In a "culture of denunciation" overwhelmed by the mindless repetition of slogans and catchphrases, Snyder asks readers to "think up your own way of speaking," which is another way of telling us not to abandon our own way of thinking. "When we repeat the same words and phrases that appear in the daily media, we accept the absence of a larger framework," he warns, just as the "shamanistic incantation" and endless repetition of a leader's rhetoric override independent thought. Speaking in your own terms is resistance against a narrowing of thought, while speaking with those beyond your own circle is resistance against a narrowing of life. "Ideas about change must engage people of various backgrounds who do not agree about everything," Snyder writes, stressing the importance of everyday, informal communication. "Make eye contact and small talk," he urges. "This is not just polite. It is part of being a citizen and a responsible member of society," and a way to "break down social barriers." This kind of conversation is more virtue than signal.

Activist Amy Siskind has come up with her own way of talking.

Her 2018 book *The List* offers a relentless tally of the unimaginable, and thus makes a unique contribution to the resistance canon. *The List* recounts every norm broken, every conflict of interest flaunted, every institution degraded, and every truth casually disregarded by the Trump administration in its first year in office. Siskind began posting her list each week immediately after the election. The first week (November 13–20, 2016) featured nine items. The second week had eighteen items. The third had twenty-six, including Trump's statement on Twitter about the "millions" who voted illegally. Soon, each week swelled to more than one hundred entries, an effort, the author explains, to provide "a trail map for us to follow back to normalcy and democracy—a journey, sadly, I suspect will take years if not decades to travel."

The book is hard to read—each chapter spans one week, and each week is a series of numbered transgressions, just a sentence or two each, all totaling more than five hundred pages—but that difficulty is the point, a reckoning with our inattention. Even for dedicated news junkies, it is remarkable how much one forgets, in the shock of the moment, about the previous shock of the moment. Reading *The List*, I realized I'd forgotten that Trump gave the announcement of his first Supreme Court nominee a reality-television, who-will-he-pick vibe (Week 12). I'd forgotten about the insidious incompetence of a $2 trillion double-counting error in Trump's 2018 budget proposal (Week 28). I'd forgotten that Trump chose his son Eric's wedding planner to oversee federal housing programs in New York (Week 31). And I'd forgotten about White House adviser Kellyanne Conway's invocation (Week 12) of the entirely fictional Bowling Green massacre (Week Never).

The List is most ruthless in its deployment of repetition and specificity. For weeks on end, Siskind reminds readers that Trump had accused President Obama, without evidence, of wiretapping

Trump Tower. "Five weeks have passed. . . . Six weeks have passed. . . . Seven weeks have passed . . ." since the initial charge, and Siskind delights in presenting virtually the same sentence each time. She charts the slow-motion fiasco of Jared Kushner's security clearance and financial disclosures. She dwells on the president's habitual scorn for essential information, including daily intelligence reports and State Department briefings prior to conversations with foreign leaders. And most of all, she details the endless ethical breaches and financial conflicts of interest that trail this White House, the family that dominates it, and the top aides and cabinet members beholden to it. It's one thing to know, but another to be reminded, in writing, over and over and over.

I'm not sure that simply detailing Trump's tumult and transgression will help lead us back to normality, not when abnormality far predated the Trump presidency, not when chaos is less a hindrance to this administration than its fulfillment. Even so, Siskind fears the risk not only of forgetting but of letting things slide. She dedicates the book to "the Resistance," and there is resistance in the simple imperative to remember.

Outrage serves the resistance against Trump. It is usually the most strident writers and activists who offer early warnings that something has gone deeply wrong. That role requires "some aggressive outrage," even a "paranoiac bent," writes Harvard law professor Noah Feldman, in the 2018 essay collection *Can It Happen Here? Authoritarianism in America*. The supply of fresh outrage appears endless, too. "As President Trump continues to mobilize his base with inflammatory rhetoric and extremist politics," Fisher writes in *American Resistance*, "he may be exactly what the Resistance needs to survive." Sometimes democracy by desperation is all there is.

But outrage is "an exhaustible resource," Hogue reminds us in *What We Do Now*. And when outrage is your only fuel, it risks becoming your only purpose. Outrage is too easily diffused, and too quickly directed at people rather than principles. It is also Trump's terrain; anger is his safe space. "Moral shocks can be an effective tool for mobilizing strangers to participate in a march or, potentially, a number of marches, without personal ties to groups that do the work of organizing, but it is difficult to sustain activism," Fisher acknowledges. The resistance books are packed with calls for the renewal of the American story but give no clear sense of how to begin rebuilding a post-Trump America. "In 2020, America will decide what story it wants to tell about itself, when the country chooses between keeping the Trump Show going or fundamentally changing the script," Reid writes at the end of *The Man Who Sold America*. But pining for a new narrative can only be your narrative for so long.

There are two essays scattered among the resistance writings that offer a different kind of warning, and an alternative means to resist. In *What We Do Now*, arts activist Nato Thompson calls on artists to explore our stark national divides rather than only calling them out or amassing forces on one side. "We must also acknowledge the nuances of our political concerns so that we don't gloss over them," he writes. "If click-bait fueled by indignance cannot capture that nuance, then our president's unhinged (and 'post-truth') tweets certainly cannot." Thompson urges artists not to retrench but to cut across ideology, party, and geography. "Their work must reject the kneejerk reaction to reject other voices—and instead take into account the serious complexities of what makes people who they are."

In *Radical Hope*, the novelist and critic Katie Kitamura confronts the hostility to independent thought and the degradation of rhetoric in Trump's America. "I need a language adequate to this impossible world, one that will help me act upon it," Kitamura writes. "But language is malleable, and it is not always on the side of truth. This is something every writer knows. Words make and unmake the world with terrifying rapidity, and they do so without moral distinction." Here Kitamura is describing Trump's words: his posts on social media, his executive orders and his denigration of people he considers less than true Americans. "The man who refuses to be accountable to his own words now wields language with the authority of a tyrant," she warns.

But Kitamura is well aware of how the president's opponents can succumb to facile speech, thought, and argument, too. In the form of a letter to her young child, she offers an urgent counterpoint to the style, substance, and self-satisfaction of the American resistance:

> *There is no time for complacency. There is no time for inaction.* This is undoubtedly true. But at the same time, we need to defend another way of thinking and being, one that allows for hesitation, for nuance and mutability.
>
> I have a distrust of certitude, even when I agree with the essential position being advocated. I don't think the urgency of our situation means that we cannot afford uncertainty. I need to believe in the value of the doubt I now feel, in its ability to create a space for the slowness of thought and conviction. . . .
>
> I worry that you will grow up in a time of ideological haste, a time of wild conviction and coarsened thought. The truth is that they have already taken so much, and they will take much more. But I promise that I will do everything in my power to keep them from impoverishing the language you are fighting so hard for right now, from reducing your world to absolutes.

Ideological haste, wild conviction, and coarsened thought—
that is a future worth resisting, too, no matter its banner. "The habit
of dwelling on victimhood dulls the impulse of self-correction,"
Snyder cautions in *On Tyranny*. He is writing about those who
succumb to nostalgic myths of restored greatness, but his warning
also fits those who counter such visions with their own exclusion,
blind spots, and sloganeering. If political resistance to the president means greater social and cultural retrenchment, then the divisions that bequeathed us Trump will only strengthen. They will
grow more resistant.

Calling Trump "not my president" is emotionally satisfying, if
politically obtuse. It is Trump—governing for his base, his family,
and himself—who made that choice long ago. Resistance should
involve rejecting, rather than deepening, the American divide on
which Trump thrives. Should he win a second term in the Oval Office, brace for a new round of How Awful I Felt on Election Night
essays and anthologies, in which the anger of 2016 is magnified,
and the despair even more so. But if he does not, I fear that four
years of resistance may not have prepared us for the task of making
"one nation after Trump" a reality greater than a book cover.

BOOKS DISCUSSED

David Cole and Melanie Wachtell Stinnett, eds. *Rules for Resistance: Advice from Around the Globe for the Age of Trump*. The New Press, 2017.

Carolina De Robertis, ed. *Radical Hope: Letters of Love and Dissent in Dangerous Times*. Vintage Books, 2017.

E. J. Dionne Jr., Norman J. Ornstein, and Thomas E. Mann. *One Nation After Trump: A Guide for the Perplexed, the Disillusioned, the Desperate, and the Not-Yet Deported*. St. Martin's, 2017.

Dana R. Fisher. *American Resistance: From the Women's March to the Blue Wave*. Columbia University Press, 2019.

Leah Greenberg and Ezra Levin. *We Are Indivisible: A Blueprint for Democracy After Trump*. One Signal Publishers/Atria, 2019.

Dennis Johnson and Valerie Merians, eds. *What We Do Now: Standing Up for Your Values in Trump's America*. Melville House, 2017.

Naomi Klein. *No Is Not Enough: Resisting Trump's Shock Politics and Winning the World We Need*. Haymarket Books, 2017.

Joy-Ann Reid. *The Man Who Sold America: Trump and the Unraveling of the American Story*. William Morrow, 2019.

Linda Sarsour. *We Are Not Here to Be Bystanders: A Memoir of Love and Resistance*. 37 Ink, 2020.

Amy Siskind. *The List: A Week-by-Week Reckoning of Trump's First Year*. Bloomsbury, 2018.

Timothy Snyder. *On Tyranny: Twenty Lessons from the Twentieth Century*. Tim Duggan Books, 2017.

Sarah Swong and Diane Wachtell, eds. *How Do I Explain This to My Kids? Parenting in the Age of Trump*. The New Press, 2017.

THREE

THE CONSERVATIVE PIVOT

Throughout Trump's 2016 presidential campaign and even early into his presidency, some conservative commentators and intellectuals hoped or fantasized that Trump would change, that the gravity of the office would mold him into something other than what he was. But there was no pivot; both as candidate and as president, Trump remained true to Trump. The only discernible pivot would come from conservatives themselves.

Three varieties of conservative have emerged in the Trump era. First are the sycophants, who through a lack of options, imagination, or shame embraced the new order and relentlessly justified that decision. Next are the Never Trump conservatives, those who declared their opposition to Trump right away and have held fast to a vision of conservatism that they hope endures no matter its dwindling power and adherents. Then there are the pro-Trump conservative intellectuals, those seeking to retrofit an ideological framework onto the whims of a man whose positions show few organizing principles beyond self-interest and self-regard.

These disparate camps regard one another with a mix of accommodation and hostility, yet they share one essential trait: even as they obsess over Trump, they are in denial about him—who he is, what he means, or how he overpowered their party and movement.

In their books, the sycophants lavish praise on Trump while fantasizing about his policies and euphemizing, or simply ignoring, his worst tendencies. The Never Trumpers write book-length breakup letters to the Republican Party and to conservatism but fail to reckon with their own complicity in Trump's rise. Meanwhile, the intellectuals sympathetic to the president want desperately to believe that there is something rational called Trumpism, not just someone crass named Trump, and they attempt to translate the president's instincts and narcissism into an ideology that can outlive him. Yet more than upholding Trump's worldview, they default to attacking his opponents, whether Democrats, establishment Republicans, civil servants, immigrants, demonstrators, or loosely defined elites. The pro-Trump intellectuals claim to support the president for his principles, but they really love him for his enemies.

What conservatism can arise from a period when Republicans in power hold few principles, and principled Republicans hold little power? Not the Never Trump conservatism that pines for a return to the pre-2016 status quo; as conservative writer George Will has put it, there are bells that cannot be unrung and words that cannot be unsaid. It may be a more narrow and divisive conservatism that promotes an ever more exclusionary American nationalism, hunkering down in the smallest of small tents. Or it may be the improbable account of revisionists who, deciding that servile loyalty is no longer politically useful or tenable, would quickly declare that they stood with Trump only to privately push back on his worst ideas—a self-sacrifice in the service of true conservatism, which, they will whisper sagely, Trump never really embodied.

Trump is the sun around which all forms of conservatism now revolve, along orbits of submission, derision, and revision. And yet the Trump era's most illuminating case for conservatism is one that barely considers him at all, that instead focuses on how to rebuild the essential political and cultural institutions that have lost both the public's trust and the conservative movement's interest—losses that Trump has exploited and deepened to his own ends.

It is pointless, even dangerous, to avoid or reimagine Trump. But it is vital to look beyond him.

Whatever the sycophants' vantage points—loyal former staffers, outside confidants, cable-news personalities—they pledge allegiance to Trump in remarkably similar terms and tones. The president's most steadfast supporters display Trumpian language, comfort with cynicism, talent for tautology, and weakness for flattery. They also recast the president's most glaring flaws as major strengths or, if necessary, just ignore them. Even for the truest believers, submission reveals itself through omission.

The coarsening of political language is one of the president's most obvious legacies, and the sycophants echo Trump's voice as well as his views. Fox News host Jeanine Pirro, among the most unctuous of the president's devotees, litters *Liars, Leakers, and Liberals* (2018) with Trump tropes, calling out "Fake News," "Crooked Hillary," and "Sloppy Steve" and coining monikers such as "Pipsqueak Papadopoulos" and "Rotten Ryan." She fawns over the president's "Kryptonite-proof aura of invincibility," which overpowers those neutered specimens populating Washington. (President Obama "didn't have the balls to stand up to anyone," former House speaker Paul Ryan "didn't have the stones" to personally challenge a controversial presidential pardon, and Jeff Sessions lacked the "prosecutorial balls" to be an effective attorney general.) When no better case is available, Pirro dismisses Trump's critics with meaningless one-liners: *Not on my watch. Give me a break. Drives me nuts. I don't think so. Don't get me started on those wackadoos.* Arguments needn't be any stronger if your objective is mindless agreement rather than engaged thought. For that, "don't get me started on those wackadoos" works just fine.

External adulation not only feeds Trump's ego but excuses his indifference to the details of governing. In the sycophant's eyes, ignorance is smart and laziness savvy. "One thing I have learned about Donald Trump is that he learns very fast—and that the speed at which he operates optimizes his learning," Newt Gingrich writes in *Understanding Trump* (2017), the first of several obsequious works on his latest patron. "So," he continues, "one of the most fascinating aspects of his presidency will be how he overcomes the gaps in his knowledge of institutional government." (Fascinating!) The former House speaker explains that Trump "places a greater emphasis on speed than mistake avoidance," which to most readers might suggest that the president rushes into bad decisions. But it turns out that forethought is unnecessary: In *Let Trump Be Trump* (2017), former 2016 campaign aides Corey Lewandowski and David Bossie don't mind the boss's lack of prep work before his presidential debates because "he had been preparing his whole life." Trump determines what is important for him to know merely through questions journalists ask him, "a talent for which he gets very little credit." To the sycophant, poor preparation is not a shortcoming to be excused but a virtue to be praised.

It was in the third presidential debate of 2016 that Clinton warned that Trump would be a puppet of Russian president Vladimir Putin, and Trump famously replied: "No puppet, no puppet. You're the puppet." This I-know-you-are-but-what-am-I comeback became a key element of both the Trump presidency and the sycophant canon. Trump is no liar; others lie about him. Trump did not collude with Russia or coerce Ukraine; the Democrats did all that. Trump does not endanger the rule of law; Robert Mueller, whistleblowers, and the House members who impeached him pose the real threat. Trump does not display authoritarian instincts; the Far Left and the "deep state" national-security and scientific establishments are the true tyrants. Trump is the lone patriot; his opponents are traitors. Trump did not fail to address the COVID-19 pandemic early on; the Obama administration left the government unprepared. Trump's offenses are always minor or nonexistent, and defending him involves little more than highlighting the supposed decadence and incompetence of his rivals and critics.

Nowhere is this sleight of hand more evident than in the treatment of truth and the press. Fact-checkers have tallied thousands of false and misleading claims by the president during his time in office, yet, in the sycophants' view, the real liars are all those mendacious journalists. "One of the continuing surprises to President Trump has been the willingness of the elite media to lie," Gingrich explains. "He was simply unprepared for the brutality and the depth of dishonesty of our national media." The president, by contrast, is the truth-teller in chief, Gingrich contends in *Trump's America* (2018), a leader who is "redefining the very structure of American political and governmental dialogue by insisting on fact-based conversations." It is the enemies in America's newsrooms, Pirro writes, who "twist words and play with facts until the American people can't tell what's true anymore."

Yet twisted words are weapons in the arsenal of Trump's defenders. In his 2018 book *The Russia Hoax*, for instance, Fox News legal analyst Gregg Jarrett argues by adverb and tautology. Criticisms of Trump are "transparently partisan" or "patently absurd," he writes, while the president's opponents are "arguably corrupt," and Hillary Clinton "plainly violated" multiple laws. Also, Trump could not have obstructed justice in the Russia investigation because, well, he is innocent. "If the president knew he did nothing wrong," Jarrett rationalizes, "it makes little sense that he would try to impede a probe into no wrongdoing." If your premise is that the president is blameless, the conclusion that he remains so does follow.

Whenever sycophants must confront particularly odious statements by Trump, they refuse to exercise independent moral judgment, preferring to sidestep the substance and stress the president's smarts and determination. When Trump, early in his first presidential campaign, did not back down after declaring that Senator John McCain was no war hero because he had been captured in Vietnam, Lewandowski marveled that he "had never seen a candidate have such courage in his convictions." (One candidate comes to mind: John McCain.) And though Gingrich concedes that Trump was "not fair" to Mexican immigrants when he branded them rapists and criminals in his opening campaign speech, he doesn't mind the depiction because Trump had "sent a signal" to voters that he would not succumb to "political correctness" on immigration. When these reinterpretations grow too tortuous, the sycophants just deny. Trump's words attacking Mexican immigrants were not racist, Lewandowski and Bossie assert; in fact, they were "as close to the opposite of racism as any words could be."

His hardest-core supporters don't only reimagine Trump's veracity and values, they fantasize about his policies. Gingrich devotes chunks of *Understanding Trump* to outlining his own pet programs and projecting them onto the president: he pictures Trump leading a detailed, piece-by-piece legislative strategy for reforming health care and the civil service, and even imagines that, "with a few breaks," Americans could reach Mars as early as the final year of a second Trump term. In his 2017 book *The Fourth Way*, conservative radio host Hugh Hewitt pictures Trump not only reforming the tax code and appointing conservative judges, as he has done, but also rebuilding infrastructure, remaking the social safety net, and even improving the nation's dental health via a network of local clinics caring for our "Trump teeth." (Chew on that one.) Most improbable is Hewitt's suggestion that this president is just the leader to bring the country together on immigration. "Donald J. Trump can do what perhaps no other American politician can do: he can reform the immigration system while regularizing the 11 million immigrants in the country without permission while also building a 'wall.' . . . He can do this without any credible number of serious critics branding it an 'amnesty' or a 'sellout.' " With such an accomplishment, Hewitt writes, Trump would "cut the Gordian knot" and hit a "political grand slam."

Maybe it's not so crazy. After all, Hewitt also writes that Trump is "not likely to casually tempt the impeachment gods. He knows the history here. He will self-regulate." Except Trump did tempt impeachment, failed to heed history, and could not control himself. That was not even Hewitt's worst prediction: he also thought Trump could govern "inclusively, energetically, joyously" and usher in a "booming, generous, open-handed Republic of Virtue."

Trump the virtuous. Trump the inclusive. Trump the generous. A good way to defend this president is to imagine him to be someone other than himself.

But most Trump sycophants do not even pretend that Trump should be—or wants to be—a leader for all Americans. Embracing the president's exclusion and division is the final requirement of the Trump groupie. Gingrich puts it most cynically in *Trump's America*, when he asserts that the nation is fighting a cultural and political "civil war," with hard-working, flag-waving citizens on one side and radical, liberal, globalist, academic, identity-obsessed, duplicitous, establishment, America-hating swamp creatures on the other. "Trump's America and the post-American society that the anti-Trump coalition represents are incapable of coexisting," he writes. "One will simply defeat the other. There is no room for compromise. Trump has understood this perfectly since day one."

Gingrich congratulates Trump for holding campaign-style rallies throughout much of his presidency—a habit that only a global pandemic could temporarily break. "It's important for him to see an arena full of people and be reminded that he speaks for them," Gingrich explains. Any effort to speak for those outside the arena falls beyond the scope of this presidency. Why bother? "The anti-Trump crowd is so adamant in their disdain," Jarrett asserts, "that no amount of reason will reach them."

So, no amount of reason is provided.

The Never Trump conservatives are in a tougher spot: Anti-Trump liberals don't trust them, Trump supporters loathe them, and the president himself alternates between mocking their powerlessness and decrying their treachery. Little wonder that so many of the conservatives who contributed to *National Review* magazine's famous "Against Trump" issue in February 2016 have long since dropped the "Never" from their bios.

Those remaining do not hesitate to call out the president's policies, values, and style, stressing the risks he poses to America's standing abroad and its freedoms at home. (They are especially skilled at getting under Trump's tan with television ads attacking his policies and character, often prompting presidential Twitter tantrums in response.) Yet the Never Trump books show special concern over the fate of the conservative movement and the Republican Party. "The [2016] election marked not only a rejection of

the Reagan legacy, but also the abandonment of respect for gradu-
alism, civility, expertise, intelligence, and prudence—the values
that were once taken for granted among conservatives," Charles J.
Sykes writes in *How the Right Lost Its Mind* (2017). He laments that
"somehow a movement based on ideas had devolved into a new
tribalism that valued neither principle nor truth."

Somehow. It's a telling word. If conservatism has been hijacked
by Trump, as these writers argue, who exactly left it so vulnerable?
The Never Trumpers hold everyone responsible for the rise of
Trumpism except, in any worthwhile way, themselves.

And when they do, it's more meh culpa than mea culpa. "Did
we—did I—contribute to this prairie fire of bigotry and xenophobia that seemed to grip so many on the Right?" Sykes asks. His
query proves largely rhetorical, however, with Sykes faulting himself at most for benign neglect. "For years, we ignored the birthers,
the racists, the truthers, and other conspiracy theorists," he writes.
They were like the obnoxious uncle at Thanksgiving, "whose
quirks could be indulged or at least ignored." Sykes indulged or at
least ignored it all in the hope that "things would not fall apart, and
principled conservatives would rise to the occasion." But things
did come undone, and conservatives didn't meet the challenge.
Now he frets over the "repudiation of the conservative mind"—a
repudiation that transpired while respectable conservatives such
as Sykes waited for someone else to yell "Stop!"

Rick Wilson, a veteran Republican campaign strategist and
vociferous multimedia Trump critic, cops to a "bit of guilt" for
helping rile the Republican base during the Obama years. "We fed
the monster and trained it," he admits early in *Everything Trump
Touches Dies*, published in 2018. "Then Trump came along. We lost
control of those tools, the party, and the movement. The monster
is out of its cage." But beyond noting that he should have seen it

coming—"let's get this mea culpa out of the way," Wilson writes—
he spends nearly all of his 300-plus pages blaming everyone else
for the outcome of his experiment.

And he does so in the crudest terms. Wilson never ceases to
insult Trump: "A monster from the laboratory of a jackass mad
scientist . . . the living, shitty embodiment of a culture that's more
Real Housewives and less Shining City on a Hill . . . a self-obsessed
Narcissus in a fright wig" with a "Liberace-meets-Saddam dec-
orating style"—and all that is just a selection from page 86. He
demeans the president's supporters: "I know you're in an oxy stu-
por much of the time, so I'll try to move slowly and not use big
words." He attacks Reince Priebus, Ted Cruz, and Mike Pence for
failing to fend Trump off and says Gingrich "started twerking [for
Trump] faster than a five-buck stripper." It's an image that is hard
to unimagine, and it is just one of Wilson's frequent sexualized
put-downs. White House adviser Stephen Miller "needs to spend
a week getting laid," the alt-right movement is a bunch of "pudgy
white boys from lower-middle-class suburbs who couldn't find a
woman's clitoris with a GPS and a magnifying glass," and Trump's
leadership amounts to "an endless exercise in self-fellation." Oblivious, Wilson laments the cruel discourse of the Trump era, with its
"endless stream of dick-joke-level insults." Write what you know,
I suppose.

Max Boot looks back on his career as a *Wall Street Journal* opinion editor and foreign policy adviser to the presidential campaigns
of John McCain and Marco Rubio and wonders: "Did I somehow
contribute to the rise of this dark force in American life with my
advocacy for conservatism?" (Again, *somehow.*) In *The Corrosion
of Conservatism*, published shortly before the 2018 midterm elections, Boot writes that Trump's ascent put him on "a painful and
difficult intellectual journey," one in which he came to regret his

advocacy for the Iraq War and worried that his support for free-market principles contributed to the economic struggles of Trump voters.

Yet Boot, now a columnist for the *Washington Post*, is caught in a contradiction he seems not to notice. He criticizes GOP leaders willing to "sell out their professed principles" to remain in the president's graces, with Paul Ryan ("a pathetic appeaser") and Rubio ("I had thought he was a man of principle") coming in for extra grief. Except Boot has also decided that those grand conservative principles were tainted and pointless. "Upon closer examination," he writes, "it's obvious that the whole history of modern conservatism is permeated with racism, extremism, conspiracy-mongering, ignorance, isolationism, and know-nothingism." With the convert's zeal (Boot switched from Republican to independent the day after the 2016 election), the author has glimpsed conservatism's dark side—and decides that the roots of Trumpism were there all along. "It's amazing how little you can see when your eyes are closed!" he writes. Boot, a self-described movement conservative who began subscribing to the *National Review* at age thirteen, confesses to have undergone a decades-long brainwashing, at times simply parroting conservative mantras with little grasp of the underlying issues. "I have spent most of my life as part of a political movement that has revealed itself to be morally and intellectually bankrupt," Boot writes. "That is a chastening lesson about the price of loyalty."

It also should be a chastening lesson on the insularity and posturing of the conservative intellectual community.

Jeff Flake, the former U.S. senator from Arizona, urges serious introspection. "We must never shirk our obligation to examine ourselves," he writes in *Conscience of a Conservative*, published just six months after Trump took office. Once the party of ideas, he writes, the GOP has instead adopted the politics of incoherence. "Call us willing accomplices," Flake admits. "The instant a flashy new novelty act came along, shredding conservative orthodoxy in the name of 'telling it like it is,' we bailed." The American conservative movement has been compromised by nationalism, populism, xenophobia, and celebrity, Flake writes, and has turned away from principles of free trade and fiscal rectitude. "We did it because it was cheap and easy and the real world is hard and defending a principled position to voters is harder still," he contends. Flake also knows of what he writes; rather than defend conservative principles to Arizona voters, he opted not to run for reelection in 2018 after a single Senate term.

"We all but ensured the rise of Donald Trump," he laments—but who is "we"? His critique is harsh but diffuse. The lone instance in which Flake reconsiders a specific and significant action of his own involves his 2008 House vote against the massive $700 billion Troubled Asset Relief Program bailout. He stood up for fiscal prudence and opposed the bailout of financial institutions, even though he privately hoped the act would pass. "At a moment of national and global crisis, that vote was an abdication of my responsibility," he acknowledges. It's a valuable insight—that maintaining a veneer of ideological purity just to score political points is a sham—but a single, decade-old anecdote seems to stop short of the courageous soul-searching Flake asks of conservatives in the Trump era.

So what kind of conservatism can survive, let alone thrive, in American politics today? The question hangs over the Never Trump conservatives and their books, and the answer depends in part on whether they regard the Trump presidency as an outlier or the logical endgame of a movement in decline.

"With hard work . . . and maybe a little luck, we will right this ship," Flake writes, calling for "a conservatism of high ideals, goodwill, and even better arguments." Boot, who is not even sure if he's a conservative anymore, considers the battle already lost. The GOP has become "the stupid party," he writes, and it does not deserve to survive. Wilson regards the future of the movement with a mix of honesty, generality, and banality. There was always "a whiff of bullshit" about Republican calls for fiscal conservatism, he acknowledges, and "we talk a good game about putting Main Street before Wall Street, but talk is all it's been." Nonetheless, he contends that Trumpism will someday seem a temporary aberration, as long as Republicans can—deep breath here—purge the conspiracy theorists, recruit ethnically diverse candidates, impose strict ethics rules for Congress, kill off crony capitalism, respect the Constitution, reduce the size of government, and uphold the rule of law. Oh, and stop hating. "We need to start telling Americans we believe in them again," Wilson writes. (His book doesn't help.)

Sykes calls for "restoring the conservative mind," yet he admits there may be little appetite for it. Despite the conservative refrain that America is at its core a center-right nation, "there has never been a strong constituency for the kind of tough budget cuts that would either limit the size of government or reduce the national debt," he writes. Sykes urges conservatives to step back from a zero-sum worldview in which opponents are demonized and the stakes vastly exaggerated. "We simply should not care about politics as much as we do," he concludes.

The Never Trumpers are engaged in a worthy exercise—yet it took the nomination, election, and presidency of Donald Trump to make it happen. In a sense, the Never Trumpers are also the Only Trumpers. Only with the rise of Trump did they think to interrogate the conservative dogma they'd long defended. Only with

Trump did they begin to reconsider their role in encouraging a frenzied base. Only with Trump did they see the need to restore or reach for higher ideals. Had Trump come close but failed to win the 2016 Republican nomination, had the party establishment and donor networks eked out one more mainstream nominee while still capitalizing on anger and conspiracy to turn out the vote, these earnest books would not exist. The conscience and corrosion of conservatism, the mind of the Right, would remain undisturbed and unexamined.

Only with Trump. Maybe they should thank him.

Many U.S. presidents have been drawn to intellectuals—thinkers who can elevate their instincts, pluck coherence from the rush of daily crises, or write the history they helped shape. But being a Trump intellectual is an entirely different task. Trump won the White House campaigning against established expertise. He doesn't dig into books or trust his briefing materials; indeed, he barely likes to read beyond a page or so. His brain trust is more *Fox & Friends* than American Enterprise Institute, his influences more Bannon than Buckley.

So, the conservative intellectuals who rush to Trump's defense often do so as much out of disdain for his opponents as belief in his project. And where they do attempt to retrofit an ideology onto Trumpism, they end up putting a movement in service of a man.

In the fall of 2016, Michael Anton, a former aide in the George W. Bush White House, published "The Flight 93 Election," a pseudonymous essay that previewed this approach with great melodrama. Voting for Trump, he wrote in the *Claremont Review of Books*, was like charging the cockpit of a hijacked plane on September 11, 2001. You might die—but if you do nothing, death is certain. A Hillary Clinton presidency would constitute an extinction-level event for freedom and true conservatism, he wrote; it would be "pedal-to-the-metal on the entire Progressive-left agenda."

The essay's hostility to establishment conservatives as well as immigrants—Anton decried America's "ceaseless importation of Third World foreigners"—no doubt made its author a strong candidate for a job on Team Trump. Anton, whose identity was later revealed by the dearly departed *Weekly Standard* magazine, served for fourteen months as a National Security Council official early in Trump's term, when then-White House chief strategist Stephen Bannon dubbed him "one of the most significant intellects in this nationalist movement."

But this significant intellect did not draw on his service in the White House to argue a concrete case for this president. Instead, in *After the Flight 93 Election*, published in early 2019, Anton reprints his original essay and appends a lengthy rumination to explain "the essences of conservatism, Americanism, and Western civilization, and to review the main threats to their survival." The system of federalism, separation of powers, and limited government bequeathed to us by the founders is under siege, Anton maintains, and the barbarians rattling the gate are the latest iteration of early twentieth-century progressives and 1960s radicals, justifying an ever-expanding administrative state with social-justice mantras of personal identity. "The post-1960s Left co-opts the language of 'justice' and 'rights' as a rhetorical device to get what it wants: the transfer of power, honor, and wealth between groups as retribution for past offenses," he writes. The result, he contends, is crime, family dissolution, and limitless government.

Trump, in Anton's telling, is the true resistance of this era, a warrior against the "revenge plot" of contemporary leftism. But Anton spends little time detailing or defending particular policies of the Trump administration; all that matters is the enemy. Hillary Clinton is no longer Anton's chief nemesis—it is the entire Left, along with sellout conservatives, who contribute to a "spiritual sickness" and "existential despair" pervading the United States and all of the West. Anton is declaring a permanent emergency; we are forever aboard Flight 93, endlessly in danger, as though Anton doesn't realize who has seized the controls.

Even a book titled *The Case for Trump* struggles to make the case for Trump. Military historian Victor Davis Hanson of the Hoover Institution at Stanford University instead spends much of his 2019 work attacking Trump's opponents. Hillary Clinton, no surprise, is resurrected for her ritual flogging: The misdeeds, real and alleged, of the 2016 Democratic nominee provided "scandal vaccination" for Trump's history of bankruptcies and sexual misconduct. Clinton's problem in 2016, Hanson explains, was threefold: she lied so much that her various deceptions could not be reconciled; she never learned from her past scandals; she thought herself exempt from accountability. The fact that this trifecta perfectly describes Trump's behavior in office is an irony that does not seem to graze Hanson's mind.

Trump did not create America's social and cultural fault lines, Hanson writes, but he "simply found existing sectarianism politically useful," as though the cynical exploitation of national divisions should just be one more hammer in a president's tool kit. Hanson marvels at the president's "uncouth authenticity" and his ability to troll and anger his critics. Any criticisms of the president are stylistic. For example, one of Hanson's go-to adjectives for Trump is "sloppy," as if the president is but a toddler coloring outside the lines. Trump had a "sloppy press conference" in Helsinki in July 2018, when he accepted Putin's denial of election interference over the conclusion of U.S. intelligence agencies. And

Trump's "sloppy administration in the detention of illegal aliens" is Hanson's fleeting reference to the inhumane policy of separating children from their parents on the southern border. The historian also fails to grapple with Trump's birther lie, his call to ban Muslims from entering the United States, or his difficulty condemning white nationalism. He simply blames Trump's predecessor for America's racial tensions. "Much of the current division in the country was deliberately whipped up by Obama," he contends. It's that simple.

Hanson envisions the president's politics as a kind of indiscriminate rejection of the norms, expectations, and traditions of American public life. Trumpism, he explains, is "the idea that there were no longer taboo subjects. *Everything was open for negotiation; nothing was sacred.*" Yes, there are times to toss away old verities. But just because nothing is sacred, does that mean everything must be profane?

For Hanson and Anton, Trump is an emergency measure. For Rich Lowry, Trump is an opportunity. In *The Case for Nationalism*, published in late 2019, Lowry attempts to reinterpret Trumpism as a lucid political program and ideology: a new nationalist conservatism that incorporates the president's views on immigration, trade, and foreign alliances. The problem, as always, is Trump himself.

Lowry would seem like one to understand the challenges here. Early in 2016, as editor of *National Review*, he published the "Against Trump" issue of the conservative magazine, with more than twenty contributors lamenting Trump's racial scapegoating, constitutional ignorance, and insufficient devotion to conservative values. (Lowry himself deemed Trump a "poor fit" for the Oval Office.) But victory has a way of tempering such concerns, and in his book Lowry urges Republicans to "thoughtfully integrate his nationalism into the party's orthodoxy."

Trump has tried to integrate the term into America's political rhetoric, though not all that thoughtfully. "I'm a nationalist, okay?" he declared at a rally in late 2018. "Nothing wrong. Use that word. Use that word!" Trump kept using the word, even if it doesn't necessarily mean what he thinks it means. "I'm proud of this country, and I call that nationalism," the president told Fox News host Laura Ingraham. Lowry fills in the blanks: Trump's nationalism involves immigration and trade policies adopted "with our own interests foremost in mind." America should protect itself with "the utmost vigilance" from external threats. And finally, "our country, not any other nation or international body or alliance, should always come first." You could almost call it—oh, I don't know—America First.

Lowry describes nationalism as flowing from a people's "natural devotion" to their homeland, and he emphasizes history and culture as the "indispensable glue" holding a nation together. He distances his project from the uglier aspects of nationalism by defining them away. Fascism may "appeal to nationalistic sentiment," but it is a "distinct phenomenon." Racism can "infect" nationalism, he acknowledges, but they are not the same thing. Europe's bloody twentieth-century conflicts were not about nationalism but about militarism and the "cult of charismatic leadership." Lowry frequently deploys such slippery formulations, suggesting that because two things are not synonymous, none should dare point out their links. Lowry prefers his nationalism "healthy," "well considered," "legitimate," and "true," while any other kind is "tainted with malign influences" and therefore not the real thing. Nationalism cannot be bad because Lowry has defined it as good, rendering *The Case for Nationalism* a book-length case study in begging the question.

The author similarly sanitizes Trump's variant of nationalism by deciding that the bad stuff doesn't count. "There isn't anything inherently nationalistic about wild presidential tweets, extreme boastfulness, excoriating attacks on the media, the browbeating of allies or even protectionism or populism," Lowry writes, adding, "Nor was there anything nationalistic about his initial reluctance to unambiguously denounce the far-right protests in Charlottesville, one of the low points of his presidency."

Except that those excoriating attacks on the news media as the enemy of the people and on political opponents as traitors are inseparable from Trump's interpretation of who belongs in the American nation—a message he amplifies with those wild presidential tweets. And when Trump said there were "very fine people on both sides" of the deadly 2017 protests in Charlottesville, he criticized the move to take down Confederate statues with precisely the kind of nationalist terminology that Lowry employs. "You're changing history, you're changing culture," the president grumbled. One of the lowest moral points of Trump's presidency was indeed suffused with Trump's vision of nationalism.

Lowry pines for a united and patriotic America, and he worries that the country is too divided over group identities to embrace a truly national one. But if national unity is your overriding concern, why promote a vision of the nation so heavy on exclusion? Lowry trashes intellectuals on the left, as well as corporate and political leaders holding antinationalist views, as not just misguided but treasonous. He appears animated by restricting immigration; on this he is joined by Anton (who worries about the United States importing ethnic separatism) and Hanson (who has "never seen a Malibu estate without a wall and gate"). Even though Lowry acknowledges that by the third generation, immigrants have largely shed their ancestral language, he notes that some Latin American

immigrants might remain skilled in two languages (¡*Dios mío!*)
and fail to assimilate.

"Accretions of culture add up over time to a national identity,"
Lowry writes, citing the eighteenth-century philosopher David
Hume. Great. So why should that process suddenly stop in the
early twenty-first century under Trump?

The irony of intellectualizing Trump's nationalism is that, despite what the president may say about nationalism in rallies or
interviews, he appears to care little for the American nation as a
whole; he governs with only his base and himself in mind. Not
even during a global pandemic, a crisis ruthlessly indifferent to
red or blue, can this president stop dividing, excluding, keeping
score, and even turning health versus economic recovery into a
culture-war standoff—all while placing his own grievances at the
center of the story. Not even during a nationwide outcry against
police brutality could he resist the desire to "dominate" the protesting Americans he considered his antagonists. Trump's nationalism substitutes the man for the nation, and his supporters for the
people.

In this light, the move toward a more nationalist conservatism
feels like something of a rescue mission for the Right, an effort
to retain relevance under a president and a base that care little
for conservative traditions. And so those traditions—which some
conservative intellectuals now deride as a "dead consensus" that
for too long prioritized free markets, small government, and the
interests of capital over labor—are being jettisoned. It is a dicey
endeavor, both politically and intellectually. A new nationalism
may give renewed energy to a post-Trump conservatism or gain
sway in a second Trump term, but it also risks turning conservatism into that oddest of intellectual movements, one that is

dogmatic and exclusionary even while proving itself utterly malleable.

"Use that word," Trump ordered. When his followers purport to be elevating his ideals, they're really obeying his commands.

Immediately following the November 8, 2016, election, some Republicans and conservatives who had opposed Trump suddenly found religion. Trump loyalists derided them as the "November Ninth Club," writes *Politico* correspondent Tim Alberta in *American Carnage*, his 2019 book on the battles inside the GOP. Should Trump lose the next presidential election, there will no doubt be a new club—made up of Republicans and conservatives insisting that they worked with Trump or supported him only to curb his worst instincts, that they were not enablers but heroes safeguarding the American experiment. Applications will far exceed the number of those deserving admission.

Yet there are conservative thinkers today who do not instinctively genuflect, look away, or insist that Trump and Trumpism are anything other than what they are. They seek to repair and reshape a post-Trump America and a post-Trump conservatism, not just repair their own reputations and shape their own career prospects.

Peter Wehner, a former official in the George W. Bush White House, hopes to restore politics as a noble calling. In his 2019 book, *The Death of Politics*, he insists that the path forward lies in moderation, compromise, and civility. Moderation calls for the humility to recognize limits and an aversion to fanaticism; "its antithesis is not conviction but intemperance," he writes. Compromise is moderation's practical side, Wehner explains; only the paranoid would call it treason. And civility is central to citizenship; without it, "everything in life becomes a battlefield." These values, already in short supply before Trump ran for office, have become quaint, almost nonexistent, in Trump's Washington.

Wehner is vague on how to fortify the values he so lionizes, especially in an environment that clearly repudiates them. "If each of us inspires or moves one or two or three other people to give politics—real politics, not just political theater—a second chance . . . then there will be millions among us," he assures, as though a feel-good, pay-it-forward strategy could really move us forward. Wehner also calls for the regulation of social-media platforms, greater focus on civic literacy and American history in schools, and reforms that restore Congress's pride of place as the first branch. All fine and nice as far as it goes, but Wehner is wary of going much further. If moderation and civility are his political values, then modesty and incrementalism are his governing ones. "We don't need to transform everyone's behavior or temperament (something no conservative would ever want to attempt, by the way)," he cautions.

But there is at least one who would attempt it. Yuval Levin, the editor of *National Affairs*, suggests that the cynicism, alienation, and mistrust pervading the country (he calls this a "crisis of connectedness") flow from the weakening of social and political institutions. It is not a new critique—among Trump-era books, Timothy Carney's *Alienated America* issues similar warnings—but Levin gets to the heart of why revitalized institutions are so critical. "Healthy institutions often function as molds for the people inside them," he writes in *A Time to Build* (2020). "We pour ourselves into our family, our church, our work, or our school, and in so doing we begin to take the institution's shape." Institutions are "inherently constraining," Levin writes, and he absolutely means that as a good thing. "They provide the people in them with boundaries and procedures, a code of behavior, standards of integrity, and formal responsibilities that help direct their ambitions and abilities toward a broadly shared purpose."

Popular culture compels us to ask: "What do I want?" Institutions urge a different query, Levin explains: "Given my role here, how should I act?" It is a relevant question—perhaps the most relevant—for this time and for this presidency. It is a question that combines personal responsibility with higher obligations, invoking conservative traditions that sycophants ignore, Never Trumpers forget, and pro-Trump intellectuals rationalize away. In posing it, *A Time to Build* becomes that rare work of the Trump era—the book I didn't realize I was hoping to read.

Institutions structure our thoughts and actions and embody our ideals, Levin writes; they *form* us. The problem of institutions today is that rather than being formative, they have become performative, functioning as platforms for individual advancement rather than molds for individual improvement. Congress displays a special lack of institutional ambition, Levin argues, with too many members posturing for partisan audiences and demonizing political opponents rather than engaging in the hard business of dialogue and compromise that should characterize a functional legislature. And Trump has enshrined the anti-institutional, performative spirit in the White House. Even in the Oval Office, he imagines himself as an outsider to it. Rather than being molded by his role—remember the pivot?—he contorts it for his benefit. "When the presidency and Congress are just stages for political performance art . . . they become harder to trust," Levin writes. That is why institutions are winning our attention even as they are losing our confidence.

In his 2019 vanity publishing project, *Triggered*, Donald Trump Jr. stakes his claim as heir to his father's political kingdom, largely on the strength of his outdoorsman persona and skills as a self-described base-rousing "shit-talker par excellence." The book is packed with insults, boasts, and deceptions; it equates success in political life merely with the ability to enrage. ("Anything that makes the veins in a few liberal foreheads bulge out is fine by me," he gloats.) The book's existence is worth mentioning only because Don Jr. appears to regard that attitude as a path to his own political advancement, and because the book embodies the anti-institutionalist ethos of the Trump era. Matters of policy or principle matter little here. The only question is: Are you with Trump or not?

In *A Time to Build*, Levin forces a different question, one that the president, the Republican Party, and the conservative movement have forgotten, if indeed they ever thought to ask it: Given your role in American democracy, how should you act?

BOOKS DISCUSSED

Tim Alberta. *American Carnage: On the Front Lines of the Republican Civil War and the Rise of President Trump*. Harper, 2019.

Michael Anton. *After the Flight 93 Election: The Vote That Saved America and What We Still Have to Lose*. Encounter Books, 2019.

Max Boot. *The Corrosion of Conservatism: Why I Left the Right*. Liveright, 2018.

Jeff Flake. *Conscience of a Conservative: A Rejection of Destructive Politics and a Return to Principle*. Random House, 2017.

Newt Gingrich. *Trump's America: The Truth about Our Nation's Great Comeback*. Center Street, 2018.

———. *Understanding Trump*. Center Street, 2017.

Victor Davis Hanson. *The Case for Trump*. Basic Books, 2019.

Hugh Hewitt. *The Fourth Way: The Conservative Playbook for a Lasting GOP Majority*. Simon & Schuster, 2017.

Yuval Levin. *A Time to Build: From Family and Community to Congress and the Campus, How Recommitting to Our Institutions Can Revive the American Dream*. Basic Books, 2020.

Corey Lewandowski and David Bossie. *Let Trump Be Trump: The Inside Story of His Rise to the Presidency*. Center Street, 2017.

Rich Lowry. *The Case for Nationalism: How It Made Us Powerful, United, and Free*. Broadside Books, 2019.

Jeanine Pirro. *Liars, Leakers, and Liberals: The Case Against the Anti-Trump Conspiracy*. Center Street, 2018.

Charles J. Sykes. *How the Right Lost Its Mind*. St. Martin's, 2017.

Donald Trump Jr. *Triggered: How the Left Thrives on Hate and Wants to Silence Us*. Center Street, 2019.

Peter Wehner. *The Death of Politics: How to Heal Our Frayed Republic After Trump*. Harper One, 2019.

Rick Wilson. *Everything Trump Touches Dies: A Republican Strategist Gets Real About the Worst President Ever*. Free Press, 2018.

FOUR

BEYOND THE WALL

Donald Trump's border wall began as a gimmick, morphed into a symbol, and grew into a war—a war on immigrants, but a culture war, too.

In the summer of 2014, Trump's advisers knew that immigration would be at the center of a potential primary bid, and they wanted to keep their guy on message. So they hit on the perfect device: Trump loves to brag about his skills as a builder, so why not pledge to construct a wall on the southern border and to cut off aid to Mexico to pay for it?

Trump tried the line out in a Des Moines speech—months before he would formally announce his candidacy by labeling Mexican immigrants rapists and drug traffickers—and the crowd loved it. "Trump was hooked," *New York Times* reporters Julie Hirschfeld Davis and Michael D. Shear write in *Border Wars: Inside Trump's Assault on Immigration* (2019). "The wall would become a permanent part of his campaign machinery and a potent symbol for everything he stood for, taking on totemic significance and shaping his presidency."

Whether or not a border wall would ever be completed was incidental. To fight for it and justify it, to revel in the fury it stokes—that is its purpose. It has never been about keeping immigrants out; it is about keeping the base all in.

The wall is like Trump: big and bombastic, more artifice than utility, a blunt solution to a complex and ill-defined problem. The wall, like Trump, is zero-sum: You are on one side or the other, you are with him or against him. But the wall also imposes order on the entire anti-immigrant project. Once you accept that some people should be shut out, that there is no room in Trump's America, that *we're full*, then whatever you do to them—separating them from their families, disregarding their claims of persecution, banning them on religious grounds, expelling them in the middle of a global pandemic—becomes permissible, even logical.

The immigration books of the Trump era seek to subvert that logic. They include heartfelt memoirs and seething manifestos, journalistic investigations of activism and policy, sober proposals groping for middle ground between seemingly irreconcilable positions, even earnest, try-too-hard novels that purport to tell the story of "voiceless" migrants. The best of them show that, unlike the wall or the president, immigration is not simple, monolithic, and zero-sum. That it can reshape America for the better, even while bringing out its worst.

These works reveal the impact of immigration on the United States, exploring how newcomers have slowly transformed the country, over time and from within, remaking its cities and economy. These books redirect the floodlights away from the southern border to show the modern migrant face, more Asian and more female than before. They emphasize not only the suffering of those enduring inhumane treatment at the border but the damage on those who inflict that treatment, too. And though some take comfort in America's immigrant tradition, insisting that we are intrinsically *better than this*, others question that premise, making plain that scapegoating, marginalizing, and dehumanizing immigrants has a long tradition here, too.

Every immigrant finds obstacles to belonging, and every generation of Americans finds new faces to mistrust. The current president is just compulsively indiscriminate in his compulsion to discriminate. With a mix of cruelty and opportunism, Trump has encouraged America's basest impulses and prejudices against outsiders. Yet in doing so he has created a new opening for writers to reconsider the history, values, and experiences of immigrants in America, and to remind us that we are better than this only when we demand it.

Implicit in the shocked responses to the Trump administration's immigration policies is a bit of national back-patting. After all, this is the United States of America. How could this happen *here*?

"The horror of child separation is not some evil perpetrated in a vicious civil war or a national campaign of genocide by a dictator in some far-off land," writes Jeff Merkley in *America Is Better Than This: Trump's War Against Migrant Families* (2019). "It is here, in America. It is perpetrated by our government, with our resources, on our land."

Merkley, the junior U.S. senator from Oregon, who visited the southern border in 2018 and saw migrants huddled in cells and families detained in what he likened to internment camps, is not just making a political or moral claim. He is arguing a case about history and self-perception. Trump's onslaught against immigrants, he writes, "demolishes the notion that we are a nation that treats people fleeing persecution with fundamental respect and dignity." As much as Merkley worries about immigrant families, he also is concerned that America is no longer what he thought it was. "The scandal of child separation profoundly disturbed me and so many people across the country both because it is wrong, unacceptable under any moral code or religious tradition," he writes. "But it also disturbs us because it undermines our own sense of ourselves—and of America—as champions for fairness, and freedom, and opportunity."

Our sense of ourselves. That phrase suggests a collective understanding, a self-assured consensus. Merkley concludes his prologue and his final chapter with the common notion that serves as his title phrase: "America is better than this." It is both lament and vote of confidence, portraying the Trump era as a deviation from some long-held American norm, as if how we've acted has no bearing on who we are.

In his 2018 memoir, *Stranger: The Challenge of a Latino Immigrant in the Trump Era*, Mexican American journalist Jorge Ramos acknowledges that the United States oscillates between welcoming immigrants and rejecting them. "This latter cycle is the one in which we are living now," he writes. Yet, like Merkley, Ramos casts Trump as anomalous. "The very essence of the United States is to be a multiethnic, multiracial, multicultural nation, a diverse and tolerant one created by immigrants under the guiding principles of freedom, equality, and democracy," Ramos asserts. And the nation's changing complexion—with minorities on track to become the majority before midcentury—will overwhelm the nativism and white nationalism that Trump has emboldened. Then, Ramos concludes, "the United States can continue with its tradition of ethnic diversity, multiculturalism, and acceptance of immigrants."

Just hold on. America will be back.

It's a soothing vision—that today's misdeeds will be overtaken by time, demography, and the eventual recognition of lasting traditions. But diversity and acceptance are far from America's only values; the arc of the moral universe may bend toward justice, or it may snap back in our faces. Erika Lee, a historian at the University of Minnesota, looks upon the past two and a half centuries and finds a parallel custom that often overpowers the mantra of inclusion: the mistrust and hatred of foreigners.

"Xenophobia has been neither an aberration nor a contradiction to the United States' history of immigration," Lee writes in *America for Americans* (2019). "Rather, it has existed alongside and constrained America's immigration tradition." Xenophobia is not purely a reaction to hard economic times, the author cautions. "It exists and flourishes during times of peace *and* war, economic prosperity *and* depression, low *and* high immigration, and racial struggle *and* racial progress."

Every new set of outsiders has suffered the same criticism: they are too numerous; they'll never assimilate; their allegiances are suspect. In the colonial era, Benjamin Franklin fretted that German arrivals "could 'never adopt our Language or Customs.'" Mid-nineteenth-century Irish immigrants were deemed Vatican loyalists and members of an inferior Celtic race. Polish, Italian, Russian, and Hungarian newcomers were judged "the most illiterate and depraved" of the European immigrants to reach these shores. Lee cites a question from a founder of the country's first anti-immigration think tank, dating to the late nineteenth century: "Do we want this country to be peopled by British, German, and Scandinavian stock, historically free, energetic, progressive, or by Slav, Latin, and Asiatic races, historically downtrodden, atavistic, and stagnant?"

Or, in more contemporary terms: Why are we letting in all these people from shithole countries?

Xenophobia is like a muscle that grows stronger with use, and the mistreatment of each new immigrant community becomes a baseline for the next. Lee highlights the Chinese Exclusion Act of 1882, which "legalized xenophobia on an unprecedented scale"; the internment of thousands of American families of Japanese

descent during World War II, which "de-Americanized" a generation of citizens; and the expulsion of Mexicans and Mexican
Americans during the Great Depression. Such episodes highlight
the links between xenophobia and race. Economic debates over
jobs and security concerns about loyalty and criminality are typical rationales for assailing outsiders, but Lee emphasizes that race
is "the single most important factor" in determining who suffers
xenophobic discrimination and who escapes it.

America for Americans shows how primed the country was for
Trump's message. Birtherism, for example, was not merely a racist
lie about the first black president but also proof of how branding
someone foreign and Muslim remains a potent means to discredit.
By the time Trump launched his presidential campaign in 2015,
anti-Latino sentiment had been "well established and normalized"
for at least a generation, Lee writes, harking back to the 1990s debates over California's Proposition 187. And the al-Qaeda attacks
of September 2001 had already fortified anti-Muslim attitudes,
rendering Trump's travel ban, initially targeting seven Muslim-
majority nations, entirely consistent with past discrimination.
"The Trump administration's immigration policies," Lee contends,
"were a logical evolution of America's xenophobic tradition."
Top U.S. officials' insistence on describing the coronavirus as the
"China virus" or the "Wuhan virus"—with Trump resorting to the
particularly denigrating "kung flu," to the cheers of his crowds—is
the latest instance in a long history.

In that history, Trump is less anomaly than affirmation.

Mi papá, no quiero que lo deporten . . .
¡Papi!
¡Mami!
Me puedo ir con mi tía por lo menos . . .

The sobs of Central American children begging for their missing parents in an unspecified Customs and Border Protection detention facility, as heard in an audio recording obtained by *ProPublica* in 2018, sum up the brutality of Trump's immigration policy. Of all the efforts to deter undocumented immigrants from entering the United States, the move to separate children from parents has elicited the most revulsion. "The darkness, the evil, of child separation damages the souls of everyone it touches," Merkley writes in *America Is Better Than This*. The policy became a source of consternation inside the White House and the Department of Homeland Security, Davis and Shear recount in *Border Wars*. Officials blamed one another for the public-relations disaster even as they sought praise from the president—right up until he signed an executive order reversing the policy. "The crying babies," Trump told Republican lawmakers, "doesn't look good politically."

If the border wall captures Trump's immigration policy at its most simple-minded, family separation reveals it at its cruelest. But it is a cruel irony, too, because family separation is already intrinsic to the immigrant experience, occurring long before anyone reaches America's borders. Recounted in countless memoirs, it is no less wrenching than the ruptures the Trump administration inflicted on thousands of families—and may even be more painful at times, since it happens voluntarily. That is, if acts born of despair can ever be described as voluntary.

"Every immigrant has left a love behind," writes Suketu Mehta in *This Land Is Our Land: An Immigrant's Manifesto* (2019). "Every immigrant has abandoned a lover or a child or a best friend. . . . Back home, the grandparents prepare extravagant meals, lay out the table in the garden, light the lamps in the evening for the children who will never come back. Back home, the children wait for their mothers to call every Sunday."

For immigrants, wherever they come from or however they enter, separation is an endless toll. That is why splitting up families as a form of deterrence is not only barbaric but foolish. All immigration involves family separation; to compound it at the border only adds more pain and uncertainty to the sacrifices immigrants already must make.

In *Dear America: Notes of an Undocumented Citizen* (2018), activist Jose Antonio Vargas reflects, decades later, on one of many letters he wrote as a child to his mother in the Philippines, after she sent him, with fake travel documents, to live with his grandparents in Northern California. "As I read it now, I don't recognize that young boy," Vargas writes. "What happened to all that love and longing I felt for the family and friends I'd left? Separation not only divides families; separation buries emotion, buries it so far down you can't touch it."

Separation also leaves immigrants wondering what might have been. In *A Dream Called Home* (2018), memoirist Reyna Grande recalls returning to Mexico and talking with her younger sister about the lifelong consequences of decisions the family made. Grande remained in Mexico as a child while her parents came to work in the United States, and later crossed the border herself as an undocumented immigrant. "Do you think things would have been different if they had never left?" her sister asks her. "Do you think we would all be together as a family?"

Do you think? Do you wonder? What if? It is a maddening game, and an inescapable one. It is the lot of every immigrant to straddle borders of all kinds and at all times, to gaze back with relief but also nostalgia, to look forward with hope and insecurity, to strive to belong even while we get the hint.

• • •

Separation marks individuals, reinvents families, transforms nations. *New York Times* reporter Jason DeParle tells the story of one
such individual, family, and nation in *A Good Provider Is One Who
Leaves* (2019), the multigenerational tale of a Filipino family dis-
persing across the globe, from Manila to Abu Dhabi to Galveston,
Texas, and so many places in between. Parents leave their children
behind for years, so they can send back earnings that are many mul-
tiples of what they previously made. Children yearn for absent loved
ones, rebelling or withdrawing without them, while the youngest
latch on to aunts and grandparents. Births, birthdays, weddings, ill-
nesses, funerals—the currents of daily life must be imagined at a
distance. Meanwhile, the government of the Philippines encourages
the exodus: one in seven laborers becomes an Overseas Filipino
Worker, a status so common it rates not just an official abbreviation
but also an industry of private middlemen and state agencies managing a sector that makes up one-tenth of the country's economy.

"The two main themes of Overseas Filipino Worker life are
homesickness and money," DeParle explains. "Workers suffer the
first to get the second." He tells the story of Emet, Tita, and their
daughter Rosalie, and the book's title is the family's unofficial
creed, a painful blend of self-affirmation and abnegation.

Emet cleaned pools in Manila, earning $50 a month, barely
sufficient to get by in the family's shantytown. When he is offered
the same job in Saudi Arabia for $500 per month, he takes it, and
his wife of fourteen years and their five children must stay behind.
"Ever since his orphaned childhood, all he had wanted was a family, but to support one, he had to leave it," DeParle writes. All five
of Tita and Emet's children would eventually work abroad, too.
Rosalie, their middle child, is the book's itinerant protagonist, not
simply because she becomes the clan's top breadwinner as a nurse

in America but because, for DeParle, she embodies contemporary
migration, far removed from presidential fearmongering about
bad hombres and terrorists marching through the desert.

Rosalie makes it through nursing school and works for several
years in Saudi Arabia and the United Arab Emirates before finally
reaching the United States, where she takes on the night shift at a
Texas hospital and adapts to suburban life. In between, she endures
separation not just from her parents but from her own husband
and children until they gather in Galveston. DeParle notes that,
over the past dozen years, the United States has attracted more
Asian immigrants than Latin American ones, with nearly half of
them arriving, like Rosalie, with college degrees. "Every corner of
America has an immigrant like her," he writes.

Migration to America has become less male-dominated than
before, in part because of the demand for caregivers in rich countries, a need met disproportionately by women. DeParle captures
the contradictions of a country that needs immigrants to fill jobs
yet treats them with suspicion, of a nation that discriminates
against outsiders and then complains that they don't assimilate
more quickly. "Unwelcomed is not the same as unwanted," he explains.

DeParle concludes that Rosalie's experience was "a triple win"
(for her, for the United States, and for her relatives in the Philippines), but he cautions against debating immigration in absolutist
terms. "The more the issue becomes part of the culture wars, like
guns and abortion, the more supporters of migration have to lose."
His reporting for this book began decades before the Trump era,
but his warning arrives under a president who has done everything possible to make immigration into a culture war. Trump
campaigned for the border wall in 2016 with violent and dehumanizing rhetoric, even likening migrants to poisonous snakes.

(*"Oh, shut up, silly woman,"* said the reptile with a grin, *"you knew damn well I was a snake before you let me in!"*) He powered fears of a caravan ahead of the 2018 midterm elections. And in 2020, he has linked immigration to a deadly infectious disease. Trump is not just rewriting immigration policies; he is seeking to edit openness to immigrants out of the American story altogether, leaving only the prejudice that has always stalked them.

Rosalie declined to pass judgment on the president. "I cannot judge what's in his heart," she told DeParle. But the author's own rebuttal is simple and should logically appeal to anyone who hopes for renewed American greatness. "It's good," DeParle concludes, "for your country to be the place where people go to make dreams come true."

Immigration fights are often reduced to a cost-benefit calculation, as if the worth of human beings were a matter of weighing the contributions they are likely to make against the expenditures they might cause—with those ending on the plus side becoming the lucky winners who gain entry.

Supporters of more open immigration buy into this idea and offer statistics stressing the industriousness of immigrant communities—how they pay taxes for government programs they cannot access and reduce criminality in their neighborhoods. "Trump, the conservative media, and the anti-immigrant groups present us as rapists, murderers, gang members, abusers, beaters, cheaters, counterfeiters, and criminals," Ramos complains in *Stranger*. "But the reality is that immigrants—undocumented and otherwise—commit fewer crimes than natural-born Americans. We are supportive and generous, we help those who need it the most, and we contribute greatly to the country that accepted us." Ramos cites a National Academies of Sciences report calculating the tens of billions of dollars immigrants have added to the U.S. economy in recent decades. Others make a more personal case: "We haven't taken a dime in welfare," Mehta writes of his relatives in *This Land Is Our Land*. "When we needed money, we borrowed from family."

But what if immigrants' contributions to the U.S. tax base declined somewhat in the coming years, or if their descendants proved no more and no less criminally minded than other native-born Americans? What if other families, less fortunate or resourceful than Mehta's, occasionally avail themselves of government benefits in hard times? Would that mean admitting them was a mistake? "Immigrants are seen as mere labor, our physical bodies judged by perceptions of what we contribute, or what we take," Vargas writes in *Dear America*. "Our existence is as broadly criminalized as it is commodified."

It is one thing to assess the impact of immigration as an aggregate economic force. But how to calculate the value of a new neighbor or a new family, of a new resident or worker or student—of a single life lived here, not there?

In *Melting Pot or Civil War?* (2018), Manhattan Institute president Reihan Salam urges Americans to bypass the "dueling spasms of culture-war outrage" over immigration and "meet others halfway." He locates that halfway point in a system that gives preference to better-educated and higher-skilled newcomers. A first-generation Bangladeshi American, Salam worries that long-standing U.S. immigration policy—which favors those with family ties—fosters too many closed-off, low-income, undereducated communities. And that's a recipe for strife, not just because native-born white Americans are increasingly nervous and angry over demographic change (another great sanitizing euphemism of our time), but because the new children of immigrants will not be satisfied with the kind of lives their parents accepted. "Just as Donald Trump's election spoke to the rage and disaffection of older whites in the heartland, the years to come may see a new populist revolt, driven by the resentments of working-class Americans of color," Salam warns. The challenge immigration poses today, he writes, is that it risks "undermining civic solidarity, producing ethnic balkanization, and breeding polarized backlash."

The author's proposals—a one-time amnesty for longtime undocumented residents, followed by more "resolute" border enforcement, as well as a more selective and skills-based system for admitting immigrants—will surely alienate all sides, making this an oddly brave policy book. Salam urges compromise, "even if that means risking embarrassment or alienating some of the members of your own cultural tribe." He hopes to neutralize the era's nativist and racialized politics in favor of a new "middle-class melting pot," strengthened by higher-skilled immigrants who, he argues, are better able to assimilate and flourish.

But measuring human worth by college degrees and earnings potential misses much about the benefits and costs of immigration; it may miss almost everything. In the 2019 study *Barrio America*, Penn State University historian A. K. Sandoval-Strausz shows how Hispanic migrants reinvigorated American cities in the latter decades of the twentieth century. Population loss, declining economic growth, fiscal deficits, and rising crime conspired to create the urban crisis of the 1970s and 1980s—and Latino immigrants and migrants stepped into the void, Sandoval-Strausz writes, "saving scores of neighborhoods from abandonment and replenishing the population in many places that would otherwise have continued to empty out."

These were not people preselected for their high earning prospects or their advanced training in science and engineering.

Rather, they "earned modest incomes and were socially marginalized, politically demonized, and sometimes undocumented," Sandoval-Strausz writes. Yet their presence provided a "large-scale urban reinvestment," while their rent payments and mortgages offered a lifeline to local housing markets. In the author's case studies of Dallas and Chicago, Latino immigrants became consumers and small-business owners, reviving commerce and boosting local tax revenues.

It's hard to determine in advance which immigrants will contribute most to America and what shape those contributions may take, to estimate up front who "deserves" to be here more. What is clear is that even heralding the economic potential of talented immigrants is not enough to ensure that they are welcome. In *The Making of a Dream* (2018), journalist Laura Wides-Muñoz emphasizes how the Dreamers—those young undocumented immigrants who arrived in the United States as children, and who have been so often depicted in their graduation caps and gowns—seem as ready as anyone to make a positive mark on the only homeland they know. Yet the DREAM Act has lingered for years, much like the Dreamers themselves, without winning full legal status. "The story of the perfect, well-mannered student hadn't worked," Wides-Muñoz acknowledges.

In *This Land Is Our Land*, Mehta shows how assessing costs and benefits can yield unexpected outcomes, depending on how far back the calculations go. "When migrants move, it's not out of idle fancy, or because they hate their homelands, or to plunder the countries they come to, or even (most often) to strike it rich," he writes. "They move—as my grandfather knew—because the accumulated burdens of history have rendered their homelands less and less habitable. They are here because you were there." Mehta sees immigration as reparations, as payback for colonialism, for the plunder of resources, for ecological and economic devastation.

For immigrants, there are always costs uncounted, benefits unrecognized, debts unpaid. Separating newcomers into good and bad, into talented go-getters and unassimilated burdens, may make sense in a wonk's paradise. But it ignores history and denies humanity.

"Americans are dreamers, too," Trump declared in his 2018 State of the Union address, slyly seeking to wrest moral authority away from the young immigrant activists. And throughout history, Americans have looked to the frontier to make those dreams real—the place and idea that, according to Frederick Jackson Turner's "frontier thesis," not only spurred America's development and propelled its borders but shaped its politics, its very meaning.

In his Pulitzer Prize–winning *The End of the Myth: From the Frontier to the Border Wall in the Mind of America* (2019), Yale University historian Greg Grandin examines the contradictions of the frontier and how Trump has turned them to his advantage. A country that believed it could endlessly expand its territory and economy (imbued with "an ideology of limitlessness," the author explains) also imagined that this expansion would wash away its contradictions on race, poverty, and inequality. "There was no problem caused by expansion that couldn't be solved by more expansion," Grandin writes, describing the prevailing attitudes of past times.

It is a clichéd American belief—that more growth and power will expand the pie, break the fever, ease the tensions. In this way, the ferocity deployed to conquer and extend the frontier, such as President Andrew Jackson's Indian Removal Act of 1830, could seem justified, Grandin writes, even "transformed into something noble." The frontier was a safety valve, a way to pretend to reconcile an America founded on "unparalleled freedom and unmatched unfreedom." But no longer. Trump's border wall, Grandin concludes, is "a monument to the final closing of the frontier," a sign that when America now gazes upon the frontier, it sees only threats, not possibilities.

"To understand the nation's current crisis—especially the way anti-migrant nativism has become the binding agent for what is now called Trumpism—one has to understand that the border, over the long course of its history, has effectively become the negation of the frontier," Grandin writes. "The long boundary separating Mexico from the United States served as the repository of the racism and the brutality that the frontier was said, by its theorists, to leave behind through forward motion into the future." It is as if all that pain and hatred now coalesce at the border, one more accumulated burden of history that Trump can draw on to encourage nationalist resentment. The safety valve has been shut, and far too tightly.

The inhumanity of U.S. border enforcement, with its "seething racism and militarized and paramilitarized cruelty," as Grandin writes, hardly began with Trump, but it is now out in the open. Grandin warns of the "nationalization of border brutalism" in the Trump era, an "extremism turned inward, all-consuming and self-devouring." When the president declared in a 2019 speech that he was building a border wall in Colorado, the mockery came quick, and Trump said he was joking. But there is a sense in which he was right. In Trump's America, anti-immigrant animus hangs over any community susceptible to prejudice, whatever its geography. The wall is everywhere.

The brief but savage controversy surrounding Jeanine Cummins's *American Dirt*, a middling novel published early in 2020 about a Mexican mother and son eluding assassins, corrupt officials, and thuggish patrols to make it across the border, exemplifies the culture war surrounding immigration, with all its rage and misdirection. The book, which earned its author a seven-figure advance, was initially promoted as the Great American Immigrant Novel of our time, notwithstanding its flat characters, weak dialogue, perplexing depictions of Mexican life, random use of italicized Spanish words, and obvious morality plays. (An evil Mexican commander dropping Trump quotes while terrorizing migrants feels a bit too on the *nariz*.) The book suffered a vicious backlash from Mexican American and other Hispanic writers who called it irresponsible and exploitative and assailed the author for fetishizing trauma. A book party for Cummins with barbed wire–themed décor didn't help.

In another time, a novel like this would not have received such hype or such condemnation—it deserves neither—but the controversy over *American Dirt* is inseparable from our current cultural politics, from publishers seeking a sympathetic, mass-market, movie-ready portrayal of the immigrant saga, and from critics feeling that the fix was in, that at this crucial moment, a flawed account would not only misrepresent the true immigrant story but threaten to erase it.

The irony is that a great American immigrant novel need not fixate on the border, as Trump would have us all do. It would depict migrants remaking cities and towns across America and across history, and being remade by them, too. It would look beyond the "good" and "bad" immigrants and the model minorities; it would privilege individuals over categorizations. It could highlight Spanish-speaking newcomers from Latin America, but it would not have to. It would explain what Trump has wrought through lesser-noticed regulations and rules that, even before the heightened immigration restrictions surrounding the coronavirus pandemic, had targeted undocumented immigrants for rapid removal, increased wait times for naturalization, delayed visa approvals, and slashed the number of refugees admitted to the United States. It would look beyond this president, grappling with what America has done for generations, absorbing immigrants and evolving with them, even while seeking to reject them.

And it would show that the burdens of demonization and brutality are borne primarily by migrants, but not by them alone. In his understated memoir *The Line Becomes a River* (2018), former Border Patrol agent Francisco Cantú recounts his time in the Southwest during the Obama administration, detaining and processing border crossers, slashing their water bottles and scattering their supplies to discourage them from going any further. "It sounds terrible, and maybe it is, but the idea is that when they come out of their hiding places, when they regroup and return to find their stockpiles ransacked and stripped, they'll realize their situation, that they're fucked, that it's hopeless to continue, and they'll quit right then and there." Rather than making your country the place where dreams come true, the job is to make it the place where hope comes to die.

Cantú, the grandson of a Mexican border crosser, studied immigration in college and joined the Border Patrol because he wanted to see it all for himself, even hoping he might bring some relief to those whose dreams he would thwart. He tries. He gives his shirt to a man who had lost his own and treats him to burgers. He warns two teenage boys not to cross again during the summer; the heat is too dangerous. He treats and bandages the blistered feet of a woman who was left behind by her companions because of her limp—a quitter, in the patrol's parlance. "Eres muy humanitario, oficial," she tells him.

But he doesn't feel humanitarian. Cantú suffers constant nightmares as the dissonance between intentions and actions becomes harder to bear. He dreams that he shoots a man and his son. He dreams of a cave strewn with body parts. He dreams of "men lost and wandering without food or water, dying slowly," he writes. Cantú finally leaves this work behind, but he can't really; he feels he is "still a part of this thing that crushes."

Before he joined the Border Patrol, his mother warned him that "the soul can buckle" in a job like this, and Cantú recalls her quietly damning assessment once he left: "You spent nearly four years on the border. . . . You weren't just observing a reality, you were participating in it. You can't exist within a system for that long without being implicated, without absorbing its poison."

We knew well what Trump was before we let him in. Nearly four years into his presidency, all of us are implicated in the costs of his assault on immigration. We have absorbed that, too.

BOOKS DISCUSSED

Francisco Cantú. *The Line Becomes a River: Dispatches from the Border.* Riverhead Books, 2018.

Jeanine Cummins. *American Dirt: A Novel.* Flatiron Books, 2020.

Julie Hirschfeld Davis and Michael D. Shear. *Border Wars: Inside Trump's Assault on Immigration.* Simon & Schuster, 2019.

Jason DeParle. *A Good Provider Is One Who Leaves: One Family and Migration in the 21st Century.* Viking, 2019.

Reyna Grande. *A Dream Called Home: A Memoir.* Atria Books, 2018.

Greg Grandin. *The End of the Myth: From the Frontier to the Border Wall in the Mind of America.* Metropolitan Books, 2019.

Erika Lee. *America for Americans: A History of Xenophobia in the United States.* Basic Books, 2019.

Suketu Mehta. *This Land Is Our Land: An Immigrant's Manifesto.* Farrar, Straus and Giroux, 2019.

Jeff Merkley. *America Is Better Than This: Trump's War Against Migrant Families.* Twelve, 2019.

Jorge Ramos. *Stranger: The Challenge of a Latino Immigrant in the Trump Era.* Vintage Books, 2018.

Reihan Salam. *Melting Pot or Civil War? A Son of Immigrants Makes the Case Against Open Borders.* Sentinel, 2018.

A. K. Sandoval-Strausz. *Barrio America: How Latino Immigrants Saved the American City.* Basic Books, 2019.

Jose Antonio Vargas. *Dear America: Notes of an Undocumented Citizen.* Dey St., 2018.

Laura Wides-Muñoz. *The Making of a Dream: How a Group of Young Undocumented Immigrants Helped Change What It Means to Be American.* Harper, 2018.

FIVE

TRUE ENOUGH

Back in the summer of 2002, long before "fake news" or "alternative facts" had infected the political vernacular, one of President George W. Bush's senior advisers mocked a journalist for forming part of the "reality-based community." Reality was for suckers, the aide explained. "We're an empire now, and when we act, we create our own reality." This was the hubris of a post–Cold War, pre–Iraq War superpower: if you exert enough pressure, events will bend to your will.

Reality-based thinking is again under attack from the White House, but the torrent of deceit that has emanated from the Trump presidency over the past four years is lazier, more cynical. It does not flow from strength but from shamelessness. It does not appear to serve any grand political strategy or ideology; it is self-serving. Its only endgame is to keep the game going.

Bush hoped to remake the world. Trump just makes it up as he goes along.

Among the battlegrounds of the Trump era, the cheapening of truth has drawn some of the most impassioned responses. Philosophers, literary critics, social scientists, cultural historians, political strategists, legal analysts, and of course journalists have published studies, polemics, and testimonials on truth in our time. Their book titles veer toward the terrifying—*The Death of Truth*, *Post-Truth*, *The Enemy of the People*, *Lying in State*, and *Gaslighting America*, among others—but their efforts to identify the prime mover behind today's political untruth can feel a bit esoteric. Is it postmodernism? Technology? The perversion of Enlightenment values, or the Enlightenment itself? Is lying just Trump's way—or just the American way?

These works succeed in finding patterns in, and methods to, the onslaught of the president's falsehoods (more than 20,000 false or misleading statements by July 2020, according to *Washington Post* fact-checkers), but even some of the most pessimistic authors have struggled to anticipate the extent of Trump's manipulations or interpret their impact. The power of his lies is not merely in their tally but in the escalating demands they make on us. First, we are asked to believe specific lies. Then, to bend the truth to our preferred politics. Next, to accept only what the president certifies as true, no matter the subject or how often his positions shift. After that, to hold that there is really no knowable, agreed-upon truth. Finally, to conclude that even if there is a truth, it is inconsequential. Lies don't matter; only the man uttering them does.

Defending Trump's lies is no longer about conviction, if it ever was. It is about allegiance. In his 1987 memoir, *Trump: The Art of the Deal*, the forty-one-year-old real estate developer happily admitted that he prizes loyalty over integrity, a point he reiterated thirty years later in the White House, with his request to then-FBI director James B. Comey: "I need loyalty. I expect loyalty." Accepting, excusing, or justifying Trump's falsehoods now functions as a test of that loyalty—a sign that you are a member in good standing of the team. The president's supporters know full well that he lies. Ted Cruz publicly called Trump a "pathological liar" during the 2016 primary campaign, before the Texas senator joined the loyalty brigade, while John Dowd, one of Trump's attorneys during the special counsel investigation into Russian election interference, described his client as a "fucking liar" in an interview with journalist Bob Woodward.

This knowledge does not seem to matter much. "Liars want their lies to be believed as if they were the truth, but it is not clear that Trump cares whether his falsehoods are believed; he seems to care only that they are affirmed," political scientists Russell Muirhead and Nancy L. Rosenblum write in *A Lot of People Are Saying* (2019). "He wants the power to make others assent to his version of reality."

Trump would love to exert power over the truth itself. He has settled for power over us.

The first fight about the decline of truth in the Trump era was over who started it.

In *The Death of Truth* (2018), literary critic Michiko Kakutani attacks Trump with a fusillade of bookish references and cultural allusions. "If a novelist had concocted a villain like Trump," she writes, "a larger-than-life, over-the-top avatar of narcissism, mendacity, ignorance, prejudice, boorishness, demagoguery, and tyrannical impulses . . . she or he would likely be accused of extreme contrivance and implausibility." (Reminder: To make it into the anti-Trump canon, a hefty dose of personal attacks is required early on—just to make clear whose side you're on.) Kakutani regards America's president as "some manic cartoon artist's mashup of Ubu Roi, Triumph the Insult Comic Dog, and a character discarded by Molière."

In its randomness and meaninglessness and indifference to consequences, Kakutani writes, America under Trump also resembles *The Great Gatsby, Fight Club, No Country for Old Men,* and even *True Detective.* To interpret this era's debasement of language, Kakutani enlists the World War II–era diaries of Victor Klemperer, while cameos by Christopher Lasch, Tom Wolfe, and Columbia Law School professor Tim Wu explain the rise of narcissistic fantasies, hedonistic vanity, and the "preening self" of the social-media age. *The Death of Truth* is a slim book but a crowded one.

You don't have to get every reference—believe me, I did not—to realize that it's all meant to be quite terrible and damning for Trump. And it is. But even though Kakutani asserts that Trump's presidency embodies "some sort of climax in the warping of reality," she does not blame him for it, or at least not him alone. Kakutani calls out lefty academics who for decades preached postmodernism, who argued that truth is not universal but malleable, a reflection of economic, political, and cultural forces as well as differences in relative power and individual positioning. In these early culture wars, centered on literary studies, postmodernists rejected Enlightenment ideals as "vestiges of old patriarchal and imperialist thinking," which opened the way to today's violence against scientific facts and political argument. "It's safe to say that Trump has never plowed through the works of Derrida, Baudrillard, or Lyotard (if he's even heard of them)," Kakutani sniffs, yet she concedes that "dumbed-down corollaries" of postmodernist thinking have been hijacked by Trump's defenders, who use them to explain away his untruths, inconsistencies, and broken promises.

The complicity of postmodernism is a recurring theme in the Trump truth literature, particularly among its more academic entries. In his 2018 book *On Truth,* philosopher Simon Blackburn chastised postmodernism's "ironical stance" toward science and worries that American politics has entered a "post-shame" environment: when the consequences of lying diminish, the frequency of lying will increase. In *Post-Truth*, also published in 2018, philosopher Lee McIntyre convincingly shows how intelligent-design proponents and later climate-change skeptics drew from postmodernism to distort public perceptions of evolution and global warming. "It's all fun and games to attack truth in the academy," he writes, "but what happens when one's tactics leak out into the hands of science deniers and conspiracy theorists, or thin-skinned politicians who insist that their instincts are better than any evidence?" McIntyre notes how pro-Trump troll Mike Cernovich, who helped popularize the Pizzagate conspiracy theory, has cited such influences. "Look, I read postmodernist theory in college," Cernovich told *The New Yorker* in 2016. "If everything is a narrative, then we need alternatives to the dominant narrative." And it is a short leap from alternative narratives to alternative facts. Postmodernism, McIntyre concludes, is "the godfather of post-truth."

While the philosophy profs and book critics target 1960s postmodernist theories, other writers argue that today's post-truth moment has a much longer lineage. RAND Corporation researchers Jennifer Kavanagh and Michael D. Rich point to the yellow-journalism era of the late nineteenth century and the rise of radio, television, and tabloids in the twentieth century as other moments that blurred the lines between facts, data, opinion, and experience. These past episodes, Kavanagh and Rich write in their 2018 book *Truth Decay*, were eventually undercut by "a revival of fact-based policy analysis or journalism and a renewed interest in holding authorities more accountable." Such a course correction is harder, however, when the journalists and government officials promoting accountability are themselves tarred as fundamental threats to truth.

For author and former *Studio 360* host Kurt Andersen, the problem is both deeper and simpler. Post-truth, Andersen writes in *Fantasyland* (2017), is congenital to a nation born in both Enlightenment ideals and religious extremism, a defect aggravated by the do-your-own-thing 1960s and the digital age. "Being American means we can believe any damn thing we want, that our beliefs are equal or superior to anyone else's, experts be damned," Andersen maintains. "People tend to regard the Trump moment—this post-truth, alternative facts moment—as some inexplicable and crazy *new* American phenomenon. In fact, what's happening is just the ultimate extrapolation and expression of attitudes and instincts that have made America exceptional for its entire history."

While writers like Kakutani worry that Enlightenment values of rationalism and empiricism have eroded under Trump, Andersen sees the Enlightenment itself as part of the problem, freeing people to "believe *anything whatsoever* about every aspect of existence," however fake or crazy or impossible. The misplaced trust in a marketplace of ideas where reason would always win out allowed peddlers of fantasy—from Cotton Mather to P. T. Barnum to Oprah Winfrey to one Donald J. Trump—to gain influence. After all, Andersen emphasizes, markets are not always efficient purveyors of optimal outcomes. Sometimes they crash.

Andersen is a smooth writer, and he offers memorable signposts of the decline of truth, noting, for instance, how once pejorative words connoting unreality such as "incredible," "unbelievable," "unreal," "fabulous," and "fantastic" became, over the course of the twentieth century, terms of the highest praise. Still, *Fantasyland* reads a bit like the work of an author who comes up with a catchy idea and then dumpster-dives his way through the American timeline for whatever might support it. The Salem witch trials, the Gold Rush, Scientology, Civil War reenactors, the tech bubble—all are evidence of Andersen's title conceit, and some variant on the word "fantasy" appears on virtually every page, just in case we might forget. His story concludes, inexorably, with the current president. "Donald Trump is a pure Fantasyland being, its apotheosis," Andersen writes, his personal unreality "a patchwork of knowing falsehoods and sincerely believed fantasies."

The mix of entertainment, news, and opinion in the public square is less a marketplace of ideas than an illusion of being informed, a "shortcut to erudition" rather than the real thing. So writes Tom Nichols in *The Death of Expertise*, published just a couple of months into the Trump presidency. "What I find so striking today is not that people dismiss expertise, but that they do so with such frequency, on so many issues, and with such *anger*," Nichols notes. And the intellectuals and writers who normally serve as idea brokers among academics, government officials, and the public are growing just as frustrated and polarized as everyone else. "When we are incapable of sustaining a chain of reasoning past a few mouse clicks," Nichols writes, "we cannot tolerate even the smallest challenge to our beliefs or ideas."

So the distortion of truth in our time derives from postmodernism, or the perversion of Enlightenment ideals, or rationalism itself, or the internet, or some combination of all of the above. Trump himself is a bit player in all this, just one more truth truther in the bunch. Still, he deserves credit for keeping a firm grasp on the nation's unhinging, for understanding when we would be ready for him. "Trump waited to run for president until he sensed that a critical mass of Americans had decided politics were *all* a show and a sham," Andersen explains in *Fantasyland*.

In that world, Trump fits right in.

Trump's untruths are so relentless and scattershot, one moment dealing with North Korea's nuclear threat, another with the cancer risks posed by windmills, and the next with the healing properties of disinfectant, that it's hard to discern any pattern. In *Gaslighting America* (2018), conservative political commentator Amanda Carpenter deftly identifies a logic—not to the lies themselves, but to how Trump unspools them.

A Trump lie, she explains, typically features five steps. First, "stake a claim," meaning own a political issue that others prefer not to touch. Second, "advance and deny"—that is, put the lie out there without claiming responsibility for it. (This is Trump's *someone should look into it* phase.) Third, "create suspense" by promising evidence that never materializes. Fourth, "discredit the opponent" by attacking the character and motives of anyone challenging the lie, thus rendering the matter controversial even when the truth is anything but. And fifth, claim a win, no matter what. Remarkably, Trump pulls off this last step even when admitting a lie: when he finally acknowledged that President Obama was indeed born in the United States, for instance, Trump accused Hillary Clinton of launching birtherism and congratulated himself for putting the matter to rest. Trump knows he can't compete in everyone else's reality, Carpenter contends, so he just creates his own.

That reality often takes the form of conspiracy theories. "No president—indeed, no national official—has resorted to accusations of conspiracy so instinctively, so frequently, and with such brio as Donald Trump," write Muirhead and Rosenblum. Millions of people voted illegally in California, Trump claims, otherwise he would have won the popular vote in 2016. President Obama wiretapped Trump Tower. The hacked Democratic National Committee server was in Ukraine, where the real election interference originated. Democrats and the press pushed a coronavirus "hoax" to undercut his reelection chances; once the virus became too real and too fatal to dismiss, it morphed into a cunning foreign plot.

Muirhead and Rosenblum argue that there is something unique about Trumpian conspiracies. They dispense with the usual intricate explanations and strained evidence that paint a damning picture of secret, dastardly acts. With Trump, "there is no punctilious demand for proofs, no exhausting amassing of evidence, no dots revealed to form a pattern, no close examination of the operators plotting in the shadows." With Trump, there is conspiracy, but no theory. This is what Muirhead and Rosenblum call "the new conspiracism," one based on nothing but innuendo and repetition, all allegation and no evidence. The new conspiracism "substitutes social validation for scientific validation: if *a lot of people are saying* it, to use Trump's signature phrase, then it is true enough." Unless a belief can be irrefutably falsified, then "it might be true," the authors explain, and these days that's plenty. Of all the norms of public life that Trump has shattered, this one may be the most ironic: he has lowered the bar even for conspiracy theories.

Yet that renders them more potent, not less. Trumpian conspiracies rely on simple, even one-word assertions—an election is "rigged," an investigation is a "hoax," a news story is "fake"—that build more power the more they are shared and repeated. Conventional conspiracies must persuade through their complexity and contrivances, but Trump's carry no such burden. Normal conspiracies, however deluded, also often uphold some principle or idealistic goal, such as unmasking a nefarious political actor or revealing stealthy threats to personal liberty. Trump-style conspiracies are wholly negative, Muirhead and Rosenblum contend, focused solely on "destabilizing, degrading, deconstructing, and finally delegitimating, without a countervailing constructive impulse." Their targets are political opponents and any independent arbiter of truth. Trump's conspiracies don't just undermine particular facts but seek to tear down the way truths are reached and agreed upon.

Muirhead and Rosenblum offer an example of this corrosion:

> We see how the longer-term process of delegitimation goes: a conspiracist president tilts against his own government—against the Justice Department, the State Department, and potentially every agency he directs. Offended by the "deep state" that he imagines plots against him, the president first ignores and then eliminates the career bureaucrats who (in his mind) impede him. Initially, these agencies look illegitimate mostly to the company of conspiracists and the president's own base. Beleaguered, ignored, harried, and underfunded, the agencies—once staffed by professionals who responsibly served whatever party is in power—are progressively gutted and demoralized. As they lose competence and capacity, they will come to look more and more illegitimate to more and more people. The steady stream of conspiracist claims has cumulative force.

In a perverse twist, the president then retroactively enlists the very federal government he is discrediting in the effort to validate his claims—the "commandeering of institutions for conspiracist purposes," as Muirhead and Rosenblum put it. Recall, for instance, the White House's commission investigating nonexistent electoral fraud, or Trump's pressure on the National Park Service to produce more favorable photographs of Trump's inauguration, or the president's urging of already overworked health and science officials to study his bizarre proposals for treating COVID-19.

A Lot of People Are Saying is among the most clarifying of the recent books in the truth genre because it captures not only the methods and intent of the president's deceit but also its appeal and impact. Some embrace the barrage of conspiracies as a sign of tribal solidarity with the president's base and to rejoice in the shock of Trump's critics. For all the mockery by Trump supporters of liberal sensitivities, Trump's untruths sell best precisely when feelings overpower facts, when America becomes a safe space for fabrication, when "true enough" is all you need. For those resisting the assault of untruth, a tempting response is simply to tune out, the authors note, "retreating into private life and distancing themselves emotionally from every bit of news about public life."

The latter response is not an option for those charged with reporting on that public life, for the journalists covering and investigating the Trump administration. As depicted in some of their books, their options involve two different sorts of tribalism—one that adheres to ingrained journalistic conventions or one that adopts a more aggressive stance, at least temporarily, confronting a president who relentlessly demeans reporters' work, honesty, and motives.

In *Gaslighting America*, Carpenter suggests that the news media "loves it" when Trump lies, because the ensuing uproar "keeps people reading the papers, watching their shows, and clicking their links." It is a cynical view, perhaps informed by the author's experience in the world of cable-news punditry. And while she is contemptuous of the sycophants defending Trump on television—people with nothing to lose, she writes, those grasping for "a sliver of a chance at stardom"—Carpenter understands the incentives involved. "For those who wanted to board the Trump train, outward expressions of belief in Trump's grand lies were required." (Only outward expressions, though; true belief remains optional.)

Journalistic fact-checking appears to exert little influence on

Trump; if anything, news media complaints about his truthfulness may enhance his appeal. "His intense commitment to his outlandish ideas is a form of virtue signaling to his base," Carpenter writes. Fact-checking in the Trump era serves the historical record—an essential task of journalism—but has less power to influence that history in real time, especially when journalists themselves, including the fact-checkers, are a target of the president's delegitimation campaign. As Carpenter puts it, it's "like trying to put out a raging forest fire with a garden hose."

The *Washington Post* had run a fact-checking operation for nearly a decade before the 2016 election, "but we had never encountered a politician like Trump—so cavalier about the facts, so unconcerned with accuracy, so willing to attack people for made-up reasons and so determined to falsely depict his achievements," the *Post*'s Glenn Kessler, Salvador Rizzo, and Meg Kelly write in their 2020 catalogue of presidential falsehood, *Donald Trump and His Assault on Truth.* Their sample size of thousands of untrue statements is so vast that readers can dip into Trump's most famous falsehoods (how Mexico will pay for the border wall, or how millions of votes for Hillary Clinton were cast illegally), sift through multiple chapters on Trump's bogus claims about himself (regarding his wealth and even his ancestry), explore his lies regarding specific policy arenas (say, the size of his tax cut), or even relive the extended dance-mix of mendacity he offered at a single 2019 campaign rally in Battle Creek, Michigan.

During the first three years of his presidency, Trump averaged some fifteen false or misleading claims each day. "But the pace of deception has quickened exponentially," the *Post* fact-checkers note. Six claims a day in 2017. Nearly sixteen per day in 2018. And more than twenty-two each day in 2019. "If he thinks a false or incorrect claim is a winner," they explain, "he will repeat it constantly, no matter how often it has been proven wrong." Most politicians back down after their lies have been publicly revealed, but not so Trump, not even when his favorite social-media platform feels compelled to fact-check his tweets. And that nonstop shamelessness prompted a debate that has bounced around America's newsrooms during the Trump presidency: When does an untrue statement deserve to be called a lie?

In *Truth in Our Times* (2019), *New York Times* lawyer David E. McCraw recalls the pressures in the newsroom during the 2016 race, when "readers demanded that we call a lie a lie." In the past, the *Times* had deployed softer terms—*misrepresented* or *misstated*—to characterize deceptions by presidents or presidential candidates. But newsroom editors eventually concluded that "the old rules could no longer hold when there was no doubt that the misstatement was knowing and willful," McCraw writes. The *l*-word made its way into *Times* headlines during the campaign, though top editors decided they would use it only sparingly lest it lose its power.

"Whether all of Trump's false statements could be considered lies is certainly subject to dispute," Kessler, Rizzo, and Kelly contend. "Many are exaggerated or factually wrong, but 'lie' suggests that a person knows his statements are false." Some of the president's statements, they decide, clearly qualify as lies, such as Trump's claim that he didn't know about secret payments to cover up his affairs. But they also submit that at times the president convinces himself that a false statement is in fact true, because Trump "lives only for the moment—what he said yesterday may be completely different from what he says today, and he sees no problem in the inconsistency." (This sounds more like indifference to truth than delusion about it, though that too depends on the president's unknowable mindset.)

Perhaps the simplest and most persuasive position on this debate appears in *Nation* columnist Eric Alterman's 2020 book *Lying in State*, a survey of presidential deceit from George Washington to Donald Trump. "A president does not have to mean to lie in order to lie," Alterman argues. "He just needs to stick to the falsehood once he learns the truth." Under this definition, a persistent misstatement becomes a lie once it is revealed as false. And because the presidency is about more than one individual, the president must assume responsibility for more than just his own words and intentions. "A presidential lie takes place when the president or someone with the authority to speak for the president seeks to purposely mislead the country about a matter of political significance," Alterman writes. "The president can remain silent while his subordinates lie for him. He can censor the truth or impede the means to discover it." Given the extent of Trump's false statements, Alterman is less concerned with divining the intentions behind particular lies than ensuring accountability for them. "Yes," he concludes, "America has a pathological liar for its president, and literally nothing he says can be taken at face value."

With a 2016 presidential candidate who threatened to weaken libel laws, the press may have anticipated the wrong battles for the Trump era. McCraw writes that he initially believed the only defenses the press needed were the First Amendment and precedents such as the Supreme Court's decision in *New York Times v. Sullivan* (1964), which made it much harder for public figures to sue for defamation. The *Times* lawyer gained a burst of fame when he wrote an October 2016 letter responding to Trump's attorneys, who had demanded that the newspaper retract a story about Trump's behavior toward women. McCraw's missive, which the *Times* posted online, not only defended the accuracy and newsworthiness of the story but argued that the lawyers' libel claim was baseless, because "nothing in our article has had the slightest effect on the reputation that Mr. Trump, through his own words and actions, has already created for himself." The letter concluded with a flourish, telling Trump's lawyers that the *Times* welcomed "the opportunity to have a court set him straight."

But McCraw soon realized that legal precedents were not enough to protect journalism in the Trump era. "I finally saw where this was heading," he explains. "Forget 1964. Forget *Times v. Sullivan*. The war over press freedom was not going to be about changing America's laws. It was going to be a fight about the very nature of truth." Legal battles become a secondary concern. After all, McCraw reasons, "why litigate when you can just lie?"

In that fight, there may not be much an in-house counsel can do—except exhort his *Times* colleagues to resist the call of resistance. The newspaper's core readers are relentless in their disdain for the president, McCraw writes, and he has worried that journalists would "set our compass" by what readers prefer rather than by the reporting the country needs. "We shouldn't be pursuing an agenda of political resistance or political change," McCraw writes. Yet while he insists that the underlying objectives of journalism should not change—"there is precious little to save democracy's day other than transparency, shining the harsh light of truth on the people in power," he writes—he acknowledges that the president's attacks on truth may have dimmed the news media's influence. "It doesn't matter how much freedom journalists have if no one believes them," McCraw concludes. "A discredited press plays no role in shaping democracy and holding power accountable."

In such circumstances, other journalists willingly adopt a more confrontational approach. "I welcome Trumpworld's hatred," CNN's Jim Acosta declares in *The Enemy of the People: A Dangerous Time to Tell the Truth in America* (2019), his memoir on covering the Trump White House. The book begins with the arrival of a pipe bomb at CNN's offices in New York (mailed by a disturbed Trump supporter) and concludes with Acosta's successful legal battle to regain his White House pass after the White House arbitrarily revoked it in late 2018, so his feelings are understandable. Acosta fears journalists may be hurt or even killed by the followers of a president who promotes hatred of journalists, calling them dishonest, disgusting, scum, thieves, sleaze, and worse. He worries that Americans are "surrendering our decency, and perhaps our humanity," under Trump, and that in attacking CNN and other outlets as "fake news" even before winning the Oval Office, Trump attacked not only professional journalists but the profession of truth.

"A different kind of president requires a different kind of press," Acosta contends, and he has grown more aggressive in the White House briefing room, even holding a testy and memorable debate with presidential adviser Stephen Miller on the role of immigration in American life. The 2017 exchange, which transcended the normal question-and-answer format, proved revealing and newsworthy, with the president's most influential voice on immigration accusing Acosta of "cosmopolitan bias" and arguing that the Emma Lazarus poem "The New Colossus," at the base of the Statue of Liberty, was only "added later" and does not speak to America's immigrant traditions. Viewers learned something about the administration's thinking and historical interpretations, which means that Acosta was doing his job right.

Acosta's adversarial approach can also veer into silliness at times. When White House press secretary Sean Spicer suspended televised coverage of press briefings, CNN's correspondent snapped a picture of his socks during a briefing and shared it on Twitter. "The Spicer off-camera/no audio gaggle has begun,"

Acosta tweeted. "I can't show you a pic of Sean. So here is a look at some new socks I bought over the wknd." In his book, Acosta notes with pride how "the sock tweet went viral." (Congrats, Jim!) He regards social media as something of an equalizing force, but the platform can also equalize pettiness. "I vented my frustrations on Twitter," Acosta admits. "Hey, if *they* can do it, my thought was, why can't *we*?"

In *The Enemy of the People*, CNN's chief White House correspondent often doubles as a political pundit. He argues that defeating Trump should have been a "layup" for the Democrats in 2016. The son of Cuban immigrants, Acosta reveals how he took the administration's immigration positions personally and how he believes U.S. presidents should always champion immigrants. "That's the American way, even if it's not Trump's way," he asserts. Indeed, in these pages, Acosta frequently passes judgment on what is and is not truly American. Trump's attacks on the news media are "un-American," while the crowds at Trump rallies are "not a true reflection of America, mind you," he explains. "They were overwhelmingly white, blue-collar, and elderly." (This, after bragging about how well he relates to the pro-Trump crowd: "I get blue-collar folks. . . . I am more like them than the man they come to the rallies to see.") Even as he assails the president and his supporters for not reflecting the country's values or complexion, Acosta is appalled that Trump has so vilified members of the press that journalists now seem "anti-American" to the president's supporters.

That vilification has had more severe consequences than even Acosta may have feared. The threat to journalism under Trump has come from more than some unhinged, violent supporter of the president. Law enforcement officers have harassed, arrested, and even assaulted journalists fulfilling their constitutional right—and professional duty—to cover protests against racism and police brutality. The rights of both demonstrators and reporters are covered by the First Amendment, yet the very agents of the state charged with protecting such rights have threatened their free exercise.

Acosta believes that the tensions between the press and the presidency can be dialed back in a post-Trump America. "As new presidents come along and return a state of normalcy to dealings with the news media, will there be as great a need to stand up for ourselves?" he asks. "Of course not." It is a confidence unsupported by the story Acosta himself tells. "A free society," he argues at the end of his book, "cannot sustain the collective weight of the kind of abuse we've endured without its institutions, and its people, undergoing a profound metamorphosis." The press is hardly immune to such transformations, which will go well beyond calling lies by their proper name or asking tougher questions at press conferences. American newsrooms are experiencing a defining, generational debate between journalists hewing to old standards of neutrality and objectivity and others more willing to confront and take public sides in battles over race, truth, and justice—battles that they see in clear moral terms. There will be no return to "normalcy," even if one were desirable, after Trump's time in the White House is over.

When Sean Spicer stood behind the podium in the James S. Brady Press Briefing Room in the White House on January 21, 2017, and insisted that the crowd on the National Mall the prior day had been "the largest audience to ever witness an inauguration, period," his lie was a conventional lie—an effort to have Americans believe a specific and verifiable untruth. But the demands on public credulity and belief did not stop there.

When White House adviser Kellyanne Conway defended her

colleague the next day on *Meet the Press*, saying that Spicer had merely offered "alternative facts" about the inauguration, she went further in degrading the truth, granting viewers permission to pick and choose among different versions of reality—truth as multiple choice. A year and a half later, when Trump addressed a Veterans of Foreign Wars convention in Kansas City, Missouri, he offered a more authoritarian version of truth, asserting that only his own preferred reality—on whatever subject—could be considered valid. "Stick with us," he urged. "Don't believe the crap you see from these people, the fake news. . . . Just remember: What you're seeing and what you're reading is not what's happening."

Shortly thereafter, when the president's attorney Rudy Giuliani explained in an August 2018 television interview why he didn't want Trump to testify before the special counsel investigating Russian interference in the 2016 election, he said he feared the president would be caught in a perjury trap if he contradicted someone else's version of the truth, because "truth isn't truth." This is truth as shrug emoji: everyone says something different, so why bother trying to figure it out?

And finally, when Republican members of the U.S. Senate argued that the Trump impeachment trial did not require witnesses because they already knew the facts of the president's misdeeds but would still do nothing about it, they went further still—in their eyes, even the knowable truth no longer mattered.

This final move is consistent with the attitudes of the party's base. "In the age of Trump, there is evidence that Republicans have grown less concerned about presidents being honest than they were a decade ago," Kessler, Rizzo, and Kelly explain. In 2007, they report, a poll found that 71 percent of Republicans, 70 percent of Democrats, and 66 percent of independents considered it "extremely important" for presidential candidates to be honest. In

2018, the percentages for Democrats and independents had not changed, but the share of Republicans had declined to 49 percent. "Many Republicans realize that Trump often lies, yet they have decided that truth-telling is less important than the message he sends about the country's sorry state and the forces he blames for its troubles."

These attitudes are inseparable from the media diet and information sources of conservative voters, which makes them inseparable from what CNN's Brian Stelter calls "the Trumpification of Fox and the Foxification of America." In his 2020 book *Hoax: Donald Trump, Fox News, and the Dangerous Distortion of Truth*, Stelter provides an obsessively insider account of the news network in the Trump era—full of backstabbing and extramarital affairs and who got which job and why. But above all, Stelter captures the reinforcing cycles of disinformation between Trump and the network, particularly between the president and prime-time host Sean Hannity, who doubles as a key informal adviser, and the morning show *Fox & Friends*, which offered Trump a platform long before he decided to run for president and which would become the Trump White House's daily sounding board.

"Trump's entanglement with Fox has no historical precedent," Stelter writes. "Never before has a TV network effectively produced the president's intelligence briefing and staffed the federal bureaucracy. Never before has a president promoted a single TV channel, asked the hosts for advice behind closed doors, *and* demanded for them to be fired when they step out of line." Stelter likens it all, fittingly, to a TV series starring "a dysfunctional White House, a delusional president, and a drama-filled network misinforming him from morning through night."

And loyal viewers suffered for that misinformation. Stelter points to the federal government's poor preparedness for the coronavirus pandemic and notes how, "when the virus was silently spreading across the United States, some of Fox's biggest stars denied and downplayed the threat posed by the virus; Trump echoed them; and they echoed back." Together, the network and the president magnify each other's distortions of truth and fact. "Through 'hoax' and 'fake news' and 'witch hunt,' Trump and Fox changed the language of politics," Stelter writes. The network's straight-news journalists struggle to retain their credibility, while shows such as Hannity's deliver "pure propaganda" in support of the president. And when an increasingly radicalized audience demands more propaganda, Fox News serves it up. A former *Fox & Friends* producer explains the logic to Stelter: "People don't care if it's right, they just want their side to win. That's who this show is for."

The CNN anchor accuses Fox News of enabling Trump's "creeping authoritarianism." And for many of the authors of the Trump-era truth literature, the fashioning of alternative realities indeed threatens America's two-and-a-half-century-old democratic experiment. "Without truth, democracy is hobbled," writes Kakutani, who warns of nihilism spreading across the country. Kavanagh and Rich argue that without consensus over facts, data and their good-faith interpretation, "it becomes nearly impossible to have the types of meaningful policy debates that form the foundation of democracy." Nichols contends that anti-intellectualism is "short-circuiting democracy," blinding us to the consequences of our choices. Muirhead and Rosenblum emphasize that the new conspiracism succeeds in "hollowing out democracy" and makes citizens believe that representative government simply does not work, certainly not on their behalf.

Despite offering such dire admonitions, their proposed fixes mostly vary from the obvious to the dutiful to overly narrow. Kakutani calls on citizens to protect the institutional checks and balances connecting the three branches of government and to stick up for an independent press. Andersen, too, urges us to "call out the dangerously untrue and unreal." Carpenter encourages readers to stop asking Trump to correct himself or apologize, which he appears incapable of ever doing. Instead, "ask him to explain himself," she suggests. "That's where he struggles." And true to their calling as social scientists, Kavanagh and Rich stop short of actionable solutions and instead serve up 114 possible question topics meriting deeper research, divided into four broad categories and twenty-two subgroups. (So RANDy.)

Muirhead and Rosenblum agree that calling out lies and conspiracies is a "moral imperative," especially for elected officials, but they are not optimistic about the ability of truth and transparency to counteract threats to the reality-based community. "Transparency can be manipulated and marketed," they caution, "and conspiracists can twist and exploit the very materials transparency makes accessible." (Consider the unending backlash against the report by special counsel Robert Mueller, which the president still seeks to discredit, rewrite, and relitigate.) However, they point to a process they call "enacting democracy" as a possible antidote. Though they dress it up in overly academic prose, enacting democracy simply means faithful attention to regular order; that is, explaining and following the standard procedures and mechanisms of political life and public decision-making. (It is reminiscent of Yuval Levin's approach in *A Time to Build*: Given your role here, how should you behave?) In the Trump era, this may be the most revolutionary tactic of all.

Enacting democracy "entails a literal articulation of how each step in the process of legislating, prosecuting, regulating or investigating (or even campaigning) adheres to fair processes," Muirhead

and Rosenblum write. It is what they call "politics as pedagogy."
This is the Trump presidency as a teachable moment for a democracy that has forgotten its civics lessons or, remembering them
still, has decided they don't matter.

In this context, for example, Mitt Romney's lone Republican
vote to convict the president for abuse of power in the Senate
impeachment trial is less notable for its effect on the outcome—
Trump was still comfortably acquitted—than for Romney's eloquent explanation of the meaning and weight of the oath he swore
when the impeachment trial began. "My promise before God to
apply impartial justice required that I put my personal feelings and
biases aside," Romney explained on the Senate floor. "Were I to
ignore the evidence that has been presented, and disregard what I
believe my oath and the Constitution demands of me for the sake
of a partisan end, it would, I fear, expose my character to history's
rebuke and the censure of my own conscience."

If democracy is a process, truth is, too, and that is one of the
more lasting lessons of these volumes. McIntyre agrees with many
of his fellow authors that official lies must be exposed and that
truth-tellers should "hit people between the eyes" with facts. But
more insidious than any one untruth the president dreams up or
repeats is "the corruption of the process by which facts are credibly gathered and reliably used to shape one's beliefs about reality."
Truth implies not instant and righteous conviction but investigation, analysis, and discernment; it is about discovery, not positioning. "Knowledge does not demand certainty," Muirhead and
Rosenblum emphasize. "It demands doubt."

In *Post-Truth*, McIntyre offers some annoying advice. "One of
the most important ways to fight back against post-truth is to fight
it within ourselves," he writes. "It is easy to identify a truth that

someone else does not want to see. But how many of us are prepared to do this with our *own* beliefs? To doubt something that *we
want to believe*, even though a little piece of us whispers that we do
not have all the facts?"

Such counsel temporarily takes the focus off Trump and his
acolytes and their lies, and casts the gaze inward, toward discom-
forting self-reflection, at a moment when argument and judgment
seem like all that matter. But that doesn't make it wrong. Or untrue.

BOOKS DISCUSSED

Jim Acosta. *The Enemy of the People: A Dangerous Time to Tell the Truth in America*. Harper, 2019.

Eric Alterman. *Lying in State: Why Presidents Lie—and Why Trump Is Worse*. Basic Books, 2020.

Kurt Andersen. *Fantasyland: How America Went Haywire, a 500-Year History*. Random House, 2017.

Simon Blackburn. *On Truth*. Oxford University Press, 2018.

Amanda Carpenter. *Gaslighting America: Why We Love It When Trump Lies to Us*. Broadside Books, 2018.

Michiko Kakutani. *The Death of Truth: Notes on Falsehood in the Age of Trump*. Tim Duggan Books, 2018.

Jennifer Kavanagh and Michael D. Rich. *Truth Decay: An Initial Exploration of the Diminishing Role of Facts and Analysis in American Public Life*. RAND Corporation, 2018.

Glenn Kessler, Salvador Rizzo, and Meg Kelly. *Donald Trump and His Assault on Truth: The President's Falsehoods, Misleading Claims and Flat-Out Lies*. Scribner, 2020.

David E. McCraw. *Truth in Our Times: Inside the Fight for Press Freedom in the Age of Alternative Facts*. All Points Books, 2019.

Lee McIntyre. *Post-Truth*. MIT Press, 2018.

Russell Muirhead and Nancy L. Rosenblum. *A Lot of People Are Saying: The New Conspiracism and the Assault on Democracy*. Princeton University Press, 2019.

Tom Nichols. *The Death of Expertise: The Campaign Against Established Knowledge and Why It Matters*. Oxford University Press, 2017.

Brian Stelter. *Hoax: Donald Trump, Fox News, and the Dangerous Distortion of Truth*. One Signal Publishers/Atria, 2020.

SIX

SEE SOME I.D.

"You're living in poverty. Your schools are no good. You have no jobs. . . . What the hell do you have to lose?" That was Donald Trump's pitch to African American voters late in the 2016 presidential race, delivered at a rally in a mostly white suburb of Lansing, Michigan. Embedded in the candidate's contempt was the answer to his question: when people are dismissed, reduced, and undifferentiated, what they stand to lose is their individual dignity.

In the Trump era, identity politics—the quest for justice, recognition, respect, or power by people coalescing around race, gender, or other overlapping characteristics—has been an energizing and polarizing force. It can be a tool for equality, or a means of exclusion. It can be a rallying cry for America's minorities, or a torch lit by its white nationalists. From Charlottesville to Minneapolis, from NFL sidelines to Lafayette Park, the terrain of identity politics is everywhere, and everywhere it is contentious. The impulse to be heard and the desire to belong are natural and necessary, but in its more dogmatic iterations, identity politics can also demonize opponents, infantilize proponents, and, as we've seen, move from a resource of the marginalized to a weapon of a resentful majority.

Hillary Clinton embraced it and lost; Donald Trump stoked it and won.

The poles of identity do not stand across the usual left-right divides. Some of the more prominent attacks on left-wing identity politics come from traditional bastions of American liberalism. In *The Once and Future Liberal* (2017), Columbia University historian Mark Lilla worries that modern liberalism is too preoccupied with diversity, too fascinated with "the margins of society," to offer a robust alternative to an ascendant right. Rather than obsess over microaggressions and cultural appropriation, Lilla argues, the Left must concentrate on winning elections and exerting power—and that means refocusing on a far broader sense of "we," on a solidarity that transcends the particularistic attachments of identity. Former *New York Times* columnist and editor Bari Weiss frames this battle in quasi-religious terms. "Worship of the group over the dignity of the individual, which we are seeing on the far left, is worship of another false deity," she contends in *How to Fight Anti-Semitism*, published in 2019. And Stanford University political scientist Francis Fukuyama, who once heralded Western liberal democracy as the last man standing among history's political ideologies, regards identity politics as a threat to liberal democracy, a diversion from problems such as economic inequality, which he believes should preoccupy the Left. How can we come together to solve anything big when we keep slicing ourselves into smaller factions? "Down this road lies, ultimately, state breakdown and failure," Fukuyama warns in *Identity* (2018).

Such authors make an alarming case, but it is complicated by the flood of recent memoirs, histories, studies, and manifestos of identity. Without a doubt, reading through the identity literature of the Trump era reveals an insular genre that at times indulges in what Lilla calls a "pseudo-politics of self-regard." Even so, in their search for new language, insistence on new vantage points, and demands for equality, these works can also propel readers toward a cause consistent with those broad-based aspirations of liberal democracy. That cause is the individual.

If the logic of identity politics divides us into smaller and smaller slivers, as its critics fear, that sequence ends, inexorably, with an identity of one, of each person. Underlying many of these books, even those arguing most stridently and effectively for group rights and representation, is an almost desperate affirmation of individuality. And the only way to protect and uphold the individual— every individual—is through universal rights and principles. So, yes, we must move toward a politics of solidarity. But for solidarity to endure, for it to mean something real for everyone, we must grapple with the politics of identity. In *The Souls of Yellow Folk* (2018), Wesley Yang writes: "Identity politics . . . when it isn't acting as a violent outlet for the narcissism of the age, can serve as its antidote, binding people into imagined collectives capable of taking action to secure their interests and assert their personhood."

That personhood is, or should be, the essence of identity politics. The margins are never marginal to those who inhabit them. Identity politics, for all its faults, is not an obstacle to an encompassing national vision. It is an obligatory and painful step toward its fulfillment.

The yearning for personal dignity rings loud in Austin Channing Brown's 2018 memoir, *I'm Still Here*, a reflection on being a black woman with a white man's name, navigating majority-white schools, neighborhoods, and workplaces. Brown recalls a childhood move from Toledo to an overwhelmingly African American neighborhood in Cleveland, a culture shock she recalls as both "glorious and terrifying." What Brown needed then was not just blackness but the freedom to live it in her own way, without the judgments and pressures of representing anyone other than herself. "I could choose what felt right for me without needing to be like everyone, or needing everyone to be like me," she writes. "Black is not monolithic. Black is expansive, and I didn't need the approval of whiteness in order to feel good in my skin."

That approval or disapproval would appear regardless. In college, she resisted the expectation of serving as a black spokesperson for the edification of white classmates, that implicit understanding, Brown writes, that "I was made for white people." Yet even her name suffers that fate. Her parents called her Austin, they explained, in the hope that she'd get more job interviews as an adult if prospective employers thought she was a white man. (Over the years, she often encountered confused white managers resetting their assumptions.) Brown craves her individuality, particularly in workplaces delighted with numerical diversity but not the diversity of ideas and culture that should follow. "I became either a stand-in for another Black female body—without distinction between our size, our hair, our color, our voices, our interests, our names, our personalities—or a stand-in for the worst stereotypes—sassy, disrespectful, uncontrollable, or childlike and in need of whiteness to protect me from my [Black] self."

Early in her career, Brown pitched a diversity training program to a nonprofit's board of directors. "Why don't we want assimilation?" the treasurer asked. "Don't we want to bring in people of diverse backgrounds and then become one unified organization?" Brown could have been answering the critics of identity politics with her exasperated, unspoken reaction: "How could I possibly explain that the unity he desired always came at my expense?"

Such moments, when individuality is overpowered by organizational, corporate, or popular culture, are ever-present in the memoirs of the identity age. As a precocious middle schooler in Los Angeles in the 1990s, Patrisse Khan-Cullors didn't fit in with the white kids smoking pot between classes or the black girls who wanted to grow up to be Whitney Houston. "People say I am weird, but I don't feel weird," she writes in *When They Call You a Terrorist: A Black Lives Matter Memoir* (2017), authored with writer and activist asha bandele. "I only feel like myself." Yet that sense of self nearly dies when Khan-Cullors is handcuffed by police in front of her classmates, suspected of carrying drugs. "That was the year that I learned that being Black and poor defined me more than being bright and hopeful and ready," she recalls. She was twelve years old.

Instead, Khan-Cullors feels forced into a collective identity she never chose, that of a generation written off by the war on drugs and on gangs, by criminalization and incarceration. "We are the post-Reagan, post–social safety net generation. The welfare reform generation. The swim or motherfucking sink generation." She watches as her older brother Monte, a boy with a "ginormous heart," is treated by police as a super-predator, that Clinton-era label that justified so much damage and offered so few chances. Monte, who suffers from mental illness, cycles between hospital and prison, two institutions that keep him just alive enough to continue the exchange. When her father is imprisoned, too, the author's loneliness highlights a long-running family separation crisis in America, far removed from any national borders. "We wonder what it means to have so much of our own relationships formed by absence," she writes. Even when they are reunited, reconnecting is a struggle. "What goes unsaid, what goes unknown, even as we try to be entirely open before each other?"

It feels almost inevitable that Khan-Cullors would become an activist and a founder of the Black Lives Matter movement—a movement forged in protest against police violence but that, to her, also encompasses the demand for decent food, housing, and health. "We deserve, we say, what so many others take for granted," she explains simply. It is not exactly the "we" that skeptics of identity politics desire, but the vision is no less inclusive.

Even some of the most relentless voices decrying ingrained racism in America are, at their core, demanding acceptance on their own terms. In *How to Be an Antiracist*, published in 2019, Boston University historian Ibram X. Kendi gives "racism" a ruthlessly straightforward meaning: a racist idea is any idea suggesting that one racial group is inferior or superior to another on any grounds, while a racist policy is any policy that creates or aggravates racial inequities. This definition targets far more than overt segregationists. In Kendi's view, "assimilationists" who argue that black Americans must be lifted up into the national (that is, white) mainstream, or that they just need to work harder or become better parents or grow more self-reliant, are racist as well. In an earlier work, Kendi's National Book Award–winning *Stamped from the Beginning* (2016), Abraham Lincoln, Frederick Douglass, W. E. B. Du Bois, and Barack Obama all fall short of this antiracist standard. To Kendi's credit, he believes that he does as well, and his new book doubles as a self-examination of his own past beliefs and actions.

For Kendi, whose books exploded in popularity during the 2020 protests following the killing of George Floyd at the hands of the Minneapolis police, one is either racist or antiracist; indifference means complicity. Even so, he declines to make broad accusations against any racial group. "Generalizing the behavior of racist White individuals to all White people is as perilous as generalizing the individual faults of people of color to entire races," he writes. For him, identity is personal. "I felt the burden my whole Black life to be perfect before both White people and the Black people judging whether I am representing the race well. The judges never let me just be, be myself, my imperfect self."

The cry for individual identity is piercing in Yang's *The Souls of Yellow Folk*, which details the "peculiar burden of nonrecognition" carried by Asian men in America, considered neither white enough to win the perks of whiteness nor victimized enough to rate full person-of-color privileges. Yang gleefully rejects the stereotypical and internalized notions of Asian Americanness. "Let me summarize my feelings toward Asian values," he begins. "Fuck filial piety. Fuck grade-grubbing. Fuck Ivy League mania. Fuck deference to authority. Fuck humility and hard work. Fuck harmonious relations. Fuck sacrificing for the future. Fuck earnest, striving middle-class servility." These are not the only labels Yang spurns. Though he is the child of immigrants, he writes, "I have never wanted to strive like one." Sometimes fending off labels becomes an identity, too.

He, too, argues that the language of identity politics can be counterproductive; the ever-expanding definition of white supremacy, for instance, only dilutes the power of the charge. In this fiercely ambivalent book, Yang recognizes that the much-mocked terminology of campus identity wars—"microaggressions" and "safe spaces" and the like—caught on precisely because they elicited a throb of recognition. "The terms were awkward, heavy-handed, and formulaic, but they gave confidence to people desiring redress for the subtle incursions on their dignity."

Language does not just defend identity; it can recognize and define it, too. Sociologist Arlene Stein, whose 2018 book *Unbound* tracks the experiences of young transgender men in the United States, notes how often her subjects cannot fully explain themselves until they encounter the right language, hear the right words. Stein tells the story of Ben, a twenty-nine-year-old transgender man who first identified as a tomboy, later as a lesbian, finally embracing the "transgender" label shortly after learning that the term existed. "Though people often experience their gender variance as an aspect of themselves they have little choice over, they exercise personal agency when they name themselves transgender," Stein writes. A reminder that claiming a group identity remains a powerful act of individual will.

Late in her book, Stein describes attending a transgender conference of academics and activists, where she felt overwhelmed by difference, nuance, and choice. "Once stable gender categories are being sliced and diced and shattered into a million little pieces," she writes. However, at the conference she found even more categories available, "so many that it often seems that our gender identity is so deeply personal that the only thing each of us can say for sure is that we alone possess it."

In July 2017, when Trump announced a ban on transgender people from serving openly in the military "in any capacity," the move was more an effort to reawaken culture warriors than to cut costs, enhance military readiness, or protect troop cohesion. Collective classifications can grant people power, but they also render them targets.

And those classifications can still clash with self-knowledge. Ben adopts the transgender label, but he finds it lacking. "Trans man, yes, that's typically the box I fit into," he tells Stein. "But does that really describe who I am? No. I think that it's more complicated than that. . . . But the act of identifying with others means that, oh God, I'm not alone. Not being alone gives me the space to think and explore those possibilities."

If identity politics is a search for personal dignity, it is a search made bearable by the support that only a group provides. It is individuality, through community.

In *The Once and Future Liberal*, Lilla doesn't seek out new words or labels; he prefers the restoration of old ones. "We must relearn how to speak to citizens as *citizens* and to frame our appeals—including ones to benefit particular groups—in terms of principles that everyone can affirm," he writes. The Franklin Roosevelt era was a time of such solidarity, Lilla writes wistfully, a collective enterprise to protect against hardship and risk. Its vision was "class based," he explains, "though it included in the deserving class people of any walk of life—farmers, factory workers, widows and their children, Protestants and Catholics, Northerners and Southerners—who suffered the scourges of the day. In short, nearly everyone (though African Americans were effectively disenfranchised in many programs due to Dixiecrat resistance.)"

Ah, that parenthetical, two quick keystrokes that say so much and offer so little! When the plight of a specific racial group can be bracketed off from the warm embrace of "nearly everyone," then the case for identity politics is clear. Lilla is right that America's "we" must grow far more capacious. But attacking identity politics for its "turn toward the self," as Lilla does, is less than fair when so many selves have good reasons to feel excluded from the whole. When they fit in a parenthetical.

The contradiction of identity politics, many critics contend, is that it aggravates the problems it purports to fix. In *How to Fight Anti-Semitism,* Weiss grapples with intersectionality, the notion that a person can experience overlapping forms of oppression due to her simultaneous membership in multiple marginalized groups (black women, for example, can suffer workplace discrimination that is distinct from that endured by white women or black men). Weiss accepts the framework but worries that in practice it replaces one oppressive hierarchy with another. "If white, straight men have historically sat at the top of the hierarchy, now those with the most oppressions (black, transgender, disabled) are located at the top, and, furthermore, are granted a greater claim to truth and morality," she contends. The result is that intersectionality "retribalizes us, preventing us from treating people as individuals."

Fukuyama, in *Identity*, hails contemporary movements such as Me Too and Black Lives Matter for "changing culture and behavior in ways that will have real benefits for the people involved," but argues that the blinders of identity politics hinder progress on other problems. "It is easier to argue over cultural issues within the confines of elite institutions than it is to appropriate money or convince skeptical legislators to change policies," he writes. Identity politics also places a lower priority on "older and larger groups whose serious problems have been ignored," Fukuyama contends, pointing, for instance, to the struggles of America's white working class. Most troubling of all, he writes, identity politics on the left has stimulated the politics of white-nationalist identity. "The right has adopted the language and framing of identity from the left: the idea that my particular group is being victimized," Fukuyama writes. Lilla criticizes Black Lives Matter as a "textbook example of how not to build solidarity," not because he disbelieves the justice of its aims but because of the reaction it can elicit. "As soon as you cast an issue exclusively in terms of identity you invite your adversary to do the same," he warns. "Those who play one race card should be prepared to be trumped by another." And there is nothing accidental about that latter verb.

Yet if you accept as valid any of the causes motivating modern identity movements—for instance, that police violence against

black Americans is disproportionate and intolerable—then worrying about a white-nationalist backlash, or about the despair of
the white working class, arbitrarily elevates the anger of one group
over another. And interpreting Black Lives Matter as a "cultural
issue" or as playing the "race card," as these authors do, rather than
as a social movement propelled by questions of justice and even
survival, may reflect a certain privilege of the academic perch.

Lilla calls for "putting the age of identity behind us." The problem is that America has always lived in the age of identity, with a
single category overpowering the rest.

That category, in the argot of identity politics, is "whiteness."
Whiteness does not mean white people, at least not necessarily.
For most identity authors, whiteness is the presumption that white
is normal, the universal standard against which all else conforms
or from which all else deviates. "Whiteness is slick and endlessly
inventive," Michael Eric Dyson argues in *Tears We Cannot Stop:
A Sermon to White America* (2017). "It is most effective when it
makes itself invisible, when it appears neutral, human, American."
For all the discussions of white privilege, this default position on
humanity's drop-down menu is the greatest entitlement of whiteness. "My story is not about condemning white people," Brown
writes in *I'm Still Here*, "but about rejecting the assumption—
sometimes spoken, sometimes not—that white is right: closer to
God, holy, chosen, the epitome of being."

Even critics of whiteness soak in it, to the point that they fail
to notice its pervasiveness. For Jennine Capó Crucet, growing up
Cuban American in South Florida—a community full of Cuban
doctors and Cuban police officers and Cuban politicians—meant
enjoying the benefits of such status. "To be Cuban in Miami was
to be a kind of white, with all the privileges and sense of cultural

neutrality whiteness affords," she writes in *My Time Among the Whites*, published in 2019.

The culture shock of student life at Cornell University compels Crucet to embrace Hispanic identity. "I became Latinx to find community, to survive," she explains, and her new perspective shifted everything, in ways that were profound, mundane, and occasionally hilarious. The beloved Disney World of her childhood, for instance, suddenly becomes a kingdom whose only magic is to manufacture a white, straight American fantasy. (When Crucet visits the theme park with her family as a college senior and spends the trip pointing out the heteronormativity, patriarchy, and bigotry implicit in every ride, her parents wonder if elite higher education had somehow ruined her ability to enjoy things.) And the wedding reception Crucet eventually plans must be made to appeal to her fiancé's white midwestern relatives, which means holding in check those qualities that would make it a more Cuban affair.

Even Crucet's first name—like that of Austin Channing Brown—grasps at the advantages of whiteness. Her parents, Cuban refugees, adapted "Jennine" from the name of a white Miss USA contestant in 1980. (Crucet reshaped this decision into a story for a fiction workshop in college, only to be admonished by white classmates that a real Cuban couple would never do that.) Crucet, now a professor of English at the University of Nebraska–Lincoln, recalls how, during her elementary school years, her mother wondered aloud why Jennine couldn't be more like a white classmate. "She just wanted better for me, which meant: whiter."

White Americans have the luxury of seeing themselves as "culture-less, as vanilla," Crucet writes, which only proves how little race intrudes on their daily lives. Whiteness is not a preoccupation when it seems ubiquitous. But that may have changed in

2016, when most white voters cast their ballot for Trump, who "essentially ran on a version of whiteness," Crucet writes. "That election compelled some white people to look at themselves, at their whiteness, and to wonder what being white—something they'd never really thought about at all—might mean."

For some, whiteness means fear, rage, and retribution for imagined offenses. In *How to Fight Anti-Semitism*, Weiss explains that white right-wing perpetrators of anti-Semitic violence believe their whiteness is "being muddied and diluted and eventually washed away by waves of non-white, non-Christian Americans and immigrants—a takeover engineered, of course, by devious Jews." Jewish Americans are caught in a "double bind" of whiteness and misperception, she laments, considered "at once white and nonwhite; the handmaidens of white supremacy and the handmaidens of immigrants and people of color; in league with the oppressed and in league with the oppressor." (Weiss was inspired to write the book after the slaughter of eleven people at the Tree of Life synagogue in October 2018, in her hometown of Pittsburgh. In his online posts, the alleged killer wrote that Jewish groups were responsible for dangerous caravans of migrant "invaders" who were coming to the United States to "kill our people.")

Others respond with guilt and shame. Even as he decries Trump's race-baiting and demagoguery, writer Thomas Chatterton Williams identifies a strain of self-loathing among liberal white Americans in the Trump era. "I've also been troubled to watch well-meaning white friends in my Twitter timeline and Facebook news feed flagellate themselves, sincerely or performatively apologizing for their 'whiteness,' as if they were somehow born into original sin," he writes in his *Self-Portrait in Black and White*, a 2019 memoir. That attitude is affirmed in the 2018 bestseller *White*

Fragility, written by anti-bias trainer Robin DiAngelo, a book that has become a cleansing ritual for white liberals on the road to racial enlightenment.

"Your parents could not have taught you not to be racist, and your parents could not have been free of racism themselves," DiAngelo tells readers, whom she assumes to be white. "A racism-free upbringing is not possible, because racism is a social system embedded in the culture and its institutions. We are born into this system." She wants white Americans to understand themselves as an inherently racist collective. "Talking about race and racism in general terms such as *white people* is constructive for whites because it interrupts individualism," she explains. In the service of identity politics, DiAngelo undermines the individual person-hood that inspires so much recent writing on identity.

The result is that *White Fragility* reads like a pharmaceutical ad for treating whiteness. "If and when an educational program does directly address racism and the privileging of whites, common white responses include anger, withdrawal, emotional incapacitation, guilt, argumentation, and cognitive dissonance," DiAngelo writes. Symptoms vary for "so-called progressive whites," she explains, who claim they need no such treatment thanks to prior immunities. All such responses are instances of white fragility, the author forewarns, because for white people, "the smallest amount of racial stress is intolerable." And if you are a white person who disagrees—well, you are just proving the point. From such circular logic do thought leaders and bestsellers arise.

Throughout her book, DiAngelo reflexively defers to people of color—a term that, ironically, has always affirmed whiteness by defining the rest of the world in reference to it. People of color, though largely powerless in her view, do hold power enough to define and litigate all racist behavior, and thus help people like

DiAngelo and her clients engage in "authentic explorations of racial realities" and improve themselves. Do better.

The outbreak of the white-nationalist "alt-right" has been the subject of multiple works in the Trump years, exploring its origins, principles, and subcultures. They suggest an identity movement with greater staying power—and a far longer history—than the tenure of any one president.

Long before the 2016 campaign, the alt-right was already gathering strength. Then came a leader with enough charisma to embolden the ranks and enough brazenness to lessen the social discomfort of open bigotry. Trump's birther campaign against President Obama, his travel ban against Muslims, his many-sided response to the murderous violence by neo-Nazis in Charlottesville, Virginia, his admonition to four new female House Democrats to "go back" to where they come from, his insistence on specifying the Chinese origins of COVID-19, his compulsion to honor the Confederate legacy, his sharing on social media of a video in which supporters cry "white power," to name just a few episodes, all granted official legitimacy to views that deserve to remain marginal. The path from "What the hell do you have to lose?" to "When the looting starts, the shooting starts" is not long.

The rise of Trump and the alt-right reinforce each other—and both derive strength from the diminished appeal of conventional conservatism. "Trump could not have captured the GOP nomination if the mainstream right was not already in a weakened state," University of Alabama political scientist George Hawley writes in *Making Sense of the Alt-Right*, published in 2017. "And the Alt-Right would similarly not be growing if more people continued to find traditional conservatism appealing."

Although its name suggests an extension of right-wing politics, the alt-right is uninterested in free markets, strong national defense, or moral traditionalism, those notions that once defined modern conservatism. Fearing the demographic transformations underway in the country, the alt-right wants the Republican Party "to embrace the hard right and push transparent white-identity politics," Hawley writes. It wants to redefine traditional conservatism; to lead, not follow. The alt-right's meme-crazed conspiracists are fueled by racism and anti-Semitism, energized by their opposition to Black Lives Matter or Me Too or to the latest spats over campus dogma. (In a rare overlap, the 2012 death of Trayvon Martin and the exoneration of his killer, George Zimmerman, appear throughout the identity literature—a force behind Black Lives Matter and an inspiration in white-nationalist circles, a singular event refracted in opposite directions through media, ideology, and emotion.)

Journalist Angela Nagle dives into the digital swamps where the white-nationalist conversation lurks, a world in which nihilism and cynicism mingled with pornography, prejudice, and misogyny to produce what she calls the movement's "taboo-breaking anti-PC style." Nagle's *Kill All Normies* (2017) pinpoints the Gamergate controversy, when female video game creators suffered online harassment and death threats, as a moment that politicized young men on the right to wage cultural wars against the Left. While the "normies" of Nagle's title is alt-right slang for white people who have yet to achieve racial consciousness, in the author's view the alt-right is about more than race. It is an indiscriminate and brutal aesthetic also targeting women, religious groups, and cultural minorities for the sake of forestalling a supposed civilizational and cultural decline. In this telling, the counterculture never died; it just switched sides. Transgression now lives on the right, dogmatism on the left.

Books such as Hawley's and Nagle's help explain this moment, but they risk making it seem solely of the moment. Chroniclers of America's recent surge in white identity politics have endless material long predating Trumpism or the rise of racist online subcultures. (You don't have to go all the way back to 1619, though I suppose you can.) In *Alt-America: The Rise of the Radical Right in the Age of Trump* (2017), journalist David Neiwert plumbs "an alternative dimension" of paranoia, conspiracy, and white resentment dating back decades, a world where the sieges of Ruby Ridge and Waco in the 1990s loom as eternal reminders of encroaching fascism, where Hillary Clinton was long an agent of the New World Order, where white Americans are invariably oppressed, and where immigrants and minority groups suck up the nation's resources. (For Neiwert, the Tea Party rallies during Obama's first term were a hinge in this history, when this paranoid universe began to overlap with mainstream, Fox News–viewing conservatives.)

Historian Kathleen Belew goes further back, tracing the modern white-nationalist movement to the aftermath of the Vietnam War. In her 2018 history *Bring the War Home*, Belew links the white-power movement to racist, sexist, anticommunist, antifeminist, anti-immigrant and religious extremist ideologies that gained currency after the war—a conflict whose outcome white nationalists regarded as a symbol of American decline and state duplicity. "All corners of the movement were inspired by feelings of defeat, emasculation, and betrayal after the Vietnam War and by social and economic changes that seemed to threaten and victimize white men," Belew writes. The result was the rise of a paramilitary-style social movement incorrectly interpreted as "inexplicable lone wolf attacks motivated not by ideology but by madness or personal animus," she writes. Timothy McVeigh is remembered this way—wrongly so, Belew contends—as is Dylann Roof, the convicted killer of nine African American churchgoers in Charleston, South Carolina, in 2015. "Because of the Internet," she writes, "Roof never had to meet another activist to be radicalized by the white-power movement, nor to count himself among its foot soldiers."

Such histories offer the best rebuttal to those who blame modern identity politics on the left for stimulating a white identity politics of the Right. White nationalism is not a product of the Trump era; Trump simply recognized, exploited, and adapted a long-running malady. To gaze upon the landscape of identity politics and conclude that *this is why Trump won*—that overzealous left-wing activism backfired and gave us the birther lie and Charlottesville and the Muslim ban and so much more ugliness—is to grant identity politics both too much power and not enough. These works can exist independently of the Trump presidency; the stories they tell often far precede this president, and the arguments they make will far outlast him.

"Unless we can work our way back to more universal understandings of human dignity, we will doom ourselves to continuing conflict," Fukuyama warns. But there is no working our way *back* to such an understanding, if we ever truly held it or lived it. There is only a lengthy path forward. Identity politics, by illuminating the inconsistencies and failings of our grand national visions, shows how far there is left to travel.

Some look upon the battlefields of identity and choose to opt out, refusing to let group categorizations overpower them. They seek individualism, and they seek it entirely on their own.

Thomas Chatterton Williams grew up in middle-class New

Jersey suburbia with a white mother and a black father, and when he was young, "blackness as an either/or truth was so fundamental to my self-conception that I'd never rigorously reflected on its foundations." But reflect he now has. In *Self-Portrait in Black and White*, he recounts his decision to become an "ex-black man"—not simply renouncing blackness but "rejecting the legitimacy of the entire racial construct in which blackness functions as one orienting pole." His decision came suddenly, upon the birth of his first child, who entered the world with blond hair, light skin, and "a pair of inky-blue irises that I knew even then would lighten considerably but never turn brown." Her face confronted Williams with the absurdities of racial classifications that could "so easily contradict, or just gloss over, the physical protestations and nuances of the body." In his book, he reconsiders just about every aspect of his life that informs his racial identity—his relationships, his relatives, his DNA test (39.9 percent sub-Saharan, 58.7 percent European, for those keeping score at home), even a single strand of light hair protruding from his clavicle—as part of his effort at "outgrowing the bounds and divisions of identity, of touching the universal."

Self-Portrait in Black and White is a counterintuitive addition to the recent identity literature, and a welcome one. But Williams does not simply want to share his journey; he insists that everyone take the same trip. "Most so-called 'black' people do not feel themselves at liberty to simply turn off or ignore their allotted racial designation, whether they would like to or not," he writes. "But that doesn't mean that they *shouldn't*." He calls on white Americans and Asian Americans to do the same, to reject the legitimacy of race, not just on biological grounds but also in the realm of ideas, where he says race has produced "a philosophical and imaginative disaster." It's a big ask, but Williams is confident that anyone can slip the bonds of identity. After all, he did.

Yet he has lived a life that renders his discernment more possible, his choices less constrained. Williams, who resides in Paris with his French wife and two young children, says he is frequently the only black person in any given room. As such, "race recedes from my lived experience and becomes something wholly cerebral." He recalls that his parents instilled in him a habit of standing apart, and that as an adult he has never suffered harm "by my appearance or lineage." Williams believes this life makes him a precursor, not an outlier. "I've been granted a view that most Americans on either side of the color line haven't had, but from a position that an increasing number will find themselves in as the mixed-race population expands."

We could do worse, I suppose, than look around decades from now and realize that Williams's self-portrait had indeed become America's. But Williams seems unaware—or disinclined to accept—that his plea for personal autonomy can also mean the power to accept group identities, and that such identities can also lead, in their own way, to individual dignity. Instead, he suggests that because identity activists accept the existence of race, even as a social or cultural force, they are somehow "in sync with toxic presumptions of white supremacism." It is not enough for him to reject race as a construct and question the ever-shifting demands of woke progressivism; he appears to reprimand anyone who recognizes race's enduring role in American life. That doesn't feel like touching the universal.

Philosopher Kwame Anthony Appiah understands the unifying power of identity. "We're clannish creatures," he acknowledges in his 2018 book *The Lies That Bind: Rethinking Identity*. But he also recognizes its tendency to pit us against one another. Identities can become "the enemies of human solidarity, the sources of war, horsemen of a score of apocalypses from apartheid to genocide," he writes. "Yet these errors are also central to the way identities unite us today."

Appiah does not reject identity politics. He does, however, reject "essentialism" surrounding race, gender, religion, nationality, class, or culture—the idea that there is some force tethering a people together, that our surface-level differences and similarities explain our deeper differences and similarities, or that they necessarily illuminate how we think or behave. He, too, prefers to dwell on the individualism within our collectives. "People may join churches and temples and mosques and announce sectarian identities, but when it comes to the fine points of belief, it can sometimes seem that each of us is a sect of one." Identities are also mutable and volatile; cultural identity, in particular, is constantly acquired, spread, transmitted. It is messy. "That it has no essence is what makes us free," Appiah writes.

This is the identity not of the group but of the individual intersecting through countless groups, whose salience varies in different circumstances. It is intersectionality, but one that does not seek to displace whiteness only to establish new social hierarchies. Reading Appiah, one ventures to conclude that there is no automatic trade-off between our individual and collective identities, between *me* and *we*, those most universal of pronouns.

Identity politics is as necessary as it is temporary, because the more accepted an identity grows, the less defining it becomes. "Culture isn't a box to be checked on the questionnaire of humanity," Appiah concludes. "It's a process you join, in living a life with others."

BOOKS DISCUSSED

Kwame Anthony Appiah. *The Lies That Bind: Rethinking Identity*. Liveright, 2018.

Kathleen Belew. *Bring the War Home: The White Power Movement and Paramilitary America*. Harvard University Press, 2018.

Austin Channing Brown. *I'm Still Here: Black Dignity in a World Made for Whiteness*. Convergent Books, 2018.

Jennine Capó Crucet. *My Time Among the Whites: Notes from an Unfinished Education*. Picador, 2019.

Robin DiAngelo. *White Fragility: Why It's So Hard for White People to Talk About Racism*. Beacon Press, 2018.

Michael Eric Dyson. *Tears We Cannot Stop: A Sermon to White America*. St. Martin's, 2017.

Francis Fukuyama. *Identity: The Demand for Dignity and the Politics of Resentment*. Farrar, Straus and Giroux, 2018.

George Hawley. *Making Sense of the Alt-Right*. Columbia University Press, 2017.

Ibram X. Kendi. *How to Be an Antiracist*. One World, 2019.

———. *Stamped from the Beginning: The Definitive History of Racist Ideas in America*. Nation Books, 2016.

Patrisse Khan-Cullors and asha bandele. *When They Call You a Terrorist: A Black Lives Matter Memoir*. St. Martin's Griffin, 2017.

Mark Lilla. *The Once and Future Liberal: After Identity Politics*. Harper, 2017.

Angela Nagle. *Kill All Normies: Online Culture Wars from 4Chan and Tumblr to Trump and the Alt-Right*. Zero Books, 2017.

David Neiwert. *Alt-America: The Rise of the Radical Right in the Age of Trump*. Verso, 2017.

Arlene Stein. *Unbound: Transgender Men and the Remaking of Identity*. Pantheon, 2018.

Bari Weiss. *How to Fight Anti-Semitism*. Crown, 2019.

Thomas Chatterton Williams. *Self-Portrait in Black and White: Unlearning Race*. W. W. Norton & Company, 2019.

Wesley Yang. *The Souls of Yellow Folk: Essays*. W. W. Norton & Company, 2018.

SEVEN

HIM, TOO

Never forget the time Donald Trump was groped at a dinner party.

"I was seated next to a lady of great social pedigree and wealth," he writes in *Trump: The Art of the Comeback* (1997), one of the forgotten sequels to *The Art of the Deal*. They were in the middle of an innocent conversation when "all of a sudden I felt her hand on my knee, then on my leg," Trump recalls. "She started petting me in all different ways. . . . The amazing part about her was who she was—one of the biggest of the big."

They moved to the dance floor, where the unnamed socialite became "very aggressive," Trump writes. "Look, we have a problem," he said. "Your husband is sitting at that table, and so is my wife." But this passion knew no bounds. "Donald, I don't care," she answered. "I just don't care. I have to have you, and I have to have you now." Trump appeased her by promising a phone call. "This is not infrequent," the future president of the United States informs readers. "It happens all the time."

The story is classic Trump, its unlikelihood rendering it even more so. It is not any anonymous woman but a rich and connected and fabulous anonymous woman—*the biggest*. The purported dialogue is impossibly tacky. Trump thinks he comes off like a gentleman, when in fact he makes clear that sexual propositions are fine if his wife isn't around. And, of course, women accosting him with pulp-romance come-ons are a recurring problem. That's just life as the Donald.

Throughout his memoirs and self-help books, Trump constantly passes judgment on women. "The smart ones act very feminine and needy, but inside they are real killers," he explains. "I have seen women manipulate men with just a twitch of their eye—or perhaps another body part." The women in his own life usually fall short for conflicting reasons: Ivana is too focused on business, Marla too fixated on home life, while references to Melania are often prefaced with "my beautiful wife," clarifying not just her appearance but her purpose. Over the years Trump has developed some insights into women. "There's nothing I love more than women, but they're really a lot different than portrayed," he concludes. "They are far worse than men, far more aggressive, and boy, can they be smart."

And boy, are they just naturally drawn to him. "All the women on *The Apprentice* flirted with me—consciously or unconsciously," he writes in *Trump: How to Get Rich* (2004). "That's to be expected. A sexual dynamic is always present between people, unless you are asexual." It's a reassuring belief system for the modern heterosexual male. If a woman resists your charms, her true longing for you must exist subconsciously, unless thwarted by a biological condition. So, go ahead and make that move! Remember, when you're a star, they're supposed to let you do it.

"I couldn't be more proud of my record with women," Trump declares in his 2015 campaign book, *Crippled America*, congratulating himself on hiring female subordinates. Yet Trump's record with women is one of the starkest contradictions of our time. Even as long-hidden truths, once revealed, have brought low powerful men in Hollywood and the news media, the Oval Office remains occupied by a man with more than a dozen accusations of sexual misconduct against him. By a man who gleefully denigrates women in public. By a man caught on tape bragging about how he assaults women because, well, he just can't help himself. *I just start kissing them. It's like a magnet. . . . I don't even wait.*

No wonder that, in the memoirs, essay collections, and reported accounts of the Me Too era, discernment, fury, and resignation come together, producing incisive books that can be utterly demoralizing to read. Reporters who covered the 2016 race recall sexism emanating from multiple campaigns. Activists dwell on the frustrations and divisions behind the Women's March and the pitfalls of collective resistance. Intellectuals emphasize how the anger propelling the Me Too revelations was so fierce precisely because it had been repressed so long. And survivors of sexual assault detail the humiliation and pain of an aftermath that never ends.

Imagine for a moment that Trump had not run for president in 2016 and America had still experienced a national reckoning about sexual misconduct by powerful men. Might not a narcissistic real-estate-developer-turned-reality-television-star with a scandalous personal history have become one of Me Too's more obvious targets? Would he have survived without an intensely loyal electoral base and a White House backdrop? The Me Too movement was a "perfect storm of female rage," Rebecca Traister writes in *Good and Mad* (2018). "Never before, in my memory, had so many white male authority figures been censured, dismissed." She muses that it was precisely the shock of electing Trump—"the ultimate, inflated embodiment of white patriarchal power abuse who had faced no repercussion for his behavior"—that helped propel that movement forward. "Then again," Traister adds, "perhaps it was simply the impossibility of containing the fury any longer."

This president is thus far exempt from the backlash synonymous with his time. He holds power despite his unceasing transgressions against women or possibly even because of them. If Me Too marks the beginning of the end for a certain kind of open secret, with Trump it has always been open. The secret is how, for him, it doesn't seem to matter.

This was not supposed to be a time of feminist revolt. In a book published during the 2016 presidential campaign, *Bitch* magazine founder Andi Zeisler argues that, over the prior two decades, the fight for gender equality had morphed into a "glossy, feel-good feminism" preoccupied with celebrity endorsements, faux empowerment, and consumer tie-ins. This "marketplace feminism," she writes in *We Were Feminists Once* (2016), is largely apolitical, a feminism that "can exist in fundamentally unequal spaces without posing any foundational changes to them."

Marketplace feminism is the feminism of self-congratulatory women's leadership conferences and of credit card campaigns marking the 150th anniversary of the Seneca Falls Convention. It is the feminism of "I did it for me" Botox injections and soap ads pitching "real beauty" along with armpit-whitening deodorant. It's debates over whether Emma Watson or Beyoncé rates as Feminist of the Year. "Simply claiming an identity that's feminist," Zeisler observes, "stands in for actually doing work in the service of equality."

Yes, it's the fate of every activist to decry the inevitable cooptation of the cause, but Zeisler doesn't just critique feminism's recent past, she heralds its near-term future. "Feminism is not fun," she writes. "It's not supposed to be fun. It's complex and hard and it pisses people off." Feminism needs to confront "deeply unsexy" problems such as wage inequality, workplace harassment, and violence, Zeisler writes, and taking them on will require more than "sweet-talking appeasements." Hillary Clinton's defeat, following a race in which sexism thumped a steady background beat, affirmed the limits of the marketplace-feminism era. The Me Too movement, by contrast, embodies Zeisler's call for a more confrontational activism, one that seemed especially necessary after the 2016 campaign.

"This election wasn't simply a political contest," writes memoirist Cheryl Strayed in the 2017 collection *Nasty Women: Feminism, Resistance, and Revolution in Trump's America.* "It was a referendum on how much America still hates women." Clinton became a magnet for that animosity—both from the Right, long practiced in the arts of Hillary hatred, and from purists on the left, who deemed her insufficiently devoted to their vision. For a certain kind of male progressive, *Nasty Women* co-editor Kate Harding contends, "the right time for women is always some day in the future, and the right woman candidate is always the hypothetical one."

In Clinton's account, the matter is clear. "This has to be said: sexism and misogyny played a role in the 2016 presidential election," she states flatly in *What Happened*, her memoir of the race. "Exhibit A is that the flagrantly sexist candidate won." Though Clinton writes mercilessly about James Comey's impact on the election—after Trump, Barack Obama, Bernie Sanders, and Clinton's family, no one gets more attention in *What Happened* than the former FBI director—she also contemplates the simple humiliations of campaigning while female. "The moment a woman steps forward and says, 'I'm running for office,' it begins: the analysis of her face, her body, her voice, her demeanor; the diminishment of her stature, her ideas, her accomplishments, her integrity," Clinton writes. "It can be unbelievably cruel."

The response to the publication of Clinton's memoir in the fall of 2017—with even members of her own party wishing that the former presidential nominee, secretary of state, U.S. senator, and first lady would just go away—did little to disprove her. Nor did the Democratic primary contest of 2020, when the talented and experienced women vying for the nomination fell out of contention, one by one. When Vice President Joe Biden pledged in March that, if chosen as the party's nominee, he would select a woman to join him on the ticket, the sense of history in the making included the whiff of a consolation prize.

Of course, no one is immune; even Clinton's campaign operation displayed its own bouts of sexism. Some riveting passages in Amy Chozick's *Chasing Hillary* (2018), a memoir on her years covering Clinton for the *New York Times*, concern the candidate's longtime male press aides, whom she identifies only with nicknames: Brown Loafers Guy, Policy Guy, Outsider Guy, and the loathsome Original Guy, "the most-devoted member of Hillary's court of flattering men." The Guys constantly mess with Chozick's head, amplifying her insecurities. "I don't care what you write because no one takes you seriously," one tells her. They suggest that a *Times* colleague is leaking her story ideas to rival outlets, and they ask if there is a male reporter they can deal with instead of her. When Chozick spars with Original Guy over whether a conversation can go on the record, he randomly paraphrases a crude line from the 2005 movie *Thank You for Smoking*, in which a female journalist sleeps with a male lobbyist for information. "I didn't know I had to say it was off the record when I was inside you," Original Guy smirks. ("The words hung there," Chozick recalls, "so grossly gynecological.")

Chozick fully acknowledges Clinton's shortcomings as a campaigner—"if there was a single unifying force behind her candidacy," she writes, "it was her obvious desire to get the whole thing over with"—but is also mesmerized by the prospect of covering the first female commander in chief. Chozick even fantasizes about sticking up for Clinton against relentless sexist attacks. "Bernie's supporters, Republicans, and garden-variety Hillary haters always told me it wasn't about gender," she writes. "They'd vote for a woman, just not *THAT woman.* . . . I wanted to scream at every critic that thirty years of sexist attacks had turned her into *that woman.* That sooner or later, the higher we climb, the harder we work, we all become *that woman.*"

Though in agreement over the causes behind Clinton's defeat, the contributors to *Nasty Women* clash over what came next: the mass female mobilization on January 21, 2017, the day after Trump's inauguration. Some of the authors and activists share their disappointment, even resentment, over the belated arrival of white suburban women—the marketplace feminists, perhaps—to the battle that others were already waging. "The march looked like a celebration, and also like boilerplate and mainstream feminism," journalist Collier Meyerson writes. "A universal angry and hostile rejection of Donald Trump's misogyny or of women's inequality writ large, it did not appear to be." She decries the memes, T-shirts, and pussy hats that became synonymous with the march, pointing out that Black Lives Matter activists did not enjoy the benefit of Nasty Women Vote posters or special headgear for their demonstrations. "Did the issues and problems facing black women need cuter packaging to translate for white women?" Meyerson wonders.

Alicia Garza, one of the founders of Black Lives Matter, opted to participate in the first Women's March despite her misgivings, joining with newer activists even if they did not grasp the specifics of her own black, anticapitalist brand of feminism. Her choice was a practical one, even though she didn't like it much. "If our movement is not serious about building power," Garza decides, "then we are just engaged in a futile exercise of who can be the most radical."

What does unite much of the female resistance to Trump—and many of the feminist writers publishing books in the Trump era— is a seething, relentless fury. Consider the titles: Soraya Chemaly's *Rage Becomes Her*, Brittney Cooper's *Eloquent Rage*, and Traister's *Good and Mad*, to name a few. All published in 2018, these books make up a trilogy of female anger, the sort of works typically reviewed and discussed by women even if they really need to be read by men. They are about anger, and they are angry themselves. As I read, I found so much that I had not bothered to know, so much that I had the luxury of not even imagining.

I didn't realize that by the time they are preschoolers, children learn that boys, not girls, are allowed to express anger. "We are not taught to acknowledge or manage our anger so much as fear, ignore, hide, and transform it," Chemaly writes. I didn't know how much physical pain women endure, simply because they are women, and how frequently that pain is minimized or dismissed. "Because Black women are viewed as preternaturally strong, our pain often goes unnoticed both in the broader world and in our own communities," Cooper explains. I hadn't fathomed quite how much time, money, and mental energy women spend avoiding and fearing rape. "Ask a man what his greatest fear is about serving jail time, and he will almost inevitably say he fears being raped," Chemaly muses. "What can we deduce from the fact that jail is to men what life is to so many women?"

And I didn't fully grasp how, throughout history, principled rage has been lionized when emanating from men but pathologized when coming from women. "We are primed to hear the anger of men as stirring, downright American, as our national lullaby, and primed to hear the sound of women demanding freedom as the screech of nails on our national chalkboard," Traister argues. She admits that, for a long time, she moderated her own tone, softening the edges of her work to make it more palatable. "I'd absorbed the message that open anger was needlessly overdramatic and unattractive—that it would be too *much*, really—and I had worked to accommodate these assumptions, tempering my fury in my writing," she explains. "So I was funny! And playful, cheeky, ironic, knowing!" No longer.

The anger of the Trump era is all the greater for having been kept in check. Just as Barack Obama could not appear to be the angry black candidate in 2008, Clinton could not channel the furious feminist in 2016. "As Hillary Clinton geared up to run for the presidency," Traister writes, "the stakes were far too high for the kind of anger that had been so openly and defiantly expressed by the activists—in suffrage, abolition, civil rights, feminism—whose achievements had, ironically, made her candidacy possible." Trump and Sanders could parade their anger, but never Clinton, not when every laugh, decibel, or inflection would be found insufficient or inauthentic.

The outpouring of female anger after the election was about more than losing; it was about losing to *him*. "The smart girl who had done her homework loses to the class clown," laments *Nasty Women* co-editor Samhita Mukhopadhyay. For Cooper, the fury was aggravated by its familiarity. "There is no other group of women who can understand just how devastating Hillary Clinton's loss was than Black women," she writes. "What might feel like a singular and stunning defeat for her is one that Black women learn to live with every day—the sense that you are a woman before your time, that your brilliance and talents are limited by the historical moment." Cooper calls out white feminists for failing to "get their people" in 2016—that is, the 53 percent of white female voters who cast their ballots for Trump—but decides that chastising white women is wasted effort. "I have too much feminist shit to do to spend my time hating white women," she explains. "Going after white women online will get you lots of clicks and likes. But you'll feel exhausted at the end."

Not everything, Cooper concludes, is worth your rage.

Even during a presidential race that resurfaced Trump's history of sexism and misogyny, the candidate could not quite control himself. In her 2017 memoir on covering the Trump campaign, Katy Tur of NBC News writes that the Republican candidate touched and kissed her—an unwanted and uninvited act—immediately before an appearance on MSNBC's *Morning Joe*. "Before I know what's happening, his hands are on my shoulders and his lips are on my cheek," Tur writes in *Unbelievable: My Front-Row Seat to the Craziest Campaign in American History*. "Fuck. I hope the cameras didn't see that," she thinks to herself. "My bosses are never going to take me seriously. I didn't have time to duck!"

As if ducking from Donald Trump's hands and lips should be Tur's responsibility. *I just start kissing them. It's like a magnet.*

There are names that will be forever tied to the Me Too era, with Harvey Weinstein and Bill Cosby just two of the most prominent. But the movement is also inseparable from Trump himself and the impunity he thus far enjoys. "One year after Donald Trump had faced no repercussion for having admitted to grabbing women nonconsensually," Traister writes, "women appeared hell-bent on ensuring that other men *would* be forced—at long last—to accept some consequence." The consequences of Me Too have included public shame, firings, even convictions and prison sentences for

some transgressors. Just no discernible consequences for the man
in the Oval Office, who has done his best to ignore, discredit, and
mock his accusers, in some cases explaining that they were not
attractive enough to assault. "You've got to deny, deny, deny and
push back on these women," Trump told a friend who had acknowledged misconduct toward women, according to Bob Woodward's *Fear* (2018). "If you admit to anything and any culpability,
then you're dead."

Opposite such denial is the power of testimony and truth long
withheld. In *She Said* (2019), Jodi Kantor and Megan Twohey, the
New York Times reporters who broke the story of the Weinstein
horrors, explain how legal and corporate cultures help silence victims of workplace harassment and abuse. It happens informally,
through threats and intimidation, and formally, via nondisclosure
agreements and financial settlements. So instead of speaking out,
the women in Weinstein's orbit quietly helped each other, trading
tips on how to protect themselves. Sit in armchairs, not on sofas,
so Harvey can't slide in next to you so easily. Wear heavy coats
even if it's warm. One young producer wore two pairs of tights as
a deterrent.

But it was never enough. Instead, the reporters identify a pattern of predatory behavior: Weinstein invited women into hotel
rooms for supposedly job-related meetings, pressured them for
massages, then escalated demands for sexual acts. "Each of these
stories was upsetting unto itself, but even more telling, more chill-
ing, was their uncanny repetition," Kantor and Twohey recall. "Actresses and former film company employees, women who did not
know one another, who lived in different countries, were telling
the reporters variations on the same story, using some of the same
words, describing such similar scenes."

She Said is an *All the President's Men* for the Me Too era, packed with reluctant sources, emotional interviews, clandestine meetings, impatient editors, secret documents, and intense show-downs with Weinstein himself. The weapons of secrecy wielded by powerful men—financial settlements between abusers and their victims—become, in the hands of journalists, tools of exposure. "Transactions that complex can never be truly secret," Kantor and Twohey explain, noting the lawyers, agents, family members and friends who inevitably learn about them. "Together the payments formed a legal and financial trail. . . . The settlements didn't pre-vent the story; they *were* the story."

But documents alone would not tell this story. Kantor and Twohey needed courageous women to speak, to defy Weinstein's threats and overcome their shame and fear. Some were unknown individuals ("I've been waiting for this knock on my door for twenty-seven years," a former Miramax assistant tells Twohey); others were famous actresses and performers who had also suf-fered at Weinstein's hands, and whose background accounts and on-the-record statements proved essential. When *Times* editors pushed Kantor and Twohey to publish an early Weinstein story after months of reporting, the writers resisted until they could per-suade more such sources to go on the record. "The Weinstein story had two strands: the producer's apparent menacing of generations of his own employees as well as of actresses who wanted parts," they explain. "Without the second—many actresses, even some top stars, said they had been harassed by Weinstein—the story would be incomplete."

When Ashley Judd finally agrees to be quoted by the *Times* ("I'm prepared to be a named source in your investigation," she informs Kantor), the reporter begins weeping. "This means the world to me as a journalist," Kantor tells her.

Note the specificity. *As a journalist.* Kantor and Twohey have authored a book that is on the Me Too movement but not necessarily *of* the movement. The Weinstein reporting became a "solvent for secrecy," they write, propelling countless women to share their stories. But Kantor and Twohey are not advocates and do not pretend to know or decide what the new rules on sex and power should be. Though they express sympathy for the imperative to believe women, they emphasize that the obligation of journalists remains to "scrutinize, verify, check, and question information." Their dedication to that obligation is what made their reporting so influential and what makes *She Said* so memorable. "If the story was not shared, nothing would change," they conclude. "Problems that are not seen cannot be addressed. In our world of journalism, the story was the end, the result, the final product. But in the world at large, the emergence of new information was just the beginning."

Among the most lasting consequences of the Me Too movement, even beyond the penalties paid by men, is the renewed ability of women to say it all out loud, to find and hear one another, to elevate their stories out of private anguish and into public memory. The memoirs of the Me Too era are so piercing that, even if they do not bring systems crashing down, they reveal the rotting foundations.

In *Crash Override* (2017), Zoë Quinn, a video game developer and anti-online-abuse activist, describes her life during the notorious Gamergate episode, a case of vicious and sustained online harassment against a woman who had the temerity to make games dealing with mental illness. In *What Do We Need Men For?* (2019), E. Jean Carroll ticks through assaults she suffered over the decades from "the Most Hideous Men of My Life," an ever-expanding list of childhood and college acquaintances, ex-bosses, an ex-husband, a former summer camp director, and, most notably and violently, a New York real estate tycoon who years later would win the White House. And in *Know My Name* (2019), Chanel Miller offers a searing and beautiful memoir, showing that being a survivor of sexual assault means not only living through the attack but fighting to survive every day after, "to transform the hurt inside myself, to confront a past, and find a way to live with and incorporate these memories." These are just three of endless Me Too recollections, too many of which, even now, will go unwritten and unspoken.

"Let me be the Virgil to your Dante as we descend through the various webrings of hell," Quinn writes in *Crash Override*, recounting how an ex-boyfriend's savage 2014 online manifesto about their relationship incited a mob of "white supremacist movements, misogynist nerds, conspiracy theorists, and dispassionate hoaxers" who got their kicks threatening and harassing her and people close to her. They encouraged her to kill herself, fantasized about raping her, and disseminated intimate images of her. Quinn witnessed it all unfold online. "This kind of behavior is not just about terrorizing you; it's about control," she writes. "It's about making you want to disappear, instilling fear, and limiting your possibilities." She watches, horrified, as the vitriol she suffered in her corner of the internet found a willing host in the larger political system during the 2016 race, with white nationalists and misogynists coming together and attracting new adherents. "There are different tactics and systems at play," she writes, "but there is always one constant: the mob needs a witch to burn."

Carroll does not read like a victim in someone's allegory. A former champion cheerleader and longtime advice columnist, she in fact relishes being playful, cheeky, ironic, knowing. "You are reading a book written by a person who was the most boy-crazy seventeen-year-old in the nation," she admits early on. *What Do We Need Men For?* chronicles her cross-country road trip—she is accompanied only by her dog, named Lewis Carroll—through small towns across the South, Midwest, and Northeast, where she asks strangers her title query. The answers she receives display a certain thematic consistency:

"So our wives will have somebody to boss around."

"To take out the trash."

"Nothing."

"Nothing."

"Nothing."

"Yard work."

Carroll's conversations—with strangers, herself, her dog, her mechanics—are bizarrely delightful, like an endless group chat that you scroll through occasionally, smiling because you can't imagine how the conversation got *there*. But this book is really about Carroll's dialogue with her own memories. Those begin with an assault during her freshman year at Indiana University at Bloomington in the early 1960s ("Get off!" she demands, to which he answers, "I *am* gonna get off") and continue in no particular order, jumping decades, states of the nation, and states of mind. The sardonic proposal of her subtitle is to get rid of men altogether, cordoning them off somewhere in the American Northwest, or at least color-coding them so it's clear who they really are. "Red for harassers. Blue for cheaters. Green for men who pay women less. Yellow for men who push back against our rising power, and so on." Under this method, the president of the United States would approximate a rainbow.

That Trump is not first on Carroll's list of hideous men—he does not even appear in the book in a significant way until the eleventh of twelve chapters—reads like an assertion of strength and independence. Not everything has to be about Trump; Carroll's life is notable for far more than what happened to her one night at Bergdorf's in the mid-1990s, following a random encounter and some flirty banter about how to buy lingerie. "I assure you that I have been attacked by far, far better men than the president," Carroll writes. But she goes into greater detail about this one hideous man than any other, and even fends off questions and criticisms she expects to face.

No, she did not report Trump to the police. Yes, she told two friends at the time. One offered to accompany her to the police station, the other urged her to keep quiet. ("He has two hundred lawyers. He'll *bury* you.") No, she doesn't have any photos or visual proof, though she wonders if the store had surveillance cameras at the time. She's not sure if she has DNA evidence. ("I never dry-cleaned the Donna Karan coatdress. It's still hanging on the back of the door in my closet.") Why hasn't she said anything before? Because she wasn't eager for death threats.

Carroll also writes that, no, she hasn't experienced mental anguish or lasting trauma from the assault. But she remembers it in detail:

> The moment the dressing room door is closed, he lunges at me, pushes me against the wall, bumping my head quite badly, and puts his mouth against my lips. I am so shocked I shove him back and start laughing again. He seizes both my arms and pushes me up against the wall a second time, bumping my head, and, as I become aware of how large he is, he holds me against the wall with his shoulder and jams his hand under my coatdress and pulls down my tights.
>
> I am astonished by what I'm about to write: I keep laughing.
>
> The next moment, still wearing correct business attire, shirt,

tie, suit jacket, overcoat, he opens the overcoat, unzips his pants, and, forcing his fingers around my private area, then thrusts his penis halfway—or completely, I'm not certain—inside me. It turns into a colossal struggle. I am too frightened to panic. I am wearing a pair of sturdy, black patent-leather, four-inch Barneys high heels. I try to stomp his foot. I try to push him off with my one free hand—for some reason I keep holding my purse with the other—and I finally get a knee up high enough to push him out and off, and I turn, open the door, and run out of the dressing room.

The whole episode lasts no more than two or three minutes.

Carroll appends one eviscerating sentence to her account, an addendum that casts doubt on her claim of having suffered no lasting harm from the experience: "I've never had sex with anybody ever again."

In *Know My Name*, Miller's story is not about Trump. Yet, almost unavoidably, it still comes back to him.

Chanel Miller was first known and unknown as Emily Doe, the anonymous victim of a sexual assault outside a Stanford University fraternity party in 2015. She has no recollection of the attack—both she and her assailant had been drinking earlier that night—but later learned that she was found partially clothed and unconscious, with her attacker, an undergraduate student-athlete named Brock Turner, still on top of her. (Two Swedish graduate students discovered the scene and tackled Turner when he tried to leave.) Convicted of three felony counts of sexual assault, Turner was sentenced to only six months in jail and served half that time. Miller's "victim impact statement," which she read in court and addressed directly to Turner, became an internet sensation, revealing the author's strengths as a writer but mainly as a human. "You don't know me," she began, "but you've been inside me, and that's why we're here today." The judge responsible for Turner's lenient sentence was recalled by outraged voters in 2018, two years after the trial.

That is what you might have known before reading *Know My Name*; that is all I knew. The memoir covers everything else—everything Miller does to continue surviving. She details the confusion of waking up in a hospital and being told by a hesitant police deputy that she might have been sexually assaulted; of suddenly being photographed naked ("to measure and document the abrasions," a nurse spells out), and of cameras snaking inside her; of latex fingertips all over her skin; and of pine needles, inexplicably, falling out of her hair. She thinks of asking the deputy where her underwear is but refrains, "because a part of me understood I was not ready to hear the answer."

Hearing, understanding, and accepting what had happened takes time; learning to live with it never ends. Miller's family and job, her sense of safety, her long-distance relationship with her boyfriend—everything suffers in the aftermath of what Turner's father would dismiss as "twenty minutes of action." Miller bifurcates herself into Emily and Chanel; the former absorbs the indignities and pain, the latter tries to move on as if nothing has happened. Miller leaves California and enrolls in art school on the East Coast but finds no respite, suffering constant street harassment from strangers. Simply walking between home and her classes becomes a nonstop exercise in avoidance, fear, and interpretation. One man strolls alongside her. *Can I walk with you? Let me walk with you. I'm just trying to start your day right.* Another pulls up in a van. *Come talk to me. I'm lonely.* These moments make Chemaly's insight about the fear of rape—"What can we deduce from the fact that jail is to men what life is to so many women?"—scream off the page.

Miller deconstructs the *Access Hollywood* video of Trump and Billy Bush talking on that bus, focusing not on Trump's vile language but on the way the two men regard their prey—the actress waiting to take them onto a soap opera set. "She was present, visible but excluded," Miller writes. "I imagine her standing outside, smiling and waiting patiently. She is the deer while we are made aware of the mountain lions lurking in the bushes, and I am whispering at her to perk up her ears. Run." When the men step off the bus, their public personas flip on: polite, confident, cheerful. That moment fills Miller with dread, a reminder of "all the ways we are unaware."

I had watched the video numerous times, but not until reading Miller's memoir did I notice some odd phrasing. "All I can see is the legs," Bush says to Trump when they spot the actress. "Oh, it looks good," Trump responds. Note that Bush says "the legs" rather than "her legs"—the extremities are somehow separate from the human being to whom they belong. Trump uses "it" rather than "she" to describe the woman awaiting them. To them, she is barely a person. *She* is an *it*.

Trump's words on the video evoked for Miller the testimony of her attacker during his trial, and she intersperses the two transcripts to devastating effect: "Trump sounded like someone I knew. *I just start kissing them. Just kiss. I don't even wait.* 'I kissed her,' Brock said. 'And you didn't ask her permission before you kissed her, did you,' my DA said. 'No,' Brock said. *I moved on her like a bitch.* 'I kissed her cheek and ear,' Brock said. 'I touched her breasts. I moved her dress down.' *Grab 'em by the pussy.* 'I took off her underwear . . . and then I fingered her.' *I did try and fuck her.*"

Though Miller hails the Me Too movement, she resents its

fundamental asymmetry, with multiple female voices needed to balance out a single male one, with women defined by what they endured and men by all they could've been. Miller recalls the congressional testimony of Christine Blasey Ford in September 2018, and how the self-effacing research psychologist defied that asymmetry when she accused Supreme Court nominee Brett Kavanaugh of a long-ago sexual assault. "She had none of the requirements society tells us we need before we dare open our mouths," Miller writes. "She had every reason to stay hidden, but stepped straight into the most public, volatile, combative environment imaginable." In Miller's case, the asymmetry lasts longer than Turner's conviction and brief jail time; it lingers even after her victim impact statement captivated tens of millions of readers. It is the asymmetry of seeing her talents as a writer understood only in the context of Turner's attack and of her status as a victim.

"Brock will always be the *swimmer turned rapist*," she realizes. "He was great and then he fell. Anything I do in the future will be by the *victim who wrote a book*. His talent precedes the tragedy. . . . I did not come into existence when he harmed me. *She found her voice!* I had a voice, he stripped it, left me groping around blind for a bit, but I always had it. I just used it like I never had to use it before."

Know My Name is an astonishing literary debut. It chronicles suffering and flows from it. The author's talent and value do not.

Lurking among the many worthy memoirs and activist anthologies, the dissections of anger and the journalistic investigations of misconduct, one book has appeared offering a broader theory of the case, almost a philosophy underlying the Me Too movement, even if it predates it, and even if the author herself would not claim the distinction.

In *Down Girl: The Logic of Misogyny*, published in November 2017, just weeks after the initial Weinstein revelations in the *New York Times* and *The New Yorker*, Cornell University philosopher Kate Manne cautions against "an obsessive focus with individual guilt and innocence" when it comes to the beliefs and behavior of misogynists. "Trying to fight misogyny primarily using juridical moral notions is a bit like trying to fight fire with oxygen," she writes. "It might work on a small scale—we do manage to blow out matches and candles, after all. But when we try to scale up the strategy, it is liable to backfire." The inevitable criticisms of the Me Too movement—*Too far? Not far enough? Men aren't mind readers!*—represent the risk built into this atomized approach.

Misogyny is typically understood as hatred, mistrust, and prejudice from one man toward all women. For Manne, this is a naive definition that restricts misogyny to the realm of emotion and psychology, where it can be particularized or even excused. Manne sees misogyny in more systemic terms. "Misogyny should be understood as the 'law enforcement' branch of a patriarchal order, which has the overall function of *policing* and *enforcing* its governing ideology," she writes. That ideology is sexism, the belief in inherent female inferiority, and misogyny upholds that belief in daily life. Manne uses too many metaphors to make her point, but her meaning is clear. "Sexism wears a lab coat; misogyny goes on witch hunts. . . . Sexism is bookish; misogyny is combative. Sexism has a theory; misogyny wields a cudgel."

In this sense, determining whether individual harassers and abusers are misogynists matters less than realizing that an environment where harassment and abuse are chronic—limiting women's safety, livelihoods, and well-being—is itself misogynistic. Misogynists expect women to provide "feminine-coded goods" such as affection, adoration, and indulgence, Manne writes, while they enjoy "masculine-coded perks" such as authority, money, and status. Women give, men take. Misogynists can love this arrangement and love their mommies, too.

Women violate this code if they call out powerful men for their misdeeds. If they talk back to the mob. If they undercut a man's perception of himself. ("She's back there, little Katy," Trump would say in his campaign rallies when Tur had a story he didn't like. "Third-rate reporter, remember that. Third rate.") If they try to take a man's job—say, the presidency of the United States. Or, really, if they just say no. "You're no fun," disgraced NBC host Matt Lauer reportedly told a new colleague who resisted his advances.

In *What Happened*, Clinton understands the transgressions that spark misogyny. "We can all buy into sexism from time to time, often without even noticing it," but misogyny is darker, she explains. "It's what happens when a woman turns down a guy at a bar and he switches from charming to scary. Or when a woman gets a job that a man wanted and instead of shaking her hand and wishing her well, he calls her a bitch and vows to do everything he can to make sure she fails."

He doesn't have to call her a bitch, though. *Lock her up* works, too. Manne recalls that incessant refrain against Clinton at Trump's rallies. The chant "obviously expressed a desire to see her punished," Manne writes in *Down Girl*. "But it also went beyond that and seemed to express a desire for her *containment*." Clinton was getting too close to power. She's no fun.

In *The Art of the Comeback*, Trump recalls how the dinner party incident with the rich, lovelorn woman supposedly ended. "I told her that I'd call her, but she had to stop the behavior immediately," he wrote. "She made me promise, and I did. When I called I just called to say hello, and that was the end of that." If only his accusers had been as fortunate.

As with so many things Trump says and does, the old story has an air of projection about it, much in the way he deflects accusations of lying and corruption by accusing everyone else of lying and corruption. I don't harass women, he is saying—look, they harass me! And yet, his attitudes toward women are not all that different from the attitude he displays with everyone, all the time.

"Nearly everything strange and disquieting about Trump—his punitive response to even mild criticism, his viscerally personal insults disguised as 'jokes,' his willingness to spread wild rumors about his targets in order to discredit or shame them, his inability to stop lashing out or degrading certain women years after they'd left his life—was also a commonly reported behavior of domestic abusers," Sady Doyle writes in *Nasty Women*. The only difference, she explains, is that Trump deploys those tactics not to wield power over one single person but to manipulate the entire nation.

That's worth remembering on the eve of the 2020 election. As Cooper writes in *Eloquent Rage*, "the deadliest time for a woman in an abusive relationship is when she decides to leave."

BOOKS DISCUSSED

E. Jean Carroll. *What Do We Need Men For? A Modest Proposal.* St. Martin's, 2019.

Soraya Chemaly. *Rage Becomes Her: The Power of Women's Anger.* Atria Books, 2018.

Amy Chozick. *Chasing Hillary: Ten Years, Two Presidential Campaigns, and One Intact Glass Ceiling.* Harper, 2018.

Hillary Rodham Clinton. *What Happened.* Simon & Schuster, 2017.

Brittney Cooper. *Eloquent Rage: A Black Feminist Discovers Her Superpower.* Picador, 2018.

Jodi Kantor and Megan Twohey. *She Said: Breaking the Sexual Harassment Story That Helped Ignite a Movement.* Penguin Press, 2019.

Kate Manne. *Down Girl: The Logic of Misogyny.* Oxford University Press, 2018.

Chanel Miller. *Know My Name: A Memoir.* Viking, 2019.

Samhita Mukhopadhyay and Kate Harding, eds. *Nasty Women: Feminism, Resistance, and Revolution in Trump's America.* Picador, 2017.

Zoë Quinn. *Crash Override: How Gamergate (Nearly) Destroyed My Life, and How We Can Win the Fight Against Online Hate.* PublicAffairs/Hachette, 2018.

Rebecca Traister. *Good and Mad: The Revolutionary Power of Women's Anger.* Simon & Schuster, 2018.

Katy Tur. *Unbelievable: My Front-Row Seat to the Craziest Campaign in American History.* Dey St., 2017.

Andi Zeisler. *We Were Feminists Once: From Riot Grrrl to Covergirl®, the Buying and Selling of a Political Movement.* PublicAffairs, 2016.

EIGHT

THE CHAOS CHRONICLES

I blame Michael Wolff.

Not just for the typos and minor errors littering *Fire and Fury*, his early 2018 bestseller on the chaos coursing through the Trump White House. Not only for the dubious versions of reality his book offers. ("If it rings true, it is true," Wolff said in an MSNBC interview on the book, a standard as journalistically appalling as it is perversely apropos of the times.) Not even for the entirely unsupported suggestion—which the author casually drops into his epilogue—that Trump and then-United Nations ambassador Nikki Haley were carrying on an affair. Haley had become a "particular focus of Trump's attention, and he of hers," Wolff writes, adding that the two had been spending "a notable amount of private time" together aboard Air Force One. (When not enough people picked up on the hint, Wolff went out of his way to draw attention to a supposed liaison in a television interview: "Now that I've told you, when you hit that paragraph, you're going to say, *bingo*.")

No, I blame Wolff above all for setting a template for so many Trump books to follow—a template that former White House aides, administration officials, and even Washington journalists far superior to Wolff have emulated to varying degrees, consciously or not. *Fire and Fury* featured so many insane moments and expletive-filled exchanges from the first nine months of the Trump presidency that even meticulously reported accounts of this White House in the years since have devolved into a contest for the most explosive, chyron-ready anecdotes—anecdotes that, while shocking in their specifics, have grown entirely commonplace in their regularity.

Reading through the Chaos Chronicles, we learn that Trump and a White House staffer sat in the president's study and compiled a list of enemies serving in his administration. We discover that Trump mused about building a moat with alligators on the southern border to fend off immigrants. (Yes, alligators. And yes, a moat.) We realize that senior aides steal sensitive documents off the president's desk, hoping he will forget about them (which he does). We are told that multiple senior officials almost quit at the same time (but didn't). And we watch as the president struggles to read portions of the Constitution out loud, stumbling over the words and complaining that they sound—metaphor alert!—like a foreign language to him.

I believe it. I believe all of it and more. That's the trouble with writing about the Trump White House, and reading about it, too: the lunacy is appalling yet unsurprising, wholly unpresidential yet entirely on-brand.

The authors of the Chaos Chronicles strive for memorable imagery to distill the events they're recounting: It's a devil's bargain! A team of vipers! It's a nervous breakdown! It's the White House as an Etch A Sketch—no, wait, as a Tilt-A-Whirl! Yes, the mayhem is integral to the Trump story, and the deployment of outlandish symbolism is understandable when one is describing an administration that gives off a reality-show vibe, that feeling, as one author puts it, "that you were watching a thing that you were not supposed to be able to see on TV—and yet here it was."

Trump, of course, has loathed the Chaos Chronicles since the beginning. "I turn on the TV, open the newspapers, and I see stories of chaos—chaos," the president complained during a White House news conference less than a month into his term. "Yet it is the exact opposite. This administration is running like a fine-tuned machine." No, it is the exact opposite of the exact opposite; on this score, the scribes of the Trump era are more credible than the president. So Trump goes on Twitter tirades about these books, only boosting their sales and confirming their narratives. For publishers, a Trump tweetstorm is a key marketing objective.

Yet White House chaos is not the full story, and it should certainly not be the only story. While well-sourced reports and insider memoirs provide a vital historical record, it is the books that tell us what the chaos means and why it matters that are most needed, even if not always most memorable. When the fire dies out and the fury subsides, what is the true American carnage wrought by and in the Trump White House? If these volumes are any indication, it is the decline of America's preparedness for truly complex crises—ones that can't be intimidated on Twitter, wished away as fake news, or redrawn with a Sharpie. It is the remaking, to its lasting detriment, of the limits and powers of the American presidency, and the degrading of our expectations for—and devotion to—public service. And it is the erosion not of personal decorum or policy process, though there is plenty of that, but of the democratic and human values to which the country should aspire.

In the Chaos Chronicles calendar, July 20, 2017, is circled in red. It is the morning of the infamous briefing in the "Tank," a high-level Pentagon affair with cabinet secretaries, top White House advisers, and the commander in chief himself, the most dramatized and dissected meeting of the Trump presidency. Think of President Kennedy's "Executive Committee" sessions during the Cuban missile crisis—but instead of worrying about Khrushchev and Castro, the assembled advisers are freaking out about their own guy.

At this gathering, Defense Secretary Jim Mattis, Secretary of State Rex Tillerson and economic adviser Gary Cohn—some of Trump's so-called adults in the room, all long since departed from the administration—hope to tutor the president on the benefits of international alliances and military deployments. The attempt backfires spectacularly, not because their arguments are invalid but because Trump's beliefs about how the world works have been cast for decades, and winning the White House by campaigning on them did little to change his mind.

Some of the best-known and bestselling books on the Trump White House, such as Bob Woodward's *Fear* and Philip Rucker and Carol Leonnig's *A Very Stable Genius* (2020), capture the scene at the Pentagon with cinematic sweep and detail. Woodward devotes nine pages to the meeting; Rucker and Leonnig go to eleven. Former Mattis speechwriter Guy Snodgrass, who witnessed the briefing from an adjoining room, spends more than a chapter on it in *Holding the Line*, published in October 2019. Eight months earlier, former Trump communications aide Cliff Sims, though not present at the Pentagon, writes about it in *Team of Vipers*, describing the president's mood when he returned to the White House. (Spoiler: Trump was psyched.) It is the kind of scene that strokes the erogenous zones of every political junkie. Generals! The president! Cursing! *A clash of worldviews!*

"There is no more sacred military space than room 2E924 of the Pentagon," Rucker and Leonnig write. The Tank is a windowless secure conference room where the Joint Chiefs discuss classified materials, a place for serious deliberations over war and peace. "Uniformed officers think of the Tank a bit like a church," Rucker and Leonnig explain. "Inside its walls, flag officers observe a reverence and decorum for the wrenching decisions that have been made here." This time, it was not about making a decision but about staging an intervention, one for a president with no reverence for the long-held assumptions of U.S. national security policies. And as in most interventions, the person at the center of it did not believe he had a problem.

Mattis and Tillerson felt "incredible pressure to educate the president," Snodgrass writes, and they decided to couch their arguments in terms that they thought would appeal to him, playing to Trump's business background (by noting the strong "return on invested capital" of U.S. diplomatic and military efforts) and his reflexive disdain for his predecessor (by emphasizing that Obama's premature withdrawal from Iraq had led to ISIS). And they would toss in sports terminology, such as explaining that stationing forces abroad means not having to protect America "on the one-yard line."

But on the day of the meeting, Trump has none of it. "Our trade agreements are criminal," the president complains, stressing that he is ready for a trade war with China. He also fixates on a Bastille Day–style parade in Washington, with troops marching and tanks rolling and patriotism pulsing. "Mattis began to shut down," Snodgrass writes, "sitting back in his chair with a distant, defeated look on his face."

Together, the various accounts offer an almost running transcript of the briefing. Trump derides NATO as worthless, free trade a scam, and Afghanistan a "loser war," Rucker and Leonnig report. "You're all losers. You don't know how to win anymore," he tells the assembled officials, who include the four-star Mattis and the chairman of the Joint Chiefs of Staff. "I wouldn't go to war with you people," adds Trump. Tillerson is the only official who comes off well in this scene in *A Very Stable Genius*, challenging the president's suggestion that U.S. troops should defend allies only if those countries pay up. (After the meeting, Tillerson delivers the sound bite heard round the world, dismissing Trump as a "fucking moron.") Woodward recounts how the president both trashes the notion of a new strategy for the war in Afghanistan ("You don't need a strategy to kill people," Trump reasons) and counters Cohn's point that trade deficits can be good for the economy ("I don't want to hear that. It's all bullshit!").

In *Fear*, the meeting is summed up in classic Woodwardian style, with a written summary by an unnamed official who spoke with people in attendance: "It seems clear that many of the president's senior advisers, especially those in the national security realm, are extremely concerned with his erratic nature, his relative ignorance, his inability to learn, as well as what they consider his dangerous views."

In other words, they feared what they already knew: they feared the very traits and habits and impulses that had prompted them to hold the briefing in the first place. Trump is who they thought he was.

Multiple people attended the meeting, including Vice President Mike Pence and senior White House adviser Jared Kushner, and the accounts reflect various sources and perspectives. Even so, the Chaos Chronicles often showcase the point of view of Steve Bannon, the ex–Breitbart News honcho who served as chief executive of the Trump campaign, the candidate's nationalist muse, and later White House strategist. Bannon's inner monologue sets up key moments in the meeting and helps guide the story. In Woodward's account: "This is going to be fun, Bannon thought, as Mattis made the case that the organizing principles of the past were still work-able and necessary." When Tillerson argues that postwar alliances had kept international peace for decades, readers of *Fear* learn that "it was more of the old world order to Bannon: expensive, limit-less engagements." In *A Very Stable Genius*, Bannon's musings are saucier: "Oh, baby, this is going to be fucking wild," he thinks as the festivities kick off.

When Trump returns to the White House, he and Bannon exult over their performance. "Steve, Steve, that was spectacular," the president says, according to Sims's *Team of Vipers*. "We had them on the ropes. Rex didn't have any idea what to say." Bannon dismisses Tillerson as "totally establishment in his thinking," and the president latches onto the phrase, as though it is some bril-liant new formulation. "That's the perfect way to put it: completely and totally establishment," Trump responds. That moment showed Bannon "at the height of his power," Sims writes.

The next month, Bannon would be out, fired by new White House chief of staff John Kelly. But much of the most dramatic ma-terial in the Chaos Chronicles transpires in year one of the Trump presidency, when Bannon still held sway with both the president and the journalists covering him. Far more than in any other vol-ume, Bannon is the spirit animal of Wolff's *Fire and Fury*, which cites him so often that the book has a "by Steve Bannon as told to Michael Wolff" vibe. (One irony: Wolff whiffs on the Tank meet-ing, even writing about inconsequential happenings on that same day.) "Interactions with Bannon often had an almost cinematic quality to them, as if he were playing out a part for a camera in the corner capturing his every utterance," Sims writes in *Team of Vipers*. He's right. Books need stories, and Bannon may have been the most gifted narrator of the early Trump era.

The trope of the genius campaign guru is ingrained in

Washington journalism, Joshua Green notes in *Devil's Bargain*, his bestseller on the Trump-Bannon relationship, which came out in the summer of 2017, when Bannon's star was at its brightest. Bannon deliberately cultivated the image of a big thinker, Green writes, one who is "able to make sense of the world and divine where it was heading." In addition, he was a talented storyteller "in the Irish comic tradition," Green notes, and candidate Trump fell for the grift. "He loved how Bannon, an avid reader of history and military biographies, fitted Trump's outsider campaign into the broader sweep of history."

The bargain at the heart of Green's account is that Bannon's hard-right nationalism and Breitbart hordes would ally with Trump's grievance politics to win the White House—at which point the new administration would enact an anti-trade, anti-immigrant, anti-interventionist agenda. (In a delightful aside, Woodward notes that when Bannon instructed the future president on populism, his student was enthusiastic, if a bit hazy on the specifics: "That's what I am, a popularist," Trump responded.) Yet Bannon's nationalist revolution was inseparable from his own exalted self-perception. "Bannon thought he was an action figure who had been stuck in a hermetically sealed package for decades until Trump finally freed him and brought him to life," Sims writes. "I couldn't help but appreciate anyone who had the stones to be that grandiose." The strategist's practical advice to Sims was revolutionary only in the most trite ways: "I want you weaponizing everything," he says when Sims joins the campaign. "F— anyone who tells you not to do something. Let's start wrecking some s—, okay?"

In Washington, all you need to do is tote around some weighty books (Bannon made sure to be spotted with *The Best and the Brightest*, Wolff points out) for journalists to start calling you a "student of history." Bannon longed to see himself featured in the great pageant of Washington power brokers, Wolff explains, and so he offered his personal running commentary on his own influence and on the unseriousness of everyone else in the White House. This commentary is well reflected in the Chaos Chronicles. Bannon's influence far surpasses his formal tenure with Team Trump because he has shaped the way the Trump story is told and remembered, serving, as Wolff puts it, as "everybody's Deep Throat."

That metaphor is wrong, of course: speaking to countless reporters on the record, on background or on the condition of easily recognizable anonymity, is the opposite of what Mark Felt did with Woodward during Watergate. Felt avoided the spotlight, denying the rumors of his role for decades; Bannon basks in his notoriety, aggrandizing his influence whenever possible. He's no Deep Throat.

But, hey, it *rings true*, doesn't it? Bingo.

Another Deep Throat candidate for the Trump era is the "senior administration official" who wrote an anonymous *New York Times* op-ed in the fall of 2018, describing an internal resistance against the president. For all the speculation it generated, the essay yielded few identifying details. The author, who as of this writing remains anonymous, claimed to be part of a coterie of like-minded bureaucrats fighting to protect America's democratic institutions by "thwarting Mr. Trump's more misguided impulses." Readers did not learn anything about the work the writer had done or which impulses, if any, had been thwarted. The article's generic op-ed-speak—its comforts were cold and its divides bitter, its observers were astute and its heroes unsung—also made it hard to identify the author. It could've been anyone, short of a decent speechwriter.

A year later, the same official published *A Warning*, a 259-page book promising to "cut through the noise" of this presidency and contending that Trump "still lacks the guiding principles needed to govern our nation." The *still* is quite a tell. Anonymous informs us that Trump is "reckless" and his management style "erratic." As if we did not know. The president, we are told, suffers from "inattentiveness," "impulsiveness," and "intellectual laziness." As if we did not know. Trump displays misogynistic behavior, embraces conspiracies, bullies his subordinates, abuses his powers, disregards briefings, and equates criticism to treason. As if we did not know. Anonymous also concedes that the thesis of the original op-ed—that the alleged adults in the room could curb Trump's worst instincts—had proved false. "Americans should not expect that his advisors can fix the situation," Anonymous acknowledges. As if we ever did.

Part of the challenge here is the author's continued anonymity. *A Warning* reads like a longer—much longer—version of the op-ed, purposely vague and avoiding major disclosures to preserve the writer's secret. Anonymity, usually granted to obtain more information, here justifies giving less. Absent hard facts, the author barrages readers with similes. Trump is "like a twelve-year-old in an air traffic control tower, pushing the buttons of government indiscriminately," we are told. He treats the U.S. military "like it's part of a big game of Battleship." Most vivid, working for Trump is "like showing up at the nursing home at daybreak to find your elderly uncle running pantsless across the courtyard and cursing loudly about the cafeteria food, as worried attendants try to catch him."

Rather than offer many instances of underlings proactively curbing presidential misconduct, *A Warning* provides an endless encore of officials expressing concern. "We all watched with a sense of doom." "We were all unnerved." "This place is so fucked up." "It was jaw-dropping." "There is literally no one in charge here."

In *A Warning*, actions are not taken; they are almost taken. In an especially dire circumstance, several top Trump officials consider resigning en masse, a "midnight self-massacre" that would draw public attention to the president's ineptitude. The move was deemed too risky, Anonymous explains, because it would "shake public confidence"—as if the eroding public confidence were not the very reason they had pondered the move. Throughout *A Warning*, at least a handful of top aides are always "on the brink" of quitting. (The Brink is a popular hangout for Trump officials.) Anonymous also wonders if Trump's response to the Charlottesville protests in 2017, when the president drew a moral equivalence between white nationalists and those Americans protesting against them, would have been the time for such a gesture. "Maybe that was a lost moment, when a rush to the exits would have meant something."

It's like *Profiles in Thinking About Courage.*

Lots of Trump insiders promise big but deliver little. In *Unhinged*, her 2018 memoir, longtime acolyte Omarosa Manigault Newman draws on her time on *The Apprentice* and in the Trump White House to conclude that her former boss is a narcissist, a racist, and a misogynist. That he loves chaos and confusion and enjoys watching people argue in front of him. That he doesn't read the legislation or executive orders he signs. That he lacks human empathy. That he has a problem with the truth. That Team Trump is "a cult of personality" in which loyalty to the leader is "an absolute and unyielding necessity."

Manigault Newman offers some occasional insights. For instance, she writes that Kelly's efforts to manage Trump's schedule and limit Oval Office access cut the president off from people he trusted, leading Trump to rely even more on cable news, Twitter, and late-night phone calls that the chief of staff could not control. But her supposed bombshell anecdote in *Unhinged*—the alleged existence of an audio tape of Trump using the n-word—remains speculative and unproven, attributed to a single, unnamed source.

In her final chapter, Manigault Newman likens the feeling of departing the White House to breaking loose from a hypnotist's spell. "For the first time in nearly fifteen years, I would be free from the cult of Trumpworld," she writes. Yet one gets the sense that Manigault Newman, who explicitly modeled herself on Trump during her villain turn on *The Apprentice*, likely would have remained forever loyal had Kelly not fired her from her amorphous job as communications director for the White House Office of Public Liaison. In an odd coincidence, she explains that she originally aspired to be that office's director, which is also the job Cliff Sims hoped to land and the perch Anthony Scaramucci originally coveted. (I suspect it is not an overly demanding post.)

Some insiders ignore the president almost entirely in their books. Mattis, who resigned as defense secretary in late 2018, publicly denounced Trump in June 2020 for his divisiveness and abuse of executive authority. But in his memoir, *Call Sign Chaos*, published in the fall of 2019, the general prefers to stand down. "I'm old fashioned: I don't write about sitting presidents," he writes. Mattis makes no mention in his book of the infamous Tank meeting; the only exchange with Trump that he cites is his initial interview for the Pentagon job. ("In our forty-minute conversation, Mr. Trump led the wide-ranging discussion, and the tone was amiable.") The rest of the book covers Mattis's distinguished military career and the leadership lessons he had distilled over the decades. Here's one that sticks out: "Leaders at all ranks, but especially at high ranks, must keep in their inner circle people who will unhesitatingly point out when a leader's personal behavior or decisions are not appropriate."

Other insider accounts, even those by former Trump aides who were humiliated at the White House and on the way out, can't help but continue to suck up, as though hoping for one more attaboy. In *The Briefing* (2018), Sean Spicer offers more of the self-abasement we saw during his run as Trump's sacrificial first press secretary. Trump is so special, Spicer gushes, that he's "a unicorn, riding a unicorn over a rainbow," an image more confusing than flattering. He explains that the real problem with the president's ban on travelers from several Muslim-majority countries, issued in the earliest days of the administration, was not its dubious legality or the lack of preparation to enforce or defend it but rather all those "liberal, activist judges" who stymied the order. In a book published one year after he departed the White House, Spicer could not stop spinning. After recalling Trump's insulting campaign comments about Mexican immigrants and about Senator John McCain, for instance, Spicer praises Trump's "relatability."

Spicer revisits his debut behind the White House press room lectern on the first full day of the new administration, when he defended the indefensible position that Trump's inauguration crowds were larger than those drawn by Obama—and he manages to make the situation even more damning in retrospect. "I didn't have hard and fast stats on attendance," he admits, "and as far as I could find out on a Saturday morning, no one else did either." But why should that stop him? "As I drafted my statement for the press, I still needed facts and figures to support the president's assertion," he writes, an admission that, from day one in the Trump White House, conclusions preceded evidence. Even so, he issued the most ironclad of statements to a roomful of perplexed reporters: "This was the largest audience to ever witness an inauguration, period."

Looking back on the episode, Spicer explains that he misinterpreted the president's wisdom: "Instead of bringing the White House press corps to heel, he had wanted a polished, nuanced argument defending his position." Improbably, Spicer adds that he assumed a Saturday afternoon briefing from a new White House spokesman litigating the size of the inauguration crowds "was not going to be big news"—a statement that makes him either a liar or just terrible at his job.

In *Team of Vipers*, Sims offers more detail on how the White House communications team crafted Spicer's message about the inauguration crowd, and polish and nuance were not their guiding principles. "How the f— are we going to find evidence to support the crowd thing?" asks Raj Shah, the deputy communications director. But Spicer, focused on proving himself to Trump, cuts short the discussion: "We don't have time to go round and round about it anymore." Spicer enlists Sims to type up his talking points, as colleagues huddle around a spare laptop and commence pulling facts out of nowhere and anywhere. "I was typing as quickly as I could," Sims recalls. "We had no idea that nearly everything we were being told was wrong." Then logistics, or fate, tried to intervene.

Suddenly, the computer made a loud beep. It'd been a long time since I had used a PC rather than a Mac, so I looked down to see if it was perhaps an audible signal that the battery power was getting low. Instead, to my great horror, the computer seemed to be going into some type of emergency shutdown. I scrambled to plug it in, thinking its battery might have run out of juice. Nothing. I frantically hit the space bar. Black screen. . . .

The draft remarks that we had collectively spent hours researching, compiling, writing, and editing had vanished forever.

If only it had been so. They pieced the material back together, Spicer went off to the press room—and the rest is embarrassing history. The crowd size episode proved to be "a senseless, unrecoverable act of self-sabotage," Sims writes, one that "did enormous damage to the White House's credibility on day one."

After reading *Team of Vipers*, I will always take heart in the notion that, just for a moment, the ghosts of press secretaries past had tried, even unsuccessfully, to kill off those remarks.

Several contributors to the Chaos Chronicles offer one overriding concept to explain the president—a single analytic lens through which his actions are explained and magnified. It is a reductionist exercise, often more clever than useful. But it *is* useful when it uncovers patterns in Trump's behavior. Trump the mobster. Trump the television star. Trump the tantrum-throwing toddler.

James Comey, the former FBI director and author of *A Higher Loyalty: Truth, Lies, and Leadership* (2018), will forever be a central character of this time. He deserves it. Comey was the first to inform Trump of the existence of the sketchy Russia dossier. (The president-elect responded by asking, rhetorically, if he seemed like the kind of guy who needs to hire prostitutes.) Comey's sacking led to the appointment of a special counsel to investigate Russia's election interference. And thanks to the lawman's compulsion to write memos on his conversations with Trump, Comey's private exchanges with the president are legend. I'm surprised that *I Need Loyalty* is not the title of yet another Chaos Chronicle.

Comey's memoir can be exceedingly pompous, even self-deluding. He tells readers that he never cut in line at the FBI cafeteria, because "it was very important to show people that I'm not better than anyone else." He is the kind of writer who doesn't just quote Shakespeare but quotes himself quoting Shakespeare. And, somehow, he still hopes that his momentous decisions in 2016—to openly chastise Hillary Clinton for being "extremely careless" in handling classified materials, and to briefly reopen the investigation into her emails with just days left in the campaign—did not influence the election.

While Comey echoes standard criticisms of Trump—he is "unethical, untethered to truth and institutional values," and his leadership is "transactional, ego driven, and about personal loyalty"—his views are rooted not just in his own dealings with the president but in the memories of his years battling mafia families as U.S. attorney in Manhattan. "As I found myself thrust into the Trump orbit, I once again was having flashbacks to my earlier career as a prosecutor against the Mob," he explains. "The silent circle of assent. The boss in complete control. The loyalty oaths. The us-versus-them worldview. The lying about all things." Ethical leaders, Comey argues, don't need to yell, inspire fear, or issue threats. "Ethical leaders never ask for loyalty. Those leading through fear—like a Cosa Nostra boss—require personal loyalty."

For Comey, the notion of a president with the instincts of a mobster is terrifying. For *New York Times* television critic James Poniewozik, it is the inevitable result of an era when Tony Soprano–style characters dominated popular culture and television audiences fragmented into opposing cultural tribes. Into this environment stepped Trump, a man whose career and presidency have been lived out on television and guided by the imperatives of the medium.

"For decades, Trump had essentially been a cable-news channel in human form: loud, short of attention span, and addicted to conflict," Poniewozik writes, in his darkly entertaining *Audience of One: Donald Trump, Television, and the Fracturing of America*

(2019). By the time Trump won the White House, "he and cable had achieved the singularity, a meshing of man and machine."

Audience of One is two books in one, outlining how television's transformation from mass-market sameness to niche-market silos has helped remake America's appetites and politics, and also explaining how Trump became a button on the nation's remote, first as a celebrity businessman and now as a president embodying the ethos of reality television. "Trump is the most influential character in the history of TV," Poniewozik writes. "He deserves a careful review."

Poniewozik is susceptible to a tendency of many Trump authors: to see in this president the fulfillment of every theory they've developed about the world. "Trump's political rise, I came to see, was the result of changes that I had been writing about as a TV critic for twenty years," he explains in his introduction. Yet the story seems to hold. The appeal of antihero shows such as *The Sopranos* and *Breaking Bad* would encourage viewers to cheer for charismatic tough guys like Trump. Reality television, with its nihilistic melding of "conflict, stereotype, the fuzzy boundary between truth and fiction," became the defining entertainment form of the 2000s and gave Trump entrée into America's homes and its politics. His character on *The Apprentice* became his own kind of antihero—impolite and exploitative—and the boardroom scenes, in which contestants knifed each other while groveling for Trump's approval, previewed the dynamics of his administration. And while it's easy to think Trump wastes valuable time as president on random battles (whether Mika Brzezinski's face, Hurricane Dorian's path, or the power of hydroxychloroquine), it's not a waste if the battles are the point. "You could say that he was doing the only job he was truly elected to do: monitoring, stoking, and embodying the cultural anger machine." Even Trump's incessant deceptions matter less in this context; with reality television, Poniewozik reminds readers, "the awareness that you were being manipulated was part of the entertainment."

Daniel W. Drezner sees Trump not as a mobster or television character but as a toddler, a comparison that is more amusing but also more alarming. Drezner, a professor of international politics at Tufts University, is best known in the Trump years as the keeper of a Twitter thread noting every time a Trump official or ally is cited in the press likening the president to a child. (He passed 1,500 instances early in the summer of 2020.) Drezner's *The Toddler in Chief* (2020) is a greatest-hits edition, a litany of examples of Trump's poor impulse control, temper tantrums, short attention span, defiant ignorance, and excessive screen time. Drezner nails the contrast by starting each chapter with a different quote from *Caring for Your Baby and Young Child*, a publication of the American Academy of Pediatrics. "Preschoolers are very eager to take control. They want to be more independent than their skills and safety allow, and they don't appreciate their limits. They want to make decisions, but they don't know how to compromise, and they don't deal with disappointment or restraint."

It's the funniest of the Chaos Chronicles, but *The Toddler in Chief* also outlines the serious risks of having a president with childlike traits. Opportunistic advisers exploit his emotions to their advantage. He doubles down on mistakes just to avoid admitting them. He makes major decisions—withdrawing forces from Syria, meeting with North Korean dictator Kim Jong Un, shutting down the government—largely on impulse. Officials briefing him on key issues are reluctant to raise his ire by presenting findings that contradict Trump's prior off-the-cuff positions. The result is a president "operating the executive branch like a bumper car, without any sense of peril," Drezner writes. "The driver is not getting any better at his job. He is just getting more confident that there is no risk to what he is doing."

The COVID-19 pandemic may not have eroded the president's confidence, but it has certainly heightened its risks. *The Toddler in Chief* was completed before the outbreak went global, but Drezner still managed to anticipate something like it, even fleetingly. "Based on Trump's behavior as cataloged in this book," he writes, "the idea of Trump coping with a true crisis—a terrorist attack, a global pandemic, a great power clash with China—is truly frightening."

Even more frightening? Such crises are not mutually exclusive.

"Prescient" is praise too generously ladled in the Trump era; countless books, movies, and other cultural artifacts have been hailed for predicting the rise of an American leader with authoritarian pretensions. (I've contributed to the genre, too. Apologies.) But among the Chaos Chronicles, Michael Lewis's *The Fifth Risk*, published in the fall of 2018, comes closest to earning the label. Not for predicting Trump, but for foreshadowing his consequences.

The book's focus—the relatively unknown tasks of the Departments of Energy, Commerce, and Agriculture in collecting data and monitoring and fending off catastrophic risks—seems less sexy than baseball or Wall Street, to name some of Lewis's past preoccupations. Yet it may be the most urgent book of the Trump years. Reading *The Fifth Risk* in the middle of a presidency obsessed with alleged "deep state" machinations feels subversive, almost countercultural. Lewis has written a love letter to the mission and dedication of America's federal workforce, the researchers and the scientists and the data geeks too easily ignored until a crisis proves their value. "We don't really celebrate the accomplishments of government employees," Lewis writes. "They exist in our society to take the blame." He wants to give them credit.

The Fifth Risk recounts the disastrous transition between the 2016 election and Trump's inauguration. An outgoing administration is required by law to help the new crew prepare to run the government, so Obama officials spent months readying detailed briefings for their successors, whomever they would be. Except Trump was not interested in planning for a transition. "You and I are so smart that we can leave the victory party two hours early and do the transition ourselves," he told former New Jersey governor Chris Christie, originally tasked with the nominal transition effort.

Much of that work by outgoing Obama officials went to waste. "We had tried desperately to prepare them," a former top Energy Department official tells Lewis. "But that required them to show up." Department of Agriculture staffers had assembled 2,300 pages of materials, but the Trump transition officials didn't arrive until a month after the election. When they did appear, Trump's teams were often more focused on ideology—asking the Energy Department for lists of staffers who worked on climate change, for example—than on learning what various agencies did all day. "There was a mentality that everything that government does is stupid and bad and the people in it are stupid and bad," one Obama official laments.

To his everlasting credit, Lewis took it upon himself to do what so many Trump transition officials didn't: he interviewed former Obama officials from those three agencies and asked what they would've told their successors if they'd had the chance. What he found is a government that seeks to manage risks so large that no one person or company could ever handle them. The former chief risk officer at the Department of Energy ticks down the five problems that keep him up at night: A nuclear weapons accident. North Korea. Iran. The vulnerability of the electrical grid. And fifth is

faulty "project management," what Lewis describes as the dangerous habit of patching up long-term problems with short-term solutions. Imagine *The Big Short*, but for the federal government.

Lewis lists some of the fast-moving, inevitable dangers that any
president must consider, such as pandemics, hurricanes, and terrorist attacks. (Yes, pandemics are first on his list.) But many risks
are longer-term and therefore easily ignored. "It is delaying repairs
to a tunnel filled with lethal waste until, one day, it collapses,"
Lewis cautions. "It is the aging workforce of the DOE—which is no
longer attracting young people, as it once did—that one day loses
track of a nuclear bomb. It is the ceding of technical and scientific
leadership to China. It is the innovation that never occurs, and the
knowledge that is never created, because you have ceased to lay
the groundwork for it. It is what you never learned that might have
saved you."

For all the president's blather about a nefarious deep state, it is
his contempt for the deep-seated expertise of the federal government that could prove most damaging. "If you want to preserve
your personal immunity to the hard problems, it's better never to
really understand those problems," Lewis explains. "There is an
upside to ignorance, and a downside to knowledge. Knowledge
makes life messier. It makes it a bit more difficult for a person who
wishes to shrink the world to a worldview."

As the Chaos Chronicles make clear, a global health and economic crisis such as the coronavirus pandemic only magnifies
Trump's political, managerial, and personal shortcomings. It demands that a leader rely on science and data, coordinate teams
across bureaucracies and agencies, communicate credibly and
clearly with the public, and demonstrate basic empathy with
Americans who suffer regardless of their party, the color of their
states, or the words on their hats. Instead, the president behaves as

he always does, and believes what he wants to believe, whether on the origins or duration of a pandemic or the proper means to fight it. In *Fear*, an exasperated Gary Cohn asks the president about his beliefs on tariffs and trade. "Why do you have these views?" the economic adviser demands. Trump's answer: "I just do. I've had these views for 30 years." Similarly, Trump instinctively regarded the virus as a border security problem, an immigration problem, a China problem, a messaging problem. He shrinks the world to a worldview.

"The office of the presidency depends on a measure of civic virtue," Susan Hennessey and Benjamin Wittes argue in *Unmaking the Presidency*, published in early 2020. Traditionally, presidents are expected to promote shared values, serve as role models, and put service to the nation above service to self. They are expected to follow the law, or at least to speak and act as if they mean to. In Trump, the authors write, America instead has a leader whose life and presidency embody "an ongoing rejection of civic virtue." Trump has made his presidency an extension of his campaign rallies, "a presidency that elevates the expressive and personal dimensions of the office over everything else." It is the presidency as vanity plate, as zinger, as pinned tweet.

This notion of the "expressive presidency" is at the heart of Hennessey and Wittes's book. In chapter after chapter, the authors contrast the norms that have grown around U.S. presidential behavior over the centuries—involving ethics, honesty, organization, rhetoric, and deference to the rule of law—with Trump's gleeful violations. The president directs policy, hires and fires officials, and addresses the nation all with one eye on his own interests and the other on the passions of his core supporters. The result is a presidency "in which the institutional office and the personality of its occupant are almost entirely merged—merged in their interests, in their impulses, in their finances, and in their public character," Hennessey and Wittes write. All the traditional functions of the office, its management roles, the execution of laws, and the "expectation of ethical conduct, truthfulness, and service," are downgraded. And Trump basically dares Congress, the courts, and the voters to do anything about it.

The irony is that governing in this way undercuts the policy effectiveness of the chief executive. Trump pays a price for announcing the withdrawal of forces from Syria so precipitously; for a travel ban that cannot pass muster in the courts; for simply tweeting out, without consultation, his decision that transgender Americans cannot serve in the armed forces. And the nation paid a price when Trump began treating the coronavirus pandemic as another opportunity for personal expression, misleading the public about the risks ("We have it totally under control"), the extent of the damage ("I like the numbers being where they are"), the availability of testing ("Anybody that needs a test, gets a test"), and the likely duration ("One day, it's like a miracle—it will disappear"). His decisions on when and how to reopen the economy seemed guided more by electoral concerns than public health considerations, and his outlandish televised briefings early in the crisis—a mix of wish fulfillment, untruth, and score-settling—seemed to embody the expressive presidency.

That is the point: coherence and effectiveness don't matter. Trump appears captivated by the theatrical, made-for-TV aspects of his job, such as press confrontations and campaign rallies. He even attempts to manufacture such moments, sometimes with disastrous consequences, as when police and National Guard members violently cleared antiracism protesters out of Washington's Lafayette Park just so Trump could stroll from the White House to St. John's Church and hold aloft a Bible for the cameras. In Trump's vision, "the presidency is emphatically not about the successful management of bureaucracies or the implementation of policy objectives," Hennessey and Wittes explain. "It is about the showmanship and flamboyance of the person and about entertaining and captivating audiences."

Unmaking the Presidency and *The Fifth Risk* help put the other Chaos Chronicles in proper context; they get at the meaning and the consequences of the disorder the others detail. These two books are also in conversation with a third one: Elaine Kamarck's *Why Presidents Fail*, a slim book published in the thick of the 2016 campaign and deserving of wider notice. Kamarck argues that presidents frequently succumb to the illusion that with just the right speech or made-for-TV moment they can overcome any political or legislative hurdles. "The obsession with communication—presidential talking and messaging—is a dangerous mirage of the media age," she writes, "a delusion that inevitably comes crashing down in the face of governmental failure." Presidents struggle to oversee the vast federal bureaucracy at their disposal, even when that very bureaucracy could prevent crises, manage them, and in various ways save presidents from themselves. The early warnings and briefings that Trump received about the impending spread of the coronavirus to the United States—which the president ignored or downplayed—provide tragic examples.

"Modern presidents," Kamarck writes, "are so distant from the government they manage that, on a regular basis, they ignore the flashing lights or fail to realize that they are even flashing."

The titles of the Chaos Chronicles are often ironic invocations of Trump's own words. *Fire and Fury* echoes the president's military threat against North Korea, but it speaks to the fury boiling over in the Oval Office. *Fear* recalls a 2016 *Washington Post* interview with

Trump, when the candidate said that fear constitutes "real power," but it underscores the distress of Trump's aides at his decisions. *A Very Stable Genius* invokes Trump's response to concerns about his mental health, a self-description that eased no one's mind. Tim Alberta's *American Carnage* cites the president's inaugural address but uses it as a metaphor for the state of the Republican Party. And Alexander Nazaryan's *The Best People* (2019) refers to Trump's pledge to hire only the most qualified officials—and then proceeds to document his scandal-ridden cabinet. I can imagine a book on Trump's rhetoric called *The Best Words*, or one on his response to the coronavirus pandemic titled *I Don't Take Responsibility at All* or perhaps *Totally Under Control*.

They're memorable, certainly, but such titles also reveal a preoccupation with the man at the middle of it all, an obsessive focus that probably appeals to this most self-centered of chief executives. So much else is happening in this administration that gets lost in the Trump glare, material that is scattered throughout the Chaos Chronicles themselves. One constant running through several of these books, for instance, is the astounding mix of arrogance and misjudgment displayed by Jared Kushner—on immigration policy, Comey's firing, the government shutdown, and much more. His misfires in the White House, including his inexplicable efforts to manage the response to the coronavirus pandemic, merit booklength investigations. And Steve Bannon, too, could prove far less noteworthy for his nationalist huff-and-puff than for his efforts to "deconstruct the administrative state," as he liked to put it, just before the country, battling for its life and livelihood, would require the services of a competent and agile state more than ever. Woodward's *Fear* could double as an indictment of the "adults in the room" argument, the illusion that some of the experienced hands serving early in Trump's term could settle him down. And though

A Very Stable Genius prompted headlines about Trump's temperament and volatility, some of Rucker and Leonnig's most memorable and damning moments center on special counsel Robert Mueller's failure to shape the public understanding of his findings. Mueller "fumbled the moment," they write, passing up multiple opportunities to influence Attorney General William Barr's portrayal of the two-year investigation.

The Mueller report itself constitutes another entry in the Chaos Chronicles, though of a very different sort.

It has its own miniseries moments. "This is the end of my presidency," Trump moans when he learns of Mueller's appointment. "I'm fucked." There's the contrast between the president's public bluster, evident in his Twitter rants, and his private diffidence, embodied in Trump's lawyerly written responses to Mueller's queries, full of "I do not recall" and "I have no recollection." There is the inevitable Nixonian reference, as when White House counsel Don McGahn refuses the president's request to instruct the deputy attorney general to dismiss Mueller, because McGahn worried about unleashing a new Saturday Night Massacre.

Despite its appendices and footnotes, its legalese and double negatives, and its river of black ink redactions warning of "Harm to Ongoing Matter," the Mueller report has nonetheless become a unique cultural artifact of our time, spawning T-shirts and buttons and memes and podcasts and poetry and graphic-novel editions. Yet in its portrayal of the Trump campaign and White House, the Mueller report reminds me of several of the Chaos Chronicles. The incompetence, disorganization, and self-interest evoke *Fire and Fury*. The mob-like mentality of the Trump team, with the president delegating dirty assignments to outside players, is reminiscent of Comey's account. There are flashbacks to Woodward's *Fear*, with top aides refusing or ignoring presidential instructions. (Imagine if Woodward could add subpoena power to his reporting tools.) And the Mueller report almost feels like a dozen anonymous *New York Times* op-eds from the internal White House resistance strung together, except far more detailed, and signed.

The report's drafters are lawyers, not stylists, but even their formal writing can be devastatingly effective. "An improper motive can render an actor's conduct criminal even when the conduct would otherwise be lawful and within the actor's authority," the report explains, a beautifully understated refutation of the argument that the president can do whatever he wants and for whatever reason as long as he technically has the right to do it. The report recognizes Trump's habit of committing wildly inappropriate acts—such as discouraging the cooperation of witnesses—right out in the open, a tendency that has perplexed journalists used to revealing misdeeds that lurk in the shadows. "That circumstance is unusual, but no principle of law excludes public acts from the reach of the obstruction laws," the report explains. "If the likely effect of public acts is to influence witnesses or alter their testimony, the harm to the justice system's integrity is the same." It might even be worse, because the openness of the offense seems to excuse its occurrence. If it's out in the open, how bad can it be, really?

Of course, the report's authority and scope have limits. The report documents Russia's "sweeping and systematic" interference in the 2016 election, for instance, but does not really reveal the impact of that interference. An omniscient narrator—"the Office"—is an essential player, but the special counsel's own actions and impressions are largely absent. And though the report offers a devastating, point-by-point portrayal of the president's efforts to interfere in the investigation against him, Mueller stops short of declaring criminality. Not because, as the attorney general initially implied, he was simply unable to make up his mind. Part of his reasoning, Mueller explains in the report, was that "a federal criminal accusation against a sitting President would place burdens on the President's capacity to govern and potentially preempt constitutional processes for addressing presidential misconduct." *Constitutional processes*—it's a nice euphemism for the impeachment remedy.

The Mueller report has two parts, as does the irony of its fate. The first is that, after so much investigation and expectation, after a damning 448-page trail of breadcrumbs showing a path forward for Congress, the ultimate articles of impeachment against President Trump would reflect none of its findings or efforts. And second, as the Chaos Chronicles show, is that those "burdens on the President's capacity to govern" have been overwhelmingly self-imposed.

BOOKS DISCUSSED

Anonymous. *A Warning*. Twelve, 2019.

James Comey. *A Higher Loyalty: Truth, Lies and Leadership*. Flatiron Books, 2018.

Daniel W. Drezner. *The Toddler in Chief: What Donald Trump Teaches Us About the Modern Presidency*. University of Chicago Press, 2020.

Joshua Green. *Devil's Bargain: Steve Bannon, Donald Trump, and the Storming of the Presidency*. Penguin Press, 2017.

Susan Hennessey and Benjamin Wittes. *Unmaking the Presidency: Donald Trump's War on the World's Most Powerful Office*. Farrar, Straus and Giroux, 2020.

Elaine C. Kamarck. *Why Presidents Fail: And How They Can Succeed Again*. Brookings Institution Press, 2016.

Michael Lewis. *The Fifth Risk*. W. W. Norton & Company, 2018.

Omarosa Manigault Newman. *Unhinged: An Insider's Account of the Trump White House*. Gallery Books, 2018.

Jim Mattis and Bing West. *Call Sign Chaos: Learning to Lead*. Random House, 2019.

Special Counsel Robert S. Mueller III. *Report on the Investigation into Russian Interference in the 2016 Presidential Election*. U.S. Department of Justice, 2019.

James Poniewozik. *Audience of One: Donald Trump, Television, and the Fracturing of America*. Liveright, 2019.

Philip Rucker and Carol Leonnig. *A Very Stable Genius: Donald J. Trump's Testing of America*. Penguin Press, 2020.

Cliff Sims. *Team of Vipers: My 500 Extraordinary Days in the Trump White House*. Thomas Dunne Books/St. Martin's, 2019.

Guy M. Snodgrass. *Holding the Line: Inside Trump's Pentagon with Secretary Mattis*. Sentinel, 2019.

Sean Spicer. *The Briefing: Politics, the Press, and the President*. Regnery Publishing, 2018.

Michael Wolff. *Fire and Fury: Inside the Trump White House*. Henry Holt and Co., 2018.

Bob Woodward. *Fear: Trump in the White House*. Simon & Schuster, 2018.

NINE

RUSSIAN LIT

"Who lost Russia?" was a self-serving query of early post–Cold War Washington. Those posing it assumed America wielded powers enough to conjure a stable Russian democracy from the ruins of the Soviet Union, but, having failed to do so, decided instead we had simply mislaid it. A quarter-century later, America found itself litigating the opposite scenario—whether Moscow, with its interference in the 2016 election, had eroded and delegitimized America's democracy, possibly even compromising its president.

From end-of-history arrogance to end-of-empire insecurity, in a single generation.

The many books exploring the ties between Russia and Donald Trump—whether links to his businesses, campaign, presidency, psyche, or some grab bag of them all—landed with great anticipation and the promise of big reveals. But more than any other genre in the Trump years, they suffered from unplanned obsolescence, each volume quickly overtaken by an upgraded version containing the newest indictments, the latest testimonies, and the most shocking leaks. These books were trapped in their moment, racing to find collusion or disprove it, to forecast the results of Russia

investigations, to discover why the man in the White House seems
so deferential to the one in the Kremlin. They attempted to tell us
where this was all going, how this would all end.

Even now—after all the books, after Trump's debasement before Vladimir Putin in Helsinki, after the Mueller report and its
misinterpretations, after the "perfect" Ukraine phone call, after the
impeachment investigation and trial—Russia still seeks to sway
the coming election, U.S. intelligence officials have warned, and
Trump still dismisses it all as a hoax. We don't yet know how, or
when, this ends.

What we can know, and must know, is how it begins.

It begins with decades' worth of business relationships between
an overstretched Manhattan real estate mogul and questionable
Russian investors, as journalist Seth Hettena details in *Trump/
Russia: A Definitive History* (2018). It begins with the smolder-
ing suspicions with which Vladimir Putin has long regarded the
United States, and the cycles of engagement and animosity be-
tween the countries, recounted in 2014 in Michael McFaul's *From
Cold War to Hot Peace*. It begins with a century of worldwide electoral interference by both Washington and Moscow, chronicled in
David Shimer's *Rigged* (2020). It begins with the erasure of historical memory in the Soviet Union, producing a nostalgic and
paranoid post–Cold War Russia, as depicted in Masha Gessen's
The Future Is History (2017). And it begins, as historian Timothy
Snyder explains in *The Road to Unfreedom* (2018), with the sus-
ceptibility of American voters to hatreds and distractions, all of
which Russia sought to manipulate in 2016, pushing Americans to
indulge our worst instincts.

How did it all begin? The quest for answers is not solely the
province of in-the-moment books on Putin and Trump, works
that, no matter how well sourced and explosive their reporting,

feel dated almost the instant they are published. Even more, it is a task for history, memoir, and memory—exercises that, in today's onslaught of myth and antagonism and untruth, are both indispensable and imperiled.

Before there was the Mueller report, and before writing books on Trump and Russia became a competitive sport, there was the Steele dossier, a thirty-five-page document packed with unverified allegations about the 2016 Republican presidential candidate. The dossier—and I will never understand why that pretentious little noun became the obligatory term—soon became the stuff of Washington lore: even those who have never read it can toss off shorthand references to its more famous and dubious contentions (think "Prague meeting" or, well, "pee tape").

In *Collusion*, published in 2017, *Guardian* correspondent Luke Harding obsesses over the dossier and its dashing creator, former British intelligence officer Christopher Steele, who makes a few appearances in the book. Steele always offers mysterious leads and enigmatic pronouncements. "It's massive. Absolutely massive," Steele says of the Trump-Russia conspiracy, and suggests to Harding that Trump's business life and personal life were both promising lines of inquiry. "The situation had a distinctly Watergate echo," Harding recalls breathlessly. "Our mission was now clear: follow the sex and the money."

Collusion is the earliest and quickest of the Trump era's Russia books, which is perhaps why it lapses so easily into Russia-themed clichés of the Trump era's Russia lit (Harding writes that Steele hoped to "unnest" the Kremlin's secrets about Trump, "like so many dolls") and plenty of analysis by italics ("Was Moscow *black-mailing* Trump? And if yes, *how exactly*?"). Even though some of the specifics of the dossier would eventually be disproved and others remain eternally unverified, Harding finds all the proof he needs to justify his book title in the June 2016 meeting at Trump Tower at which Donald Trump Jr., Jared Kushner, and campaign manager Paul Manafort sat down with a Kremlin-linked lawyer to discuss supposed dirt on Hillary Clinton, a scenario the author decries as "the textbook definition of collusion." Harding also suggests that Trump's reliance on Russia-friendly advisers and officials, such as Manafort, Secretary of State Rex Tillerson, national security adviser Michael Flynn, and Commerce secretary Wilbur Ross, formed a "discernible pattern" of collusion, "like stars against a clear night sky." When the title of your book is *Collusion*, you find it even in the heavens.

Veteran journalists Michael Isikoff and David Corn, who collaborated on a 2006 book about the U.S. decision to go to war in Iraq, are well versed in the Washington threads of the story. In 2018 they published a book called *Russian Roulette*—because of course someone had to use that title—in which they offer a fuller account of the Trump-Russia ties than Harding does, and a more opinionated and damning one. Russia is "the original sin" of Trump's presidency, Isikoff and Corn assert, a historic transgression that threatened to delegitimize his tenure. "Trump's Russia scandal posed a fundamental challenge for the American political system," they write. "Never before had a president's election been so closely linked to the intervention of a foreign power." Yet they move beyond dossiers and conspiracies to assess the U.S. response to Russia's involvement, blaming the Obama White House for not countering Putin more aggressively and calling the administration's inability to anticipate Moscow's social-media disinformation a significant "intelligence failure." Isikoff and Corn express little uncertainty about Trump's true motives, dating back to before his presidency. "What could possibly explain Trump's unwavering sympathy for the Russian strongman?" Their answer: "The opportunity to build more monuments to himself and to make more money."

Those financial opportunities are best covered in Hettena's *Trump/Russia* (2018), a painstaking look at the business entanglements among Trump and Russian interests, a book that merited more attention than it received. A former Associated Press investigative reporter, Hettena links shady Russian investors to a host of Trump properties over the decades. Beginning in the 1980s, he writes, Trump Tower attracted a "rogue's gallery of embezzlers and money launderers" from Russia and elsewhere who purchased units in the Manhattan building to park illicit profits. Trump's Taj Mahal in Atlantic City "catered to a Russian clientele," the author explains, with entertainment including acrobats and dancing bears from the Moscow Circus, Russian pop stars, and an act called "Moscow on Ice." Trump also licensed his name to a South Florida seaside condo development known as Trump Towers Sunny Isles Beach, in a town nicknamed "Little Moscow" because of its influx of Russian buyers.

After his business struggles in the 1990s, "Trump owed his comeback in large part to wealthy Russian expatriates," Hettena writes. Trump's longtime obsession with opening a Trump Tower in Moscow, an effort that the world later learned lasted deep into his presidential campaign, flows naturally from this history.

Together, these books read like a Google Doc of scandal, a collaborative, aggregated work that is constantly rewritten and updated, all leading to the conclusion that Trump's misdeeds were significant and self-evident. By consistently denying the fact of Russian interference, Trump "aided and abetted Moscow's attack on American democracy," Isikoff and Corn determine. His "no collusion" refrain was "hollow and fake," Harding writes. And

Hettena decides that the president "is either hiding something when it comes to the Kremlin, or simply one of its useful idiots," adding that "neither conclusion is comforting."

The authors seem to anticipate Mueller's eventual report as deliverance, a proof-of-concept moment for their work and suspicions. In this they resembled those Americans for whom, during nearly two years, the mere word "Mueller" conferred an oracular aura, a mix of rectitude and relentlessness that had to be protected from the machinations of the president and his allies. Consider the mix of faith, certainty, and inconclusiveness with which they wrap up their books:

Harding: "Mueller's investigation was far from over. The agony of Donald J. Trump was just beginning."

Isikoff and Corn: "Trump's own unsettling conduct guaranteed the Russia scandal was far from over—for Mueller, Congress, and the American people."

Hettena: "So far, the only wall that is being built is the legal one that Special Counsel Robert Mueller is erecting around the White House, and it increasingly seems too high for America's forty-fifth president to escape."

Mueller was America's security blanket—until the blanket was ripped off by a special counsel displaying an excess of legalistic reservations and an attorney general who had too few of them.

In *The Apprentice: Trump, Russia and the Subversion of American Democracy* (2018), *Washington Post* reporter Greg Miller spans the major elements of the saga: Russia's hacks and social-media disinformation efforts, the contacts between Trump campaign staff and Russian interests, and the FBI and Mueller investigations—all punctuated by the tirades, tweetstorms, and threats of a president unable to get out of his own way.

Yet even though his book title reads like a dig at Trump's insecurities, Miller remains circumspect on whether the Trump team deliberately colluded with Russia, and he does not pretend to assess definitively whether Kremlin interference swayed the vote. Rather, he stresses that the most scandalous aspects of the story are rarely the most important. The Steele dossier, for instance, may be remembered for its more salacious bullet points, but its central contention—that Russia had embarked on a covert effort to disrupt the 2016 election and damage Hillary Clinton—proved "accurate and prescient," Miller writes. Incessantly dismissed by Trump as a hoax cooked up by sore-loser Democrats, Russian interference in the election was confirmed by U.S. intelligence agencies in early 2017 and affirmed by a bipartisan Senate report in April 2020. If it was a hoax, then everyone but Trump and some Fox News personalities was in on it.

Running through *The Apprentice* is a persistent mystery: Why is Trump, who manages to insult heads of state even by accident, so consistently obsequious toward Russia's leader? "He praised Putin, congratulated him, defended him, pursued meetings with him, and even when talking tough, fought virtually any policy or punitive measure that might displease him," Miller writes. His conclusion is not especially nefarious, even if it is appalling. "Trump's admiration for Putin was grounded in envy of the way he ruled," Miller decides. "Putin faced none of the annoyances that Trump complained about most, including the recalcitrant press, haranguing political opposition, and the disloyal ranks of the 'deep state.' " In Trump's eyes, Putin held absolute authority—the kind of power he imagined a president should wield, the kind he still wishes he enjoyed.

This mix of solicitude and admiration came alive in Helsinki in July 2018, when the American president stood next to Putin and publicly sided with the Kremlin over his own intelligence agencies, which had concluded that Russia interfered in his favor in 2016. "I have great confidence in my intelligence people, but I will tell you that President Putin was extremely strong and powerful in his denial today," Trump said at the press conference. *Strong* and *powerful* are aspirational terms for Trump; they are how he wants to be regarded. He took Putin at his strong and powerful word. "He just said it's not Russia," Trump stated. "I will say this, I don't see any reason why it would be." In that moment, Putin proved his mastery over the American president.

Miller considers various theories concerning Trump's subservience. Is Moscow in possession of compromising sexual material on Trump, as the Steele dossier hinted, or is Trump seeking to hide his longtime financial entanglements with Russia, of the sort Hettena outlines? Miller suggests that Trump appears "beyond shame" when it comes to sex or money, and so he cites a simpler possibility: "Russia's leverage on Trump, and the collusion between them, has always been hiding right in front of us."

The author imagines secret communications between a major political candidate and a foreign power, including statements of praise and requests for campaign help. He imagines the national security establishment collecting evidence that foreign spy agencies had intervened on the candidate's behalf. He imagines that, once in office, the candidate secretly tries to limit intelligence and law enforcement investigations into the interventions. "All of this happened," Miller points out. "It was just that, rather than transpiring across encrypted channels, much of it was in plain sight, on the global stage of a presidential campaign and from the White House." In their joint press conference, Putin admitted that he had wanted Trump to win in 2016, but he continued denying the reality of Russian interference. "That may be all the leverage that

Putin needs," Miller concludes. "If Putin had gone one step further in Helsinki, blurting out that he had ordered active measures to elect Trump on a scale that could easily have tipped the outcome, it would have deprived Trump of his last hold on that lie." And Trump, obsessed with safeguarding the legitimacy of his election and his office, needs that story to persist.

As always, the scandal with Trump happens out in the open.

Such journalistic dives into Trump and Russia—with their ominous red-and-black dust jackets in the style of Soviet-era propaganda posters—are useful but partial, stressing the U.S. side of the story. Other scholars, historians, and diplomats dip the story in history to trace Putin's opportunism, Russia's anxiety, America's vulnerability.

McFaul, the architect of President Obama's "reset" policy toward Russia and later the U.S. ambassador in Moscow, looks with longing on past instances of rapprochement between the two sides. The historic meetings between Ronald Reagan and Mikhail Gorbachev. The buddy comedy of Bill Clinton and Boris Yeltsin. Even the brief soul-gazing between George W. Bush and Vladimir Putin. To this tally McFaul adds Obama's relationship with Dmitry Medvedev, Russia's president from 2008 to 2012.

The Obama administration's initial efforts to reengage with Russia were premised on the belief that Washington could deal constructively with Moscow "without checking our values at the door," McFaul explains in *From Cold War to Hot Peace*. It would be possible to work with Moscow on arms control or Iran policy, he thought at the time, while still promoting democracy and wagging a finger about human rights. Guiding the efforts would be Obama and Medvedev, both young lawyers shaped by the post–Cold War world and sharing an analytical style and a reformist self-image. "I quickly concluded that this relationship was going to click," McFaul recalls. And initially, it did, delivering the New Strategic Arms Reduction Treaty, sanctions against Iran, and expanded access to supply routes for U.S. forces in Afghanistan. "In the early days of the Reset," McFaul writes, "it seemed as if all good things could go together."

Except they couldn't, at least not for long. McFaul refers to Russia's "Medvedev era" as if one truly existed, although he knows better. "Even if Medvedev was a closet liberal—a second Gorbachev—he was operating in a very constrained environment," McFaul admits. "He worked for Putin." And when Putin ran for president again in 2012 and needed an enemy to rally support in a time of social protests, the choice was easy. "He revived an old Soviet-era argument as his new source of legitimacy—defense of the motherland against the evil West, and especially the imperial, conniving, threatening United States."

The expansion of NATO and the war in Serbia. The invasion of Iraq. The color revolutions in Eastern Europe. They all buttressed Putin's account of America's malign intentions. The Russian leader also "despised" Hillary Clinton, blaming her for encouraging domestic demonstrations against him in 2011. "Putin wanted revenge," McFaul explains. And in the 2016 election—with the hacks, the propaganda, the bots, and the trolls—he exacted it. "Did Putin make Trump president?" McFaul asks. "Of course not. American voters did that. Did Putin help Trump win? Maybe."

It is an endless argument: Yes, Russia interfered in the election, but how decisive was its role? In her 2018 book *Cyberwar: How Russian Hackers and Trolls Helped Elect a President*, Kathleen Hall Jamieson, director of the Annenberg Public Policy Center at the University of Pennsylvania, makes a forceful case that foreign interference was indeed a major factor. Russian social-media operators sought to anger and mobilize voters whom Trump needed by aggravating American tensions surrounding immigration, religion, and race—always against the backdrop of a duplicitous, untrustworthy Clinton. With an unusually high proportion of the electorate alienated from both major parties and making their choices in the final weeks of the campaign, voters were especially susceptible to such external manipulation. The author does not make a case for collusion between the Republican candidate and Moscow, even if she slyly notes the "mutually reinforcing nature" of the Trump campaign's themes and Russia's social-media blitz.

More consequential, in Jamieson's view, was Russia's hacking of emails from the Clinton campaign and the Democratic National Committee. At critical moments in the 2016 race, the stolen material was made public and "infected the news agenda" against Clinton and in favor of Trump. The final two televised debates between the candidates included questions about leaked excerpts from the Democratic nominee's paid speeches, questions for Clinton that were possible only because of Russian cybertheft. "Too often," Jamieson laments, "the press served as a conveyor belt of stolen content instead of a gatekeeper."

Trump deservedly received much criticism for inviting Russian hacking during the campaign—"Russia, if you're listening, I hope you're able to find the thirty thousand emails that are missing," he said in a July 2016 press conference—but we should not forget the line that came next: "I think you will probably be rewarded mightily by our press." On that point, he was largely correct. American journalists could not resist reporting on the contents of the hacked documents, even if doing so played into Putin's game. There would be plenty of time for media mea culpas after the campaign.

Jamieson does not settle the debate over whether the Russians tilted the election; at most, she makes a good case that they might have done so. Nor did the intelligence community reach a conclusion one way or the other, a result Trump would recast as validation of his great, untainted victory. What is clear is that Russia exploited some of the best of America—its respect for free markets and free speech, its competitive press, its communications technologies—to bring out some of its worst: prejudice, fear, extremism.

The key question about Russian involvement, historian David Shimer writes in *Rigged: America, Russia, and One Hundred Years of Covert Electoral Interference* (2020), may be less about its methods and impact than about its lessons. What conclusions will Moscow and Washington draw from the operation, and how will that affect the way they approach future elections?

"An interfering actor whose preferred candidate triumphs naturally feels all-powerful," Shimer explains. That's what occurred after the CIA sought to tilt the 1948 election in Italy, using money, propaganda, and get-out-the-vote efforts to support the Christian Democrats over the left-wing, Soviet-backed coalition. "In Washington's collective imagination, the CIA had rescued Italy's democracy," Shimer writes, and the operation became a template for future U.S. efforts in Italy and elsewhere.

The Soviet Union, which had long manipulated elections in Eastern Europe and supported friendly candidates around the world, tried to influence American contests, too. The strength of Shimer's book is in the wealth of current and former officials who speak with him on the record; *Rigged* is essentially an oral history of election interference, including the U.S. vote in 2016. His conversations with former KGB general Oleg Kalugin—who served as acting station chief in Washington and the head of the KGB's counterintelligence operations—provide glimpses into Soviet efforts to sow discord, undermine hostile candidates, and promote favored ones in the United States during the Cold War.

Nikita Khrushchev attempted to persuade Adlai Stevenson to run against Richard Nixon in 1960 ("because we know the ideas of Mr. Stevenson, we in our hearts all favor him," the Soviet premier wrote in a letter), and Moscow's ambassador to Washington offered Hubert Humphrey financial support in 1968. Both times the Soviets were rebuffed. Concerned about the presidential possibilities of Senator Henry "Scoop" Jackson, a hawkish Democrat, the Soviets tried to propagate rumors that he was gay. They also sought to discredit American democracy by stressing its racial divides, even sending fake Ku Klux Klan letters to African diplomats in New York. None of it accomplished much. "A gap existed between the intent of Soviet leaders—to disrupt and direct America's process of succession—and their actual capabilities," Shimer explains. "In the pre-digital age, the Kremlin lacked the means to shape public discourse, target voters on a personal basis, or reach the American population at scale."

Decades later, thanks to the internet and Vladimir Putin, those capabilities would be massively upgraded, and the gap narrowed, even as key Washington officials, preoccupied with the battle against terrorism, took their eyes off Moscow. "If I have any sin to confess of my directorship at CIA, it is that I didn't pay any attention to Putin," Michael Hayden, who led the agency from 2006 to 2009, tells Shimer.

Though Russia's tools in 2016 were new, its objectives and methods were "a direct continuation of old ideas," Shimer argues. The Russians attempted to spread division and disinformation by exploiting fissures in American society and culture—a technique out of the old Soviet playbook. Whether it worked is less important than whether Russia thinks it did. "The degree to which Putin believes he succeeded will instruct his policy making" in 2020 and beyond, Shimer writes. Just as Washington's sense that it had successfully swayed Italy's vote in the mid-twentieth century led the CIA to intervene in other countries' elections for a generation, "Moscow, emboldened by Trump's victory, may be headed in the same direction," Shimer concludes.

Of course, the United States was not Putin's first or only target. When Russia invaded Georgia in 2008, Georgian news agencies were hacked and internet traffic blocked, historian Timothy Snyder recounts in *The Road to Unfreedom*. Similarly, Russia's 2014 military offensive in Ukraine—which Putin denied with a wink early on—featured a massive cyberoffensive that included fictitious reports about Ukrainian atrocities in Crimea. And Britain's 2016 Brexit vote was influenced by Russian bots spreading anti–European Union propaganda.

But the U.S. election was Putin's "grandest campaign" of deceit, as Snyder puts it. He outlines the stages of Trump's ascent, beginning long before the presidential race: Russian money rescued him from financial collapse, thus enabling the reality-television fantasy of Trump the successful businessman. That character became a spokesman of the birther fraud, propelling Trump's political career and presidential ambitions, which were in turn further supported by Russian propaganda. "Fiction rested on fiction rested on fiction," Snyder writes. "From a Russian perspective, Trump was a failure who was rescued and an asset to be used to wreak havoc in American reality."

That havoc has persisted throughout the Trump presidency, forging new parallels between the two nations and the two leaders. Back home, Putin's lies are not meant to fool anyone "but to create a bond of willing ignorance with Russians, who were meant to understand that Putin was lying but to believe him anyway," Snyder writes. Putin's mockery of facts is then reported as just one more "side of the story." Such lies, the author explains, are "not meant to convince in a factual sense, but to guide in a narrative sense," reinterpreting reality in ways that always benefit the boss. Trump's thousands of instances of presidential untruth are little different.

Not so different, too, is Putin's pledge of stability for his people, when he in fact delivers the opposite, an institutionalized uncertainty of shifting rules, arbitrary decisions, and designed unpredictability. "A constant state of low-level dread made people easy to control, because it robbed them of the sense that they could control anything themselves," Gessen writes in *The Future Is History*. Russians still feel that dread. Under Trump, Americans have gotten a taste of it, too.

Several of the volumes on Trump and Russia emphasize that Putin's interference against the United States, however bold and daring, backfired, failing to deliver specific policy outcomes that the Russians desired. Just as Trump longed for the kind of unfettered power Putin wielded, the Russians believed he would have it and use it to their benefit. "They had a poor understanding of U.S. institutional politics," Harding writes. "They failed to appreciate the separation of powers or the constraints on a president—any president." McFaul agrees that Putin "did not receive the payoff he expected" from Trump's election, such as relief from U.S. sanctions or recognition of Crimea as part of Russia.

But in a symbolic sense, Trump's victory and presidency have indeed served Putin's interests, the former ambassador contends. Long-standing Western alliances and trade relations have deteriorated under Trump, as have the reputation, example, and influence of the United States. All this helps Putin argue that "the United States is not exceptional," McFaul worries, "that American democracy is no different from Russia's political system, and that we have no moral authority to preach to other countries about their behavior."

None of this means Russia is masterminding some unwitting American transition to authoritarianism. Despite all these books, Putin should not receive top billing in our national drama. "Americans were not exposed to Russian propaganda randomly, but in accordance with their own susceptibilities," Snyder emphasizes, and were meant to feel even greater outrage against the things and people they already fear or hate. Or, as Shimer puts it, referring to Russia's online troll factory, "[W]ho needs the Internet Research Agency when the president is sowing racial discord so openly?"

But Trump doesn't merit all the credit or blame, either. Our news silos, the erosion of faith in common facts and truths, the demonization of opponents, and the extremism of our politics, especially on the right—all were underway long before Trump announced his candidacy. Snyder also highlights the weakening of key provisions of the Voting Rights Act, maintaining that "when Russia acted against American democracy, the American system was already becoming less democratic." Whatever is happening here, we were ripe for it.

Looking back on the legacy of the USSR, Gessen dwells on the life and death of the mind. "The Russian intellectual landscape was populated by the barely articulated ghosts of once vibrant ideas," Gessen writes. The Soviet authorities had robbed their people of the chance to live freely and also of the ability to "understand fully what had been taken from them, and how." The Soviet regime's goal, so necessary for its survival, was to "annihilate personal and historical memory." This condition persisted into the early post–Cold War years. By the mid-1990s, Gessen reports, less than 10 percent of Russians believed that the end of the USSR had been a good thing. The author recalls a 1990s television channel devoted to showing nothing but old Soviet programming. It was called Nostalgia.

It is easy to conclude that something similar has happened to America in the Trump years, that the president's lies and insults and incompetence and nativism and performative cruelty are enough to make Americans throw up their hands in exasperation, rant in self-righteousness, or simply look away in fear or confusion. But the works on Trump and Russia are an antidote, however imperfect and untested, to the erasure of memory. They are just a start—as Hettena's subtitle suggests, it is *a* definitive history, not *the* definitive history, with so many more to come—but their cumulative power is significant.

In *Russian Roulette*, Isikoff and Corn recall the educational impact of official U.S. inquiries into past political misdeeds, such as the Teapot Dome scandal, Watergate, and Iran-contra. In the face of a deadlocked Congress and a Republican Senate majority that has abdicated its oversight of the executive branch, the investigations of the Trump era, and the journalism and literature on Trump and Russia, are standing in, however partially and imperfectly, for such an education today.

Gessen wrote *The Future Is History* to tell "the story of freedom that was not embraced and democracy that was not desired" in the author's native Russia. If freedoms eroded and democracy squandered prove to be the story of our nation and our time, let it be recorded with similar discernment, should it be written at all.

BOOKS DISCUSSED

Masha Gessen. *The Future Is History: How Totalitarianism Reclaimed Russia.* Riverhead Books, 2017.

Luke Harding. *Collusion: Secret Meetings, Dirty Money, and How Russia Helped Donald Trump Win.* Vintage Books, 2017.

Seth Hettena. *Trump/Russia: A Definitive History.* Melville House, 2018.

Michael Isikoff and David Corn. *Russian Roulette: The Inside Story of Putin's War on America and the Election of Donald Trump.* Twelve, 2018.

Kathleen Hall Jamieson. *Cyberwar: How Russian Hackers and Trolls Helped Elect a President—What We Don't, Can't, and Do Know.* Oxford University Press, 2018.

Michael McFaul. *From Cold War to Hot Peace: An American Ambassador in Putin's Russia.* Houghton Mifflin Harcourt, 2018.

Greg Miller. *The Apprentice: Trump, Russia, and the Subversion of American Democracy.* Custom House, 2018.

David Shimer. *Rigged: America, Russia, and One Hundred Years of Covert Electoral Interference.* Alfred A. Knopf, 2020.

Timothy Snyder. *The Road to Unfreedom: Russia, Europe, America.* Tim Duggan Books, 2018.

TEN

IN PLAIN VIEW

The Trump era has generated so many books about the dire risks facing government of, by, and for the people that their titles sound like they are talking to one another, a spoken-word poetry of political breakdown:

How Democracies Die . . . On Tyranny.
How Democracy Ends . . . Trumpocalypse.
What Is Populism? . . . The New Class War.
The Soul of America . . . Trumpocracy.
Surviving Autocracy . . . These Truths.

Though the authors of such books often insist that Trump is not their sole preoccupation, the president's glare looms over every volume. "This is not a book about Donald Trump, not by any means," Harvard University's Cass R. Sunstein protests too much in the introduction to his 2018 edited collection *Can It Happen Here? Authoritarianism in America.* Then he adds, "But there is no question that many people, including some of the authors here, think that Trump's words and deeds have put the can-it-happen-here question on the table." It's a bit of a Trumpian conceit—*many people are thinking!*—but let the record reflect that, less than four months later, Sunstein published an essay in the *New York Review of Books* titled "It Can Happen Here." No question mark needed.

Trump may be the muse of the death-of-democracy bookshelf, but it is not a distinction he carries alone. Degraded norms and disenfranchised voters, Chinese ambition and Russian revanchism, unprincipled political parties and unequal administration of justice—these are among the many maladies of democracy in our age. The scholars and analysts writing such books are, so far, better at diagnosing ailments than proposing treatments. It is almost as if, daunted by the scale of the problem, they have downsized their designs, as though our democracy is now so weakened that even mild medicine might prove too taxing.

Such caution is unnecessary and self-defeating. The challenges to democracy that these books outline are integral to this moment but also eternally present, aggravated by Trumpism but inherent in the American experience. The United States at its most heroic—striving to meet its promise of equality and liberty—is also the United States at its least inspiring, as it fails, repeatedly, to get there. "A nation founded on ideals, universal truths, also opens itself to charges of hypocrisy at every turn," the Harvard University historian Jill Lepore writes in *This America* (2019). Hypocrisy and inconsistency are such recurring features of American democracy that they are less its hindrance than its definition.

That's why histories connecting the Trump era to the long arc of America's democratic struggle feel particularly essential now, and they read that way, too. Remembering the history of the nation for all time is critical to writing the history of the nation in our time, which is why Trump seeks to remake not only today but yesterday, too. "Nations, to make sense of themselves, need some kind of agreed-upon past," Lepore explains. "They can get it from scholars or they can get it from demagogues, but get it they will."

With so many thinkers across so many arenas pointing, retroactively, to the inevitability of a leader like Trump emerging in America—congratulations, you all saw it coming—it is refreshing to find someone who admits he truly had no idea. "I never imagined that democracy *here* could be in danger," writes Larry Diamond in *Ill Winds*. It is a remarkable statement coming from a founding editor of the *Journal of Democracy* and a frequently cited authority on the subject, though it also may simply underscore how the establishment is often the last to realize when its time has come.

To his credit, Diamond saw lots of other stuff coming. Well before Trump's election, the world had plunged into a "democratic recession," he writes, with the rise of illiberal movements in Europe, the autocratic backlash against the Arab Spring, and the avid attempts by Russia and especially China to undermine free societies. "The problem with Russia is managing the anger, insecurity, and resentments of a former superpower; the problem with China is managing the ambitions, swagger, and overreach of a new one," Diamond explains, capturing America's foreign policy dilemma with a pithy contrast. But beyond those two powers, wannabe autocrats across the globe are belittling the free press, rigging elections, politicizing their states' civil service and security apparatus, and undercutting legislative and independent efforts at accountability. It is authoritarianism not by coups or tanks but by the deliberate erosion and co-optation of the rules. Diamond believes that only Washington can offer a counterweight against these trends. "Without U.S. leadership," he warns, "the democratic recession could spiral down into a grim new age of authoritarianism."

Instead, Washington joined the party.

Trump is "the new American Caesar," Diamond decries, a "highly abnormal and dangerous president" contemptuous of the nation's democratic traditions, eager to exert a corrupting influence on law enforcement, dismissive of oversight and preferring to mimic, rather than face down, the rise of authoritarianism. Any efforts to address democracy's decline beyond U.S. shores will have to wait until someone else occupies the Oval Office, he writes. "The longer that Trump stays in power, the deeper and more lasting will be the damage."

The reason Diamond failed to anticipate Trump's threat to democracy at home is that he, like so many, thought America's institutions were strong, its norms of political behavior resilient and embedded. Yes, "norms" have become dutiful shorthand when explaining Trump's transgressions, but they deserve that distinction. By so easily violating multiple standards of presidential behavior—by lying incessantly, even about matters of settled fact; by refusing to release his personal financial information; by disclosing classified intelligence to foreign officials on a whim; by accusing political rivals of unspecified crimes; by dismissing or berating inspectors general and other officials charged with oversight of federal agencies—Trump has shown that those standards are matters of habit and mutual accommodation, not of law or obligation.

In 2018's *How Democracies Die,* Steven Levitsky and Daniel Ziblatt emphasize four warning signs of incipient authoritarian leaders: they reject the democratic rules of the game, deny the legitimacy of rival politicians, tolerate or encourage political violence, and announce their willingness to limit the civil liberties of opponents, particularly the press. Trump, the authors note, checked all four boxes even before taking office—and he's the type who would. "What kinds of candidates tend to test positive on a litmus test for authoritarianism?" Levitsky and Ziblatt ask. "Very often, populist outsiders do," the leaders who claim to embody the people, standing firm against a corrupt, selfish, and loosely defined elite.

When Trump, in his speech at the 2016 Republican National Convention, declared "I am your voice" and "I alone can fix it," he was both speaking to his base and laying bare his populist credentials. In his brief, illuminating book *What Is Populism?*, published less than two months later, Princeton University political theorist Jan-Werner Müller summarizes the key tenet of populism: "Only some of the people are really the people." Governing with only his core supporters—with some of the people—in mind, rather than the nation in full, Trump has violated the most essential of presidential norms.

Of course, Trump has proved himself a recidivist norm-breaker, uninterested in or uninformed about the rules and traditions of democracy. He doesn't just break a norm once; he comes back and stomps on it to make sure. "In plain view, Trump was flaunting, ignoring, and destroying all institutions of accountability," Masha Gessen writes in *Surviving Autocracy* (2020). "In plain view, he was degrading political speech. In plain view, he was using his office to enrich himself. In plain view, he was courting dictator after dictator. In plain view, he was promoting xenophobic conspiracy theories, now claiming that millions of immigrants voting illegally had cost him the popular vote; now insisting, repeatedly, that Obama had had him wiretapped. All of this, though plainly visible, was unfathomable."

Levitsky and Ziblatt don't detail every Trumpian transgression—it would be hard—but rather highlight the two norms without which every other norm, and democracy itself, begins to unravel. The first is *mutual toleration*, the understanding that political competitors and rival parties should regard one another as legitimate despite their differences over policy or ideology. The second is *forbearance*, the notion that political leaders should exercise restraint in the use of their official powers, that just because it is technically legal to do something doesn't mean you should. These inextricable norms "undergirded American democracy for most of the twentieth century," the authors write.

Trump constantly delegitimizes his opponents, real and perceived, in the political arena, the judiciary, and the press, offering himself as the true and rightful representative of the people. No surprise that, during the president's Senate impeachment trial, one of his lawyers argued that if Trump believes his reelection is in the public interest, then whatever he does to further that end (such as soliciting Ukrainian assistance in undermining former vice president Joe Biden) cannot be impeachable. No surprise, either, that the president and his defenders frequently invoke the chief executive's "absolute right" to do just about anything—close the border, interfere with Justice Department investigations, pardon himself, spill intelligence to foreign powers—regardless of whether it's a good idea, of whether a president should eviscerate standards of behavior just because he can. That is how these norms work together, and fail together. "As mutual toleration disappears, politicians grow tempted to abandon forbearance and try to win at all costs," Levitsky and Ziblatt write.

Early in the COVID-19 crisis, Trump claimed absolute power over state decisions on loosening health-related restrictions and reopening the economy. "When somebody's the president of the United States, the authority is total, and that's the way it's got to be," he declared at a press conference. Later, during the 2020 mass protests against racism and police violence, the president pledged that if governors failed to quell the unrest, "I will deploy the United

States military and quickly solve the problem for them." Trump eviscerates any sense of forbearance, claiming all manner of authority, and changing course only when doing so is politically expedient, not when it is institutionally or legally advisable.

Why should Trump care if he jeopardizes the political system? He was elected to dismantle it. In *Surviving Autocracy*, Gessen says that Trump is "probably the first major party nominee who ran not for president but for autocrat," so brazen were his aspirations to absolute power and indifference to restraint. And while so much has been debated, and so much written, about why certain American voters are attracted to him, the authors of the democracy volumes focus on a different group that could have reconsidered Trump long before his name appeared on a ballot. It is a group whose leaders, initially alarmed by a populist and nativist candidate, opted to collude with him rather than shun or restrain him.

That is the Republican Party.

"Put simply, political parties are democracy's gatekeepers," Levitsky and Ziblatt explain. Throughout the nation's history, the Democratic and Republican establishments have often succeeded in rooting out or isolating the extremists within, preventing them from reaching power. America's true protection against would-be autocrats has been as much the discipline of its parties as the wisdom of its voters. But this filtering function has posed a dilemma. "These dual imperatives—choosing a popular candidate and keeping out demagogues—may, at times, conflict with each other," the authors admit. "What if the people choose a demagogue?"

The Republican Party faced this conundrum in 2016. Rather than fight it, they chose to embrace it. In Trump's rise, the unpredictable met the deliberate; shock met opportunity. A GOP establishment that comparison-shopped among an uninspiring

Jeb Bush, an unappealing Ted Cruz, and an untested Marco Rubio eventually found a bargain-basement deal in Donald Trump.

David Frum has written a pair of books on the Trump years: *Trumpocracy*, published in 2018, and *Trumpocalypse*, out in mid-2020. A longtime conservative author and former speechwriter for President George W. Bush, Frum is particularly fixated on the GOP's capitulation to Trump. "Gullibly or cynically, resentfully or opportunistically, for lack of better information or for lack of a better alternative, a great party has slowly united to elevate one man into a position of almost absolute power over itself," he writes in the first volume. If Trump was ever in position to break or bypass norms of politics, decency, and honesty, he got there with "the complicity of his allies among the conservative and Republican political, media, and financial elite." Other writers have outlined a devil's bargain between once-fringe nationalist forces and Trump's populist appeal, but the bargain Frum describes is more straightforward. Uninterested in the policy specifics that animated Republican lawmakers, Trump merely sought their inaction on his conflicts of interest, ethical shortcomings, and corporate entanglements. "*We'll protect your business if you sign our bills*," Frum writes. "That was the transaction congressional leaders offered Trump."

In exchange for backing the president at nearly every turn, Republican Party leaders won tax reform, deregulation, and conservative judicial appointments, and perhaps they've decided it's been a good deal. For all the focus on supposed collusion between Trump and Russia, Levitsky and Ziblatt highlight the "ideological collusion" between a strongman and his party, "in which the authoritarian's agenda overlaps sufficiently with that of mainstream politicians," making him an attractive gamble. But the cost can be steeper than anticipated, and the payment stream unending.

"Unwilling to pay the political price of breaking with their own president, Republicans find themselves with little alternative but to constantly redefine what is and isn't tolerable," the co-authors write. Once you've made an endless string of concessions, it is hard to stop, and you risk becoming that which you thought you were merely accommodating. As Frum puts it in *Trumpocalypse*, "A party dependent on the votes of the alienated and the resentful will find itself articulating a message of alienation and resentment."

The party decides, we were once told; now, it merely abides.

Of course, it is too much to lay the institutional and political wreckage of the Republican Party solely at Trump's feet. "Our republic's sickness has its roots in decades of rising political polarization that has turned our two parties into something akin to warring tribes, willing to skirt bedrock principles of fairness and inclusion for pure partisan advantage," Diamond writes. But he and other authors recognize that one major party has been more polarizing than the other. The Republican Party has been "the main driver of the chasm between the parties," Levitsky and Ziblatt point out. For years, it has behaved "like an antisystem party in its obstructionism, partisan hostility, and extremist policy positions." The dismissiveness of truth and fact, the latent nativism, the opposition for its own sake—all of this was apparent long before Trump propelled his political career with the birther fraud and launched his 2016 campaign with a speech trashing Mexicans and calling the Affordable Care Act a "big lie." If Trump hijacked the Republican Party, as is often said, he has steered it in a direction it was already pursuing.

Even with another presidential election victory, the GOP would be "wrecked forever," Frum contends in *Trumpocalypse*. That's because, to win again in the face of massive health, economic, and social crises, Trump will need to wage culture wars and suppress minority voters, all for a narrow electoral college majority to offset what could be another loss of the popular vote, the third such out-come in twenty years. "What will be the character of such a politi-cal party after such a history?" Frum wonders. "Not a democratic political party, that's for sure. It will have degenerated into a caudi-llo's personal entourage."

The default position of Republican senators during Trump's impeachment trial—*we know he did it, but it's not really that bad*—is a sign of this degeneration. It resurfaced in Attorney General William Barr's decision to drop the case against former Trump national security adviser Michael Flynn, even though the defen-dant had pleaded guilty to lying to the FBI about his contacts with Russian officials. And we saw it yet again in resistance against ex-amining the White House's management of the COVID-19 crisis. In the spring of 2020, Republicans were already cautioning against a post-pandemic "blame game," while Trump, even though he claimed absolute authority, washed his hands of any accountabil-ity. "I don't take responsibility at all," he declared in a press confer-ence on March 13. Those words, Frum concludes, "are likely to be history's epitaph on his presidency."

And an epitaph for those who nodded in assent.

The death-of-democracy canon includes plenty of fixes for the GOP and for the American experiment writ large. But they are often small-bore, even admittedly so. Or they are tautological. Or they threaten to adopt, rather than fight, the tactics of democracy's op-ponents, simply in the service of an alternative ideological project.

In *Ill Winds*, appearing in mid-2019, Diamond longs for a Republican savior to arise and defy the president's hold over the party, calling upon some brave party standard-bearer to launch a serious primary challenge to Trump. He name-checks Bob Corker, Jeff Flake, Nikki Haley, Larry Hogan, John Kasich, Mitt Romney, and Ben Sasse, suggesting that, even in defeat, such a candidate would "be rewarded by the verdict of history." Romney's courageous and instructive vote to convict Trump in the Senate impeachment trial will make the first paragraph of the Utah senator's obituary, no doubt, while Hogan's steady competence as Maryland governor during the coronavirus crisis has offered its own kind of rebuke to Trump—but I don't think those are the sort of challenges Diamond has in mind. He also encourages more administration insiders to reveal what they have seen of the president behind the scenes, as though a few more installments of the Chaos Chronicles will make the difference.

Diamond also calls for simplified voting registration, an end to the electoral college and voter suppression, and the creation of a Public Integrity Protection Agency to uphold anticorruption laws and standards. He urges Americans to elect more senators and representatives who are "ideologically moderate or at least flexible enough to compromise" and, why not, admonishes "people of all ages to be more civil and thoughtful on social media." His proposals are more a picture of workable democracy than a path to getting there. "What is the culture of democracy?" he asks. "How do we build it and keep it strong? The paramount component is democratic legitimacy—the resilient and broadly shared belief that democracy is better than any other imaginable form of government." It is an irrefutable argument; if democracy declines, it must be that its legitimacy declined, and if it endures, then clearly its legitimacy did, too.

In *Trumpocalypse*, Frum hopes that a Trump defeat in 2020 could propel a host of political reforms, much as the sins of Watergate led to self-examination and new oversight. But several of his proposals, while important and necessary, feel partial. They include ensuring that presidential candidates make their tax returns

and financial assets public, killing the Senate filibuster, and passing a new federal voting rights law that addresses "the abuses of the
present, not the memories of the past." What Frum desires above
all is a process of post-Trump reconciliation, and of all his proposals, that one might be hardest to achieve. The president deserves
the full penalty of the law, and his enablers in politics and the press
deserve contempt, but his voters are "our compatriots," Frum emphasizes, and Democrats won't defeat or move beyond Trump unless they can build an America with "room for all its people." So be
nice to the president's supporters, Frum urges. "The resentments
that produced Trump will not be assuaged by contempt for the
resentful," he writes. This advice echoes that of the authors of *Rules
of Resistance*, except in this case it comes from a writer whose very
book title suggests a dire, apocalyptic view of what Trump voters
have brought upon the country.

Anti-Trump conservatives love to offer campaign strategy and
political advice to Democrats, an enemy-of-my-enemy magnanim-
ity that is rarely welcome on the left. Frum urges progressives to
moderate their tones and policies, to stop being *so woke*—he loves
saying "woke"—and to quit offending people by calling out their
racism. "Trump is president not only because many of your fellow
citizens are racists, or sexists, or bigots of some other description,
although surely some are," he argues. "Trump is president also because many of your fellow citizens feel that accusations of bigotry
are deployed casually and carelessly." After so much mockery of
the supposed sensitivities of the Left, it turns out that the feelings
of Trump supporters are no less fragile. "Even if plague and recession topple Trump from the presidency," Frum writes, "the core
Trump base will remain, alienated and resentful."

Rather than follow such advice, some activists and thinkers on
the left are inclined to examine how the Right has undermined

democracy—and then retrofit those tactics for their own benefit. In *The Democracy Fix* (2019), Caroline Fredrickson offers a plan for the defense and renewal of democracy at home, but one that primarily serves progressive visions of government. She draws inspiration from the "Powell Memo," a 1971 document drawn up by tobacco industry lawyer and future Supreme Court justice Lewis Powell that became, as she describes it, "the road map for conservative dominance of public policymaking."

Fredrickson, a former president of the American Constitution Society, is an ex–general counsel of NARAL, a onetime special assistant to President Bill Clinton, and an unabashed progressive, and she looks upon the American Right with a mix of contempt, jealousy, and grudging admiration. Powell's memo, written for the U.S. Chamber of Commerce, proposed a sustained response to growing environmental regulations and consumer protection initiatives that threatened corporate power. *The Democracy Fix* is, in large part, the story of how that memo inspired the creation of corporate philanthropies, conservative think tanks, a right-wing media machine to counter and discredit the mainstream press, and a pipeline of conservative jurists to fill federal and state courts. "What Powell grasped," Fredrickson writes, "is that policy victories come *after* gaining control of the levers of power—and not before."

She is persuasive in making connections that span decades, explaining how right-wing think tanks drive pro-corporate political narratives and groom personnel to enter key government policy roles; how legal activists work diligently to discourage corporate litigation and to influence the appointment of friendly judges at all levels, including the Supreme Court; and how political operatives and funders focus on key legislative races that will help the Republican Party control the redistricting process and thus entrench legislative power. Whether the Powell Memo truly unleashed all this (some writers suggest that its historical influence has been exaggerated) becomes less relevant as the chapters progress. What does matter, Fredrickson emphasizes, is that the Right had a long-term plan, and the Left didn't.

However, it often seems that Fredrickson is more interested in boosting progressivism than in strengthening democracy, or that she blithely assumes the two goals necessarily go together. She wants "good judges," she writes, a formulation that later morphs into "good, progressive judges." It is not enough to declare originalism suspect as an interpretation of the Constitution; the case must be made that the document is inherently progressive. Much as some of the resistance writers expressed admiration for the Tea Party's tactics and organizing abilities, by the end of her book Fredrickson is hailing Powell as a "visionary" to be emulated, rather than explaining his memo as a cautionary tale of how political activists can hijack a democratic system. "We've been screwed for too long," she laments. "It's time to grab the pen and write our own rules." So she appends a public memo of her own, addressed to "Progressive Americans" and calling for a well-funded infrastructure on the left, reformed voting laws, and, of course, more of those good judges. Fredrickson may be correct in her political analysis, but *The Democracy Fix* seems like more of a fix for American progressivism.

For writers such as Michael Lind, the problem with the Democrats is not that they have failed to twist the rules in their favor but that they have succeeded, only in the service of a new "managerial elite" of business, government, and media oligarchs. The Democratic Party "is now a party of the affluent native white metropolitan elite, allied with immigrants and native minorities brought together by noneconomic identity politics rather than by class politics," he writes in *The New Class War* (2020). The "technocratic neoliberalism" of the Left is failing American democracy, because it no longer channels and supports the institutions—such as labor unions, mass-membership parties, and religious and civic organizations—that once gave voice to working-class people. Instead, Lind writes, managerial elites are a self-serving class that enjoys "near monopolies of expertise, wealth, and cultural influence," and that refuses to acknowledge the persistence of class disparities. It offers only "palliative reform" such as education and redistribution, without questioning liberalized policies on trade, immigration, and labor rights. Trump-style populism is the natural if regrettable reaction to this abdication by the Left.

Lind proposes a new "democratic pluralism," a power-sharing arrangement in which labor and capital can reach accommodations, with government a broker between them. He is hazy on the specifics of how to make it happen, and his depictions of the oligarchical Left sometimes veer into caricature. But *The New Class War* is a helpful corrective to the simpleminded belief that the Left merely need copy and redirect the antidemocratic strategies of the Right. The outcome of such a standoff is grim, Lind concludes, "a future of gated communities and mobs led by demagogues at their gates."

The horror or disdain with which many citizens regard the Trump presidency is premised, in part, on the notion that its problems are unprecedented and its moral shortcomings antithetical to longstanding American values. Critics of Trump's immigration policy, as we've seen, have been particularly susceptible to such reactions. This is why "normalizing" President Trump has become our era's mortal sin, and "that's not who we are" a battle cry for those who see today's antidemocratic and nativist impulses as aberrations along that long arc toward justice.

But what if this *is* normal for America? What if it *is* who we are or, at least, who we have too often been? Jon Meacham's *The Soul of America*, published in 2018, finds that national soul in the enduring attempts to expand liberty and opportunity. "It is a belief in the proposition, as Jefferson put it in the Declaration, that all men are created equal," Meacham writes. "It is therefore incumbent on us, from generation to generation, to create a sphere in which we can live, live freely, and pursue happiness to the best of our abilities." But at the same time he points to that "universal American inconsistency"—even as we uphold life and liberty for some, we restrict them from others, those deemed undeserving, untrustworthy, unequal.

Slavery. The Klan. Jim Crow. The Klan again. The internment of Japanese Americans and the expulsion of Mexicans and Mexican Americans. Gender discrimination and scientific racism. The Southern Strategy. Mass incarceration. All this leads to a president whom Meacham considers "an heir to the white populist tradition," a president whose only abnormality is that he manages to embody so many recurring maladies of American public life.

It is impossible to read Meacham's descriptions of politicians such as Senator Joseph McCarthy and Governor George Wallace without feeling the shadow of Trump. In his call for segregation now, tomorrow, and forever, Wallace "brought something intriguing to the modern politics of fear in America: a visceral connection to his crowds, an appeal that confounded elites but which gave him a durable base," Meacham writes. And in stoking the Red Scare, McCarthy was "a master of false charges, of

conspiracy-tinged rhetoric, and of calculated disrespect for conventional figures . . . McCarthy could distract the public, play the
press, and change the subject—all while keeping himself at center
stage." Meacham quotes McCarthy's comments to his young chief
counsel, Roy Cohn, before the televised congressional hearings in
1954 investigating a conflict between the Wisconsin senator and
the U.S. Army: "People aren't going to remember the things we say
on the issues here, our logic, our common sense, our facts. They're
only going to remember the impressions." Cohn would later become Trump's lawyer, and McCarthy's logic—privileging emotions
over facts, employing media technologies not to illuminate but to
obscure—would become part of the Trump ethos.

Meacham means to hearten his readers. Abraham Lincoln and
Franklin Roosevelt are recurring characters in *The Soul of America*, because "the most consequential of our past presidents have
unified and inspired with conscious dignity and conscientious efficiency." These qualities do not spring to mind when considering
our forty-fifth commander in chief, and Meacham likes to remind
us of better times. "The good news is that we have come through
such darkness before," the historian assures, and we've made it to
the other side. "All has seemed lost before, only to give way, after
decades of gloom, to light."

Of course, if you happen to inhabit those decades of gloom,
awareness of historical patterns bestows only limited consolation.
Yet Meacham stresses how those who have fought to expand American democracy have done so by emphasizing its shortcomings but
also by envisioning its possibilities, and by insisting that America
live up to its stated aspirations. He recalls the words of Martin Lu-
ther King Jr. addressing a mass meeting on the Montgomery bus
boycott: "We are here this evening—for serious business," King

said. "We are here in a general sense, because first and foremost—
we are American citizens—and we are determined to apply our
citizenship—to the fullness of its meaning."

Meacham concludes *The Soul of America* with a rousing affirmation that, "for all of our darker impulses, for all of our shortcomings, and for all of the dreams denied and deferred, the experiment
begun so long ago, carried out so imperfectly, is worth the fight."
Reading him and others, I would offer but one amendment: the
American experiment is not just *worth* the fight, it is synonymous
with it. That is the fullness of its meaning. With passions always
strained, the bonds of affection always near the breaking point,
the pursuit of freedom and prosperity and belonging is an endless
American struggle, an enterprise in equal measures exhausting,
exasperating, and exhilarating.

That is the message infusing *These Truths*, by Jill Lepore, a
hefty single-volume history of the United States published in 2018,
as well as the following year's *This America*, a slim summary of,
addendum to, and justification for the earlier work. For Lepore,
the fundamental question of America is whether it has lived up to
those self-evident truths of the Declaration of Independence: political equality ("all men are created equal"), natural rights (which
are "unalienable"), and government through popular sovereignty
(that is, "the consent of the governed"). The Declaration was "an
act of extraordinary political courage," Lepore writes in *These
Truths*, yet its failures were also self-evident from the start. Even
as it affirmed human dignity and political equality, it ignored en-
slaved Africans and their descendants—an omission Lepore decries as a "colossal failure of political will."

That failure would give us the Civil War, "a revolutionary war
of emancipation," as Lepore puts it, whose aftermath would pose
fundamental questions about citizenship, suffrage, and race. The

reckoning would be postponed with *Plessy v. Ferguson*, the Supreme Court's 1896 decision that narrowing, contradicting, or simply ignoring the meaning of the Declaration and the Fourteenth Amendment, gave the federal imprimatur to Jim Crow. "In one of the most wrenching tragedies in American history—a chronicle not lacking for tragedy—the Confederacy had lost the war, but it had won the peace," Lepore asserts.

In this light, asking whether authoritarianism can take root in America feels vaguely absurd. "Discussions about whether 'it could happen' in the United States sometimes overlook that it did happen in the United States," law professor David A. Strauss writes in his contribution to Sunstein's *Can It Happen Here?* "From roughly the late nineteenth century to the mid-twentieth century, parts of the United States were ruled by an undemocratic, illiberal, racist regime" under which African Americans were denied the vote and violently suppressed.

To Lepore, the truths of the Declaration are real but also eternally aspirational, "fought for, by sword and, still more fiercely, by pen." They are always with us, shaming and inspiring at once. "A nation born in revolution will forever struggle against chaos," she writes. "A nation founded on universal rights will wrestle against the forces of particularism. . . . And a nation born in contradiction, liberty in a land of slavery, sovereignty in a land of conquest, will fight, forever, over the meaning of its history."

Americans, Lepore concludes in *This America*, are bound together not only by the power of our common ideals but by "the force of our disagreements."

In a democracy, there are disagreements, and then there are efforts to inhibit those who might disagree from even expressing themselves. This is revealed, starkly, in Carol Anderson's *One Person,*

No Vote (2018), a history of voter suppression tactics spanning the American timeline. Anderson, a professor of history at Emory University, details the devastating effectiveness of poll taxes, literacy tests, voter registration rules, and other restrictions on voting that have targeted black Americans and other minority groups, all under the guise of racially neutral concerns such as fiscal responsibility, administrative efficiency or, most popular, the prevention of voter fraud. Such devices are "variations on a theme going back more than 150 years," Anderson writes, always cloaked in "feigned legal innocence."

The Voting Rights Act of 1965 was critical to protecting the enfranchisement of African Americans because it mandated federal intervention to uphold the franchise, "not because the racism that required the law in the first place had stopped," Anderson points out. In fact, it confronted a racism in which both major parties had long been complicit. As Levitsky and Ziblatt write in *How Democracies Die*, the "context of exclusion" underpinning America's democratic norms had helped white Democrats and Republicans coexist without coming to regard each other as existential threats. The effort to truly democratize the country with the Civil Rights Act of 1964 and the Voting Rights Act the following year would upend that balance, they explain, "posing the greatest challenge to established forms of mutual toleration and forbearance since Reconstruction."

That challenge came alive with *Shelby County v. Holder*, the 2013 Supreme Court case that overturned the Voting Rights Act mandate that any changes to election laws in states with a history of discrimination had to be cleared by the federal government. The consequences of holding national elections without such federal protections soon became clear. "The rash of voter ID laws, purged voting rolls, redrawn district boundaries, and closed and moved polling places were the quiet and barely detected fire that burned through the 2016 presidential election, evaporating millions of votes," Anderson writes. In a close contest, such tactics can make a critical difference, as much as or more than any foreign interference.

The prospect that a more minority-heavy American electorate could prove politically advantageous to Democrats had caused consternation among Republicans after the 2012 election, so much so that the Republican National Committee wrote the so-called autopsy report—officially known as the Growth and Opportunity Project—which proposed renewed outreach to Hispanic, Asian, and African American voters.

Or, rather than letting demography become destiny, you could just keep it from voting.

That is the story Stacey Abrams tells in *Our Time Is Now* (2020), a work that extends Anderson's history into the present, where it remains fully alive. Abrams, an African American voting-rights activist and former Georgia state legislator, lost a close gubernatorial race in 2018 to a Republican candidate who, as secretary of state, was also in charge of overseeing the electoral process. Abrams refused to offer a conventional concession speech; instead, in remarks she delivered more than a week after the election, Abrams only acknowledged that she had no remaining legal remedy against a process she believed had been tainted with widespread voter suppression. "The system worked as manipulated," she writes.

Abrams looks back on constitutional amendments ending slavery and expanding suffrage, landmark court decisions such as *Brown v. Board of Education*, and legislation such as the Voting Rights Act, but recognizes each as a step, not an end. "We often see these historical moments as flash points with instant gratification;

however, with most movements, the new laws, the new rules, only herald possibility. More must be done to make it so." For Abrams, that "more" involves her battle for expanded voting rights, and her book mixes her experiences as a lawmaker, candidate, and activist. Voting is "a leap of faith," she writes, but the faith is always tested. "Modern-day suppression has swapped rabid dogs and cops with billy clubs for restrictive voter ID and tangled rules for participation," she writes. Partisans who imagine that America's ongoing demographic transformation into a majority-minority country will eventually deliver a new progressive coalition are too optimistic, she concludes. "Demography is not destiny," Abrams writes. "It is opportunity."

The authors in the death-of-democracy genre often warn that a major catastrophe—a war, an insurgency, an act of terrorism— can spur attacks against the rule of law. "Would-be autocrats often use economic crises, natural disasters, and especially security threats . . . to justify antidemocratic measures," Levitsky and Ziblatt write. Citizens, suddenly fearing for their safety, are more tolerant of authoritarian encroachments. In *Ill Winds*, Diamond sounds the same caution but in more specific terms: "Just imagine what Trump might propose in the wake of a mass-casualty jihadist attack on U.S. soil."

Under Trump, America has suffered mass shootings, witnessed an emboldened white-nationalist movement, waged a trade war with China, traded nuclear threats with North Korea, belittled democratic allies, and sucked up to authoritarian leaders. And that was all before the COVID-19 pandemic reached our shores, our airports, our nursing homes, our workplaces, our communities, our lives.

It was not an insurgency, terrorist strike, or war, but it is nonetheless the greatest crisis of the post-9/11 era. By June 2020, its national death toll had more than doubled that of U.S. forces in the Vietnam War, and its job losses soon elicited Depression-era comparisons. The onset of the coronavirus pandemic was, by any definition, a mass-casualty event, and its economic, health, social, and cultural effects will endure for years to come. But the crisis only seemed to deepen Trump's defiance of, and disregard for, political and democratic norms. It underscored his particularism, with the president seeking to assist governors depending on their fealty to him. It heightened his disdain for accountability; "I am the oversight," the president declared, dismissing legislative efforts to oversee the disbursement of stimulus funds. It allowed his administration to push through new restrictions, particularly on immigration, that it had long sought. It created new opportunities for voter suppression, with Trump immediately resisting moves to facilitate voting by mail. And it allowed Trump to temporarily replace his rallies with a stream of press conferences in which he misled the public on testing, treatments, and his administration's efforts to fight the virus—all while bragging about his television ratings and denouncing his critics.

It was performance masquerading as governance. As Gessen puts it in *Surviving Autocracy*, the pandemic enabled Trump to "govern in precisely the manner to which he aspired . . . with the eyes of the nation riveted to him."

The intersecting crises of 2020—the coronavirus, mass unemployment, social upheaval—managed to stay true to the inequalities of the American story. The pandemic afflicted African Americans, Hispanics, and low-income and elderly citizens worse than others, and it made clear the disparities in health care access, job security, and wealth that still beset us. And nearly 250 years after we declared political equality a self-evident right, inequality before the law persists. In this context, restoring and protecting democratic norms is only the beginning of the task before us. "Those norms must be made to work in an age of racial equality and unprecedented ethnic diversity," Levitsky and Ziblatt emphasize. "Few societies in history have managed to be both multiracial and genuinely democratic. That is our challenge."

It is a challenge we've always faced yet never fully met. "The United States, rebuked by all those left out of its vision of the nation, began battling that contradiction early on, and has never stopped," Lepore writes in *This America*. "In the United States, the nation *is* that battle."

The Trump era and its aftermath, then, present but the latest fight. The only difference is that, this time, it's our fight, with many more books to come judging how well we wage it, and how well we understand it.

BOOKS DISCUSSED

Stacey Abrams. *Our Time Is Now: Power, Purpose, and the Fight for a Fair America.* Henry Holt, 2020.

Carol Anderson. *One Person, No Vote: How Voter Suppression Is Destroying Our Democracy.* Bloomsbury, 2018.

Larry Diamond. *Ill Winds: Saving Democracy from Russian Rage, Chinese Ambition, and American Complacency.* Penguin Press, 2019.

Carol Fredrickson. *The Democracy Fix: How to Win the Fight for Fair Rules, Fair Courts, and Fair Elections.* The New Press, 2019.

David Frum. *Trumpocalypse: Restoring American Democracy.* Harper, 2020.

———. *Trumpocracy: The Corruption of the American Republic.* Harper, 2018.

Masha Gessen. *Surviving Autocracy.* Riverhead Books, 2020.

Jill Lepore. *These Truths: A History of the United States.* W. W. Norton & Company, 2018.

———. *This America: The Case for the Nation.* Liveright, 2019.

Steven Levitsky and Daniel Ziblatt. *How Democracies Die.* Crown, 2018.

Michael Lind. *The New Class War: Saving Democracy from the Managerial Elite.* Portfolio/Penguin, 2020.

Jon Meacham. *The Soul of America: The Battle for Our Better Angels.* Random House, 2018.

Jan-Werner Müller. *What Is Populism?* University of Pennsylvania Press, 2016.

Cass R. Sunstein, ed. *Can It Happen Here? Authoritarianism in America.* Dey St., 2018.

TWELVE BOOKS

"Over the past four years, I have thought and spoken and written about Donald Trump almost more than I can bear," David Frum confesses in *Trumpocalypse*. "You probably feel the same fatigue."

David, you have no idea.

I did not expect, when I became a book critic at the *Washington Post* in 2015, that I would spend so much mental energy on Donald Trump, much less that something called "the Trump era" would be immediately recognizable shorthand for a nation suffused with conflict, crudeness, and mistrust. But with that fatigue also came a growing hunger for insight and comprehension. For me, books have been a way to satisfy it.

"What should I read to understand what's going on?" I've gotten this question a lot during the Trump presidency. A useful answer seems impossible, so dependent is it on each reader's needs, interests, curiosities, and blind spots. Instead, the best I can do is highlight the books that have upended my own assumptions and shifted my vantage points. I don't mean to proclaim these the *best* books of the Trump era, the most beautifully written or deeply reported, though some may indeed merit such praise. Only that these are the works that have best helped me make sense of this time, the ones I suspect I'll revisit long after the Trump era has become a subject for works of history.

We're Still Here: Pain and Politics in the Heart of America, by Jennifer Silva

Memoirs such as J. D. Vance's *Hillbilly Elegy* and Sarah Smarsh's *Heartland* provide memorable testimonials of working-class life, while studies such as *Alienated America* by Timothy Carney and *Deaths of Despair and the Future of Capitalism* by Anne Case and Angus Deaton bring a crucial cultural and economic lens to the subject. In *We're Still Here*, Silva manages to do both. This book expands my notions of who belongs to the heartland, and of the obstacles to belonging in our national politics.

On Tyranny: Twenty Lessons for the Twentieth Century, by Timothy Snyder

It's one of the earliest and slimmest of the resistance volumes, yet still the one I turn to most often. Snyder's historical context and stark warnings ("think up your own way of speaking"; "do not obey in advance") feel more powerful for having come so early. Published barely a month into the new administration, it could only picture what was to come, so it draws on the author's scholarship to warn of post-truth, heedless conformity, and institutional abdication. The effect is timeliness and timelessness at once.

A Time to Build: From Family and Community to Congress and the Campus, How Recommitting to Our Institutions Can Revive the American Dream, by Yuval Levin

This is an almost countercultural book—a call for personal and institutional restraint in public life, for a politics that forms us rather than performs for us. Levin writes from a conservative perspective, but his admonition applies broadly: "Given my role here, how should I act?" It is a question too easily forgotten, and a burden too easily shed.

America for Americans: A History of Xenophobia in the United States, by Erika Lee

This is a hard book to read but a necessary one, especially for anyone who looks upon our ongoing battles over immigration and concludes, with such confidence, that "we are better than this." We may strive to be better than this, but Lee's methodical and merciless history of American prejudice against outsiders shows how often we have failed to be better—how *better than this* is an eternal aspiration, not a natural condition.

The End of the Myth: From the Frontier to the Border Wall in the Mind of America, by Greg Grandin

This book is history as argument, and Grandin tackles a big one: the frontier and its presence in the American imagination. A young country that long deluded itself into believing that relentless expansion across the continent would pay for its own moral and human costs now obsesses instead over its border, "a monument to the final closing of the frontier." *The End of the Myth* helps us understand why, when Americans look at the border today, so many see threats rather than possibilities.

A Lot of People Are Saying: The New Conspiracism and the Assault on Democracy, by Russell Muirhead and Nancy L. Rosenblum

"Hoax." "Rigged." "Fake." Conspiracy is one of the defining elements of the Trump era, and these authors show how the president's unique style of conspiracy—single-word attacks lacking any intricate evidence or connected dots—gains power through ceaseless repetition, and is aimed not at persuading Americans of any one lie but at slowly undermining all independent arbiters of truth.

When They Call You a Terrorist: A Black Lives Matter Memoir, by Patrisse Khan-Cullors and asha bandele

Among the many memoirs of this identity age, *When They Call You a Terrorist* beautifully captures the tensions between individual and group identities, the power of marrying personal turmoil to collective struggle. "We have come to say that we can be more than the worst of the hate," explains Patrisse Khan-Cullors, one of the founders of the Black Lives Matter movement, in an unforgettable distillation of her life and project.

Report on the Investigation into Russian Interference in the 2016 Presidential Election, by Special Counsel Robert S. Mueller III

When I reviewed the report in the *Washington Post* in April 2019, I called it the best book so far on the inner workings of the Trump presidency. That assessment still stands. Despite its clunky legalese, the report combines authority, analysis, and on-the-record details in its assessment of Russia's electoral interference and the president's efforts to impede or delay the investigation. The report also doubles as a cultural artifact of its time, and the controversies surrounding its interpretation and impact make it even more so.

Know My Name: A Memoir, by Chanel Miller

A strength of the Me Too movement is its testimony, even if testimony alone is never enough. Miller's account of pain, law, and daily survival after a sexual assault outside a college dorm party in

2015 stands with the most unforgettable memoirs of trauma and loss. Her anger at her assailant is magnified when Miller explains how even her literary talent, so evident in this debut, is subsumed by the story of all that her attacker could otherwise have become.

The Fifth Risk, by Michael Lewis

With everyone fixated on the chaos inside the White House, Lewis gazes across the federal government to find the catastrophic risks that agencies and dedicated bureaucrats have long sought to manage. The task is harder under an administration that prizes loyalty over expertise, under a leader who, as Lewis writes, "wishes to shrink the world to a worldview." Before the coronavirus crisis, this book was merely prescient. During the pandemic, it is prophetic.

Unmaking the Presidency: Donald Trump's War on the World's Most Powerful Office, by Susan Hennessey and Benjamin Wittes

This is a book for everyone who has developed an unexpected nostalgia for political "norms" during the Trump years. Hennessey and Wittes look across presidential history to show how those norms accreted over time, and why Trump's "expressive presidency"—in which the personality, preferences, and impulses of the commander in chief consume the office's institutional duties—threatens to obliterate them. Other books on the Trump White House expertly detail the mayhem inside; this book builds on those works to detail its consequences.

One Person, No Vote: How Voter Suppression Is Destroying Our Democracy, by Carol Anderson

A history of efforts to hinder Americans' right to vote would be timely even without a presidential election bearing down on us.

Anderson underscores the "feigned legal innocence" that always accompanies voter suppression, as its architects cloak their designs in benign-sounding justifications, especially the always popular crusade to prevent alleged (and largely nonexistent) voter fraud. Trump decried the 2016 election as rigged, and he won that one—and he has already called into question the legitimacy of the coming vote. *One Person, No Vote* is almost fated to be relevant once again, in our next election and in more to come.

ACKNOWLEDGMENTS

I get to read and review books for the *Washington Post*—a dream job that I still can't quite believe is mine. Many thanks to Marty Baron, Kevin Merida, Cameron Barr, and Tracy Grant for giving me that opportunity. Thank you to Adam Kushner, my editor at the *Post*, for indulging my interests, sharpening my ideas, extending my deadlines, and generously granting me time to work on this project. The arguments developed in this book began with essays and reviews of mine that Adam published in the *Post*'s Sunday Outlook. I am grateful to Steven Levingston, an indispensable guide to the publishing world, for his friendship and steady advice, and for always finding new books and authors that intrigue me. And thank you to Jeff Bezos and Fred Ryan for keeping the lights on, especially when times are dark.

Simon & Schuster was the ideal home for this book, and Priscilla Painton an ideal editor—patient, encouraging, and engaged, always telling me how much she loved each draft right before explaining how I had to rethink it. My gratitude to Janet Byrne for expertly copyediting the manuscript and steering me away from my worst writing habits. Thank you to Sara Kitchen and Hana Park for guiding this book through to publication, reminding me of every deadline, and fielding all my questions along the way. I am especially grateful to Jonathan Karp, the CEO of Simon & Schuster, for trusting a first-time author with a vague idea for a Trump book about Trump books.

This book would have remained that vague idea without Gail Ross and the team at the Ross Yoon Agency. Thank you, Gail, for your belief, reassurance, and reality checks. I can't wait for our next lunch.

Moisés Naím gave me my first journalism job two decades ago and has granted me unconditional friendship and wise counsel ever since. Mil gracias, Moisés. Thanks to James Gibney for teaching me how to be an editor. (I always hear your voice—*what does this lede accomplish?*—when I sit down at my keyboard.) Thanks to many friends and colleagues for their support and advice: Marie Arana, Peter Baker, Dan Balz, Warren Bass, Marisa Bellack, Phil Bennett, Nancy Birdsall, Lisa Bonos, Marcus Brauchli, Carrie Camillo, Rajiv Chandrasekaran, Ron Charles, Chris Cillizza, Robert Costa, Tim Curran, Jill Drew, Rachel Dry, Amanda Erickson, Emilio García-Ruiz, Susan Glasser, Jeffrey Goldberg, Tom Kellenberg, Anne Kornblut, Wesley Lowery, Chris Rukan, Greg Schneider, Jennifer Senior, Julie Tate, Alvaro Valdez, Scott Vance, Scott Wilson, and Jonathan Yardley.

A special shout-out to my neighbors in Bethesda, Maryland, for their camaraderie and good cheer, to the families of St. Edward's Hall, for their friendship over the decades, to the members of the Pulitzer Prize Board, for inviting me to join the world's greatest book club, and to my journalism students with the University of Notre Dame's Washington program, for a decade's worth of conversations on writing and politics.

My eternal gratitude to Dana Milbank for suggesting the title of this book, and to Jennifer Morehead, a wonderful copyeditor and better friend, for reviewing the manuscript with the same care she gives to my essays in the *Post*.

The Carnegie Endowment for International Peace granted me shelter as a journalist in residence to work on this book. Thank you to William Burns and Thomas Carothers for your enthusiasm regarding this project. I hope that next time a global pandemic won't cut short our time together on Massachusetts Avenue. Thank you as well to the good people of the Little Falls Public Library and their well-lit, spacious quiet room.

I am particularly grateful to the authors of all the books discussed in *What Were We Thinking*. Whether I was critical of your work or rapturous about it, you made me think more deeply. Please keep writing; I will keep reading.

Finally, my family. All my love and gratitude to my mother, Maya, for her love and kindness, for teaching me resilience and always bringing joy into my life. My love to my father, Elías, for instilling in me a passion for literature, and for giving me books I was far too young to read. My love and admiration to my sister Rosi, whose example makes me strive to be a better son, father, and brother. Thank you to our departed sister Marilu, whose kindness and imagination are treasures in my memory. Thank you to Papapa Carlos and Mamama Ernestina, for setting the bar so high.

All my gratitude to my love, Kathleen McBride, for her belief and patience, for listening to me rant about whatever I'm reading, for persuading me—against her best interests—to add one more chapter, and for assuring me this book would be good because it was mine. And thank you, with all my heart, to our children: Jamie, Fiona, and Finn. This book is for you, so that when you're grown and trying to understand what happened in your country in this time, your daddy might, I hope, still be of some help.

INDEX

ABOUT THE AUTHOR

CARLOS LOZADA is the nonfiction book critic of the *Washington Post*. He won the Pulitzer Prize for Criticism in 2019 and has received the National Book Critics Circle's Nona Balakian Citation for Excellence in Reviewing. During his fifteen years with the *Post* he has also served as Outlook editor and overseen news coverage of economics and national security. An immigrant from Lima, Peru, Lozada is the former managing editor of *Foreign Policy* magazine and an adjunct professor of political journalism at the University of Notre Dame.